A Fresh Cup of Tolerance

A Fresh Cup of Tolerance

Universalism: The New Religion of Tolerance

Thomas L. Norris

Edited by Cate Norris

RESOURCE *Publications* • Eugene, Oregon

A FRESH CUP OF TOLERANCE
Universalism: The New Religion of Tolerance

Resource Publications
An Imprint of Wipf and Stock Publishers
199 W. 8th Ave., Suite 3
Eugene, OR 97401

www.wipfandstock.com

PAPERBACK ISBN: 978-1-6667-3009-8
HARDCOVER ISBN: 978-1-6667-2116-4
EBOOK ISBN: 978-1-6667-2117-1

11/09/21

Dedication

There are two women in my life who have been my greatest inspiration, and this book reflects their deep spiritual values and the unqualified support they have always given me. I dedicate this book to my mom, Ginny Norris, where it all began for me; and my wife, Cate, for being a great friend, partner, contributor, and editor who believed in me and this work. Finally, I cannot leave out the two greatest joys in my life, Dan and Alexandra, my children, who made it all worthwhile. Thank you.

Dedication

Contents

List of Figures

Acknowledgements

HAVING WRITTEN THIS BOOK, it would be easy to call it "my book," but that would not be accurate. I had a lot of help, so more accurately, it is "our book." I have a lot of skills, experience, and knowledge, but that was not enough to create this particular narrative. Almost on a nightly basis, I experienced the presence of something beyond me as I sat down to write. Many times, whole chapters poured out in one sitting. Fresh ideas and concepts emerged as I wrote. I had not contemplated many of these before they hit the computer screen, or they had been percolating for years but never quite made it to the written page until now. Either way, they came together perfectly, at just the right place and time. Sometimes, I was distinctly aware of who was helping me and, other times, I only felt a vague sense of guidance. So, these acknowledgments must begin with my etheric collaborators: the Ascended Masters, spiritual guides, angels, and archangels who truly inspired this work. It is a message from all of us, our gift to all of you.

Just as significantly, there is no way that this book could or would have been written without the love, support, and encouragement of my wife, Cate, who is more than a partner. She is truly my best friend. Cate is also one hell of a tough editor. Many of her ideas and suggestions are interspersed throughout the book, so she truly has been a contributor and not just an editor. More than once, I felt a particular section was missing something, but I couldn't quite put my finger on it. When I read the section to her, she invariably found the missing piece and where it belonged. Of course, this was not always appreciated as it inevitably signified a rewrite, new pages, and even new chapters.

Writing a book is like giving birth. The gestation period seems to go on and on and on. The labor is tiring, arduous, and painful. There is a final push near the end when there is hardly enough energy to write another word, much less finish the last chapter. And then, out pops a beautiful bouncing baby book only to then be exposed to the harsh elements of proposals, editors, publishers, critics, and readers. Yet, like all new parents, there is an ineffable joy in the process and completion of creation. Thank you, Cate, for being the midwife throughout.

Rev. Dr. Laurie Kraus headed my dissertation team and Rev. Dr. Reginald Eldon was my dissertation mentor at the Florida Center for Theological Studies in Miami. In 2004, when I was unsure what to research and write about for my doctoral dissertation, they suggested looking at the Universalist Church and developing this new theology. It could not have been done without their support and encouragement. From that dissertation, this book emerged. Just as significantly, I was assisted in discussing, expanding upon, and reviewing draft chapters by my Doctoral Project Site Team. They are members of the Universalist Church, including Iliana Alvarado, Scott Gerard, Deborah McGinnis, Dr. John Raffel, Elisa Rossi, Lorraine Sheldon, Fernanda Valle, and Dorothy Wawa. Their input clarified many blurry areas, and their support helped me through the last months of dissertation exhaustion.

Of course, I wish to thank all the church members and all my students who, through their many questions and numerous debates over the years, helped shape these ideas. Pastor Russell Greene of Good Faith Lutheran Church in Norwalk, Connecticut was also a marvelous inspiration and role model for a shy, gawky teen. Both Deborah Hellman and Barrett Eaglebear have been terrific spiritual mentors along the way as well.

Preface

Birthings

CATE, MY WIFE AND best editor, pointed out that the reason she reads a preface is to hear why the author felt the need to write the book. It certainly made sense and was something I had completely overlooked. It is odd that I would miss that because writing a book is an intensely personal experience. It literally becomes your baby. Add that to my absolute passion for the subject and my undying hope for our young species, and she is right.

There are so many books on the market. Perhaps if I explain how this book was conceived and why I felt it significant enough to put on paper, you will understand why I had to write it. The best way to spell it out is through the several vignettes in my life that first led me to this new theology.

I'll start with my religious upbringing. My family moved around a lot when I was a kid. My parents were not terribly particular about which Protestant church denomination they attended, just that they enjoyed the pastor and the church. As an infant, I was baptized at Emanuel Lutheran Church in St. Paul, Minnesota. Until the age of eleven or twelve, I attended House of Hope Presbyterian Church in St. Paul and sang in their church choir from the age of five. I was later confirmed in the United Methodist Church in Stamford, Connecticut, and I briefly attended a Congregationalist Church in Norwalk. I returned to the Lutheran Church at the Good Shepherd Church in my teens, where I was an acolyte and Sunday school teacher. When I reached high school, I attended Grace Methodist Church in Wilmington, Delaware, and later was president of the Methodist Wesley Foundation at the University of Delaware. I recite this litany of congregations and denominations only to point out the power they had in forming my early opinions about religion. In all of these various churches and Protestant denominations, I never noticed a fig's worth of difference between them. They were all northern liberal denominations, and they all looked and sounded the same. I had to attend a Christian seminary for my advanced degrees to learn the doctrinal differences between these various denominations—most of which still seem to be as narrow and insignificant as the 13th century academic debate about how many angels could dance on the head of a pin. It was the beginnings of my Universalist leanings, unknowingly assisted by some excellent pastors and Sunday school teachers along the way.

In 1980, my girlfriend encouraged me to attend an ashram on Miami Beach where a famous swami was going to speak. I didn't even know what an ashram[1] was back then, but nonetheless, she was into that "stuff" and I attended out of curiosity. It was a moving, entirely new, and even alien experience. I sang the mantras (*Om Namah Shivaya*), meditated for the first time, received *Shaktipat* (awakening energy) from *Muktananda* (*Baba*), and listened to him give a short lesson in Hindi. His young translator later became *Guru Mahi*, the only female guru of a major Hindu sect, *Siddha Yoga*. I had no idea how famous *Muktananda* was at the time, but in addition to the incredible, revitalizing energy I felt for the next month, I carried one precious gem out of the service. In his homily, he stated that the reason we should love ourselves is because we are part of God and loving ourselves means that we also love God. My head was swimming with this new concept—something I surely never heard in my Christian sermons. It was also a critical lesson for someone struggling with self-esteem issues from their childhood. You mean it was okay to love yourself? I had always been taught that was "selfish," akin to "bragging on yourself." Another Universalism seed was planted.

Next, it was August 1992, just after Hurricane Andrew, and like everyone else, I had never known so intimately the destructive force of Mother Nature. It was an interminable night with howling winds, cracking walls, and frightened children and kittens huddling in the bathroom under my worried care. A few days later, we were still reeling from the dreadful devastation visited upon southern Miami-Dade County. I worked alongside a University of Miami pediatrician, under the shelter of a bank drive-in lane next to a tomato field, as lightning bolts crashed all around us. We were handing out Pedialite to the long lines of mothers standing in the driving rain and wind squalls so their babies would

1. An Ashram is a spiritual center where the teachers (gurus) and students live together in community.

not get diarrhea and become dehydrated. Wherever he gazed, he said it looked just like the aftermath of a B-52 bombing raid in Vietnam.

I worked with the VA Mental Health Team for about a week. We did what little we could for people who had lost everything—homes, dogs and horses, cars, growing fields, family picture albums, friends, and hope. What I noticed in the first week was the tremendous outpouring of help and compassion from around the nation. Truckload after truckload of supplies from all over kept pouring in. The people in the community helped each other with food, shelter, money, electric generator hookups, a shoulder—even when they had nothing themselves. We truly became a community. It lasted a little over two weeks and then started to fall apart. By three weeks, shotgun brigades were guarding shattered neighborhoods against looters, although there were few instances of looting. From that time on, thousands of people from north Miami-Dade County and Broward County, largely intact communities with open shopping centers and services, flooded into the food distribution centers. They were taking boxes of food that were needed by the locals affected most severely by the hurricane. There were fights in the food lines, unheard of in the first week. In the stiflingly hot, humid weather, people lived in tents and gutted houses without air conditioning or electricity. Domestic violence and child abuse cases skyrocketed. Con artists proliferated, and greed raised its ugly head as thousands of people from around the country poured into the area, hoping to profit by finding work in construction. The region became a divided community once again.

This is a pattern repeated throughout history. The reasoning behind this dichotomous shift in behavior—from initial compassion to eventual dissolution—has always been an enigma to me. It intrigued me and inspired me to question dogmas and revisit history with a wide open lens. I invite you on this journey.

CHAPTER 1

The Spiritual Masters Conference

Picture a week-long roundtable conference at the Los Angeles Sheraton Gateway. Attendees include Buddha, Jesus, White Buffalo Calf Woman, Moses, Kuan Yin, Muhammad, Isis, Mahavir (*Jain*), Krishna, Quetzalcoatl (*Mayan*), Ceridwen (*Druid*), Gandhi, Mother Theresa, Martin Luther King, Jr., Malcolm X, Grandmother Twyla (*Seneca*) and many other great spiritual masters and shamans humanity has looked to over the ages for answers, support, and comfort. The roundtable topic is *Applying the Great Truths of All Time to the 21st Century.* It is a daunting task, but they are excited and enthusiastic about the opportunity to update all of their hard work and potent messages. Fortunately, unlike some of their followers, one cannot imagine any of these commanding teachers raising a hand to the other, even in the midst of their most heated, passionate debates. Rather, we observe an earnest, collegial atmosphere of respect throughout—with a healthy dose of humor—whether there is agreement or disagreement. Why would they fight and argue? They know they are all messengers of a higher truth from a higher source. The challenge is bringing this truth down to earth, which is the purpose of the conference. Are these truths still useful, helpful, relevant, and timely?

The conference begins as various panels address transitioning from the Old Age to the demanding postmodern New Age realities at the beginning of this millennium. The conference then dives headfirst into the deeper waters of theology with a number of intensive seminars entitled:

- On the Nature of God
- On the Nature of Revelation

- On the Nature of Humanity
- On the Nature of Love and Community
- On the Nature of Good, Evil, Sin, and Suffering
- On the Nature of Illusion
- On the Nature of Liberation
- On the Nature of Divine Purpose

Although much of humanity might be surprised, it is to no one's surprise at the conference that they reach a general consensus on a new theology of Universalism. The conference participants are amazed that their various followers never really "got it," although the words and signs were everywhere. Anyone delving into any of their teachings and work could not possibly miss the familiar themes of loving the Creator, loving the gifts of creation, and loving each other. They wonder how people could have missed the point that Muhammad would never kill another messenger, even of a faith different from Islam, any more than Buddha would harm a mosquito or Jesus would fail to turn the other cheek. The attendees emphatically agree it is long overdue for this world to actually start practicing what they had been preaching and teaching for millennia: tolerance, love, justice, compassion, and peace. After all, it was their love for humanity and all of creation that inspired these teachings in the first place. They believe in us and in our world! From this conference emerged a unanimous *Spiritual Manifesto of Universalism.*[1] Each signer pledges their full support to help humanity finally understand and accomplish their God/Goddess potential. They embrace Jesus' words, "You are gods!" (Psalm 82:6 and John 10:34) and "Very truly, I tell you, the one who believes in me will also do the works that I do and, in fact, will do greater works than these . . ." (John 14:12). They acknowledge the Buddhist truth that each of us is already a Buddha, even if we don't know it yet. They affirmed our promise and potential.

The conference (and this book) might happily have ended there on such a high spiritual note. However, the spiritual teachers realize the subject is incomplete if they only cover the need for dialog and the new theology. This new religion is not just a pleasant philosophy of love. It is not just an airy-fairy philosophy of life or theology of belief. It is a living, growing, changing dynamic, one that cannot be imprisoned within rigid

1. See *A Universalist Spiritual Manifesto* in Appendix A.

words (scriptures), beliefs (dogma and doctrine), or practices (rituals). It is a faith-in-action theology. Consequently, as weary as they are, the spiritual masters engage in two final decisive seminars, combined and entitled as *Praxis* (Living Practice). First is the *Praxis of Light Living*, noting that fancy words and declarations are not enough. How do we translate a theology of bringing light into the world—into our homes, our families, on the street, to the battlefield, and into our communities? And so, begins the writing of a blueprint for loving ourselves and others that can only lead to a happier, healthier life and world.

Part two of the last seminar, the most difficult in light of our global corporate economy, confronts the *Praxis of Light Working*. As employers and employees, bosses and subordinates, owners and workers, the 1% and the 99%, how do we bring the great spiritual truths into the office and workplace? How do we move organizations, companies, governmental agencies, Mom and Pop stores, and corporations to a higher standard of quality, integrity, honesty, and respect? In Hinduism, this is called *Dharma*. The conference participants are astounded once again that humanity, with all its advancements, still has not figured out that these spiritual principles will serve to enhance profits and abundance in ways that allow all to finally participate in the vast bounty of creation. And so, again, the creation of a spiritual blueprint begins. It outlines a means for the marketplace and the workplace to also be a place of light—again, with the realization it can only lead to a happier, healthier life and world for all.

The conference members complete their task with the sense of a job well done. As they embrace and say their goodbyes, they each leave with the renewed hope that the men and women of this planet will hear their words and their vision for a New World of Love, Tolerance, Hope, Peace, Joy, and Plenty. Their work is done. Now it is up to us. Such is the task of *A Fresh Cup of Tolerance*.

CHAPTER 2

A New Day

Now let all rejoice. Seek the Light that the power of the stars which is in you, may live.

JESUS, *THE PISTIS SOPHIA*

Dawning

A NEW DAY IS upon us. Some are calling it the New Age, others call it Postmodernity or Poststructuralism. Whatever the name, this millennial dawn brings mighty winds of change, even revolution. We are undergoing a vast revolution in technology and science, but of equal importance is the profound revolution in thought and perspective that is the landmark of postmodern beingness. Like all revolutions, this one has its battlefields—Absolutism vs. Relativism, Secularism vs. Religiosity, Objectivity vs. Subjectivity. And we cannot forget all the old schools of racism, colonialism, classism, sexism, heterosexism, ageism, handicappism, patriarchy, and religiocentrism versus the new schools of pluralism and Universalism. Lest you think this is just a metaphor, some of these battlefields are still killing fields. As these words are being written, men, women, and children are being tortured, maimed, and murdered on the front lines of hatred, prejudice, and fanaticism. These issues are deeply involved in the wars in Iraq and Afghanistan; the civil strife in Iran, Syria, Pakistan, and Northern Ireland; the Arab Spring uprisings; the rise of the fanatical ISIS movement; the war of the Taliban in Afghanistan and

Pakistan against educating women, which has led to death and violence against schoolgirls, their families, and teachers; violence against women in schoolyards, homes, streets, fields, and offices around the world; genocide in Darfur, Sudan; the Arab-Israeli Conflict of the past seven decades, the rise of domestic terrorism in the U.S.—and we could go on and on. There are far too many examples of this war between the old and the new, between feudal cultures, the still powerful vestiges of Modernity, and the newly emerging Postmodernity. Sadly, these age-old wars have always been the enemy of true community, and if there is anything that defines the heart and soul of this book, it is the quest for community.

The potential for true community is always present; it's in our spiritual DNA, but continuity in community is much harder to attain. We have seen the same pattern repeat itself over and over—after 911, Hurricane Katrina, the Tsunami in Indonesia, the earthquake in Haiti, the worldwide pandemic. In a crisis, our best nature surfaces—but we seem unable to sustain this sense of community and remain in the heart of compassion for more than a few weeks of intense CNN coverage. For many years as a social worker and psychotherapist, I worked with victims of child abuse, domestic violence, trauma, and sex crimes. When I entered the ministry, it became my spiritual priority to seek a means to sustain a loving community for longer periods—whether it is within the family, the church, or the larger society. A theology of Universalism offers a pathway of hope.

This book addresses these issues head on, but in an explicitly postmodern way. It is certainly not a deconstructionist postmodern treatise that attempts to question everything from before and then tear it down limb by limb. Instead, it lays down a constructionist postmodern challenge, which asks us to question, revise, overcome, change, and even revolutionize what has come from the past—without tearing it all down. The past centuries are neither good nor bad in and of themselves; they are simply what they are. Sometimes, terrible things happened in those times, and we might choose to judge the people who carried out those actions. However, we either did not live then and do not know how we would have acted with the moral knowledge and social programming of those days; or we did live then (via reincarnation) and must bear some karmic responsibility for those days. Moreover, the past got us from there to here, and I am grateful for many of the accomplishments of the Modern Age. I enjoy air conditioning in South Florida, and I really don't want to travel by horse twenty-five miles to my university campus to teach my classes.

Perhaps one thing that will become clear from this book is that the old Aristotelian model of "either-or" thinking is not a postmodern attribute.

As the book's subtitle asserts, Universalism is the new theology of tolerance, even with regard to the past. It proposes a new way of spirituality very much built upon the learnings and teachings of the Old Age, the past. Nor is it the only New Religious Movement (NRM) out there by any stretch, for one of the defining characteristics of postmodern activity is its tremendous diversity. Yet, by exploring the Universalist spirituality, much is learned about traditional religion as well as related NRM movements, notably the transition from modernity to postmodernity.

This book was created to thrust all of us outside the restrictive box of our standard social, religious, and societal programming. It aims to push us to rethink our values, belief systems, and perspectives on life, creation, Creator, and created. This re-evaluation often strengthens the underpinnings of our values and belief systems. It allows us to own them, as we have now thought through the implications of what we have been taught. We can truthfully say we have used our God-given brains and discerned what works for us and what does not—a very postmodern, individualistic vantage point. At times, the book unabashedly presents an emotional and passionate discourse on contemporary life and religion, so it clearly moves beyond the academic world into the gritty plane of the home, office, and street. In this way, perhaps, we can strengthen the transition from the Old Age to the New Age. We can build upon the many prophecies of hope; that this coming age will be one of harmony, understanding, knowledge, tolerance, and peace.

A Fresh Cup of Tolerance is broken down into four parts over nineteen chapters. Part I, *The Dialog*, begins the discussion of what the Universalist movement is about, from a historical perspective and as a postmodern spiritual venture. Part II, *The Theology*, takes a systematic theology approach as it explores Universalism from all angles, covering chapters like:

- Just Who is this God Guy or Gal Anyway? (On the Nature of God);
- AskGod.Com (On the Nature of Revelation);
- Ye are Gods! (On the Nature of Humankind);
- Pandora's Box (On the Nature of Good, Evil and Suffering);
- Seeing Through a Glass Darkly (On the Nature of Illusion);
- All You Need is Love (On the Nature of Love and Community);

- Free at Last, Free at Last! Thank God Almighty, We are Free at Last (On the Nature of Liberation); and
- All the World's a Stage (On the Nature of Purpose).

Part III, *The Praxis—Light Living*, begins a journey through spiritual ethics and practice. How does one implement and live a Universalist way of life (Lifeway)? Finally, Part IV, *The Praxis—Light Work*, travels beyond the individual and challenges us to envision a society and human organizations that live by these pluralistic and tolerant ways of living; Universalism in the workplace.

All of us in the field of theology and religious studies owe a great debt to Ninian Smart. He proposed viewing and analyzing religion from seven dimensions: ritual, doctrinal and philosophical, mythic and narrative, experiential and emotional, ethical and legal, organizational and social, and material and artistic.[1] Although we do not follow his dimensional analysis method exactly, you will see each of these dimensions poking their heads up throughout the book. Additionally, I have added a few other dimensions for consideration as well: psychological, geographic, socio-economic, socio-political, gender, and environmental. To be effectively universal, a Universalist theology must naturally embrace such an all-encompassing approach.

1. Ninian Smart, *Dimensions of the Sacred* (Berkeley: University of California Press, 1996), 10–11.

PART I

The Dialog

How do we begin the conversation? This book starts by addressing contemporary, fundamental religious issues and strains in the world. How are our postmodern visions engaging these deadly spiritual trials, including the new movement of Universalism? We initiate the discussion about the desperate need for tolerance in a world of nations and peoples at war with each other and within themselves. Upon that foundation, we can move to *The Theology* (Part II), which lays out the structure of a new Universalist theology. Finally, we finish by envisioning how that theology can be put into living practice in *The Praxis—Light Living* (Part III) and *The Praxis—Light Work* (Part IV).

CHAPTER 3

A New 21st Century Earth

For my house shall be called a house of prayer for all peoples.

ISAIAH 56:7

I am a Muslim, I am a Hindu, I am a Christian, I am a Jew.

MAHATMA GANDHI

Renewal

HOW MANY TIMES THROUGHOUT history have we heard a prophet or an oracle thunder dire warnings foretelling horrendous tragedies to befall humankind, followed by belated promises that it does not have to end that way? How many times has a great spiritual leader—a Jesus, a Buddha, a White Buffalo Calf Woman, a Muhammad, a Temple Doors[1], or a Gandhi—come along to guide us to a better way? How many dreamers, utopianists, philosophers, and idealists have described a vision of a better world? From the very first inkling of human thought five million years ago, how many opportunities have we had to choose a different

1. Hyemeyohsts Storm, *Lightningbolt* (New York: Ballantine, 1994), 312–16. According to Native American history, Temple Doors was the great General-Priestess who led her people from their lands in Central America to Northern Mexico and the American Southwest some 2000 years ago. Today, we call them the Pueblo peoples (Zuni, Hopi, Anasazi, Taos, and so on). They had a great influence on Native American culture as a democratic, egalitarian society, especially as their colonies spread northward.

path? When we weren't beheading or belittling them, how many times have we listened to these visionaries about their visions of hope? Forget the big picture of our life journey; have we even attempted to incorporate their hopes and dreams into the simple, ordinary moments of our day? For most of us, the answer is no, or at best, a very inconsistent yes. But will there be a time when they might finally be heard, and that we might finally listen? Will there be a time when their visions might finally be imagined and fully realized? Will there be a time when we might begin to finally live up to our promise as individuals and as a species—the promise that we are capable of being so much more? I say yes, and why not now!

There comes a time when the old is renewed, and the new is really new. There comes a time to harvest the human wisdom of five million years. There comes a time when evolution in heart, mind, and spirit demands creative new ways of believing, thinking, and being. There comes a time when the choices before us are so compellingly clear that only the most spiritually blind and ignorant could possibly miss the signs. There comes a time for the evolution (or revolution) of heart and soul to finally emerge, to become more than potential. Has the time not come for us to finally grow up?

What doubt can there be that we desperately need transformation in a world still ravaged by religious hatred and intolerance? Just in the past two decades, we have witnessed Muslims blowing up Jews in Israel and Jews blowing up Muslims in Palestine and Lebanon; Americans launching another perceived Christian Crusade against Muslims in Iraq, Afghanistan, and Iran; Muslims attacking Christian "Great Satan" America; Muslims and Buddhists at war in Thailand and India; Protestants shooting Irish Catholics and Irish Catholics bombing Protestants in Northern Ireland; Hindus and Muslims murdering each other over remote, mountainous Kashmir; Shia slaughtering Sunni Muslims and Sunni butchering Shia Muslims in Iraq and Syria; White Nationalists and Supremacists warring with people of color and immigrants; and indigenous peoples everywhere losing their homelands and their traditions as the contemporary world casually rolls over them with nary a backward glance. Fortunately, these battle zones do not represent the mainstream views of most people in the world, who generally follow a more moderate path. So, there is hope. Even as I wrote this section, two extremists and long-time foes, the Rev. Ian Paisley, representing the Protestant Democratic Unionist Party (DUP), and Gerry Adams of the Roman Catholic Irish Republican Army (IRA), sat down at a table together for the first time. They finally agreed to cooperate and form a coalition Protestant-Catholic government in Northern Ireland. We can only hope this attempt bears sweet and lasting fruit after so many centuries of the barren soil and bitter harvest of failed negotiations and unremitting violence. However, this type of good news is few and far between. Most often, it is the loud extremist, nationalist, and fundamentalist voices that capture the media's attention and trumpet the messages of intolerance. Amazingly, their planetary impact far outweighs their numbers, and their minority, radical message far overshadows the more moderate, tolerant, peaceful stance embraced by most people on the planet.[2] Our God is better (or bigger) than your God. Our soul is superior to your soul. Our way is the "right" way. Our way is the only way. We are the Chosen. We are better than you. We are good and you are evil. Them and Us. Us and Them. Them and Us. Us and Them.

Do we figure it out or do we destine ourselves to the living nightmare of future generations saddled with unending religious intolerance, hatred, and bigotry? Do we stay stuck in the soul-sucking quicksand of Us vs. Them, or do we free ourselves from the muck and discern there is no Us vs. Them, only Us and We. Moreover, if we remain mired in religious intolerance, egoism, and bigotry, we soon ascertain that it carries over into every significant challenge facing the planet today—poverty, environment, health, globalization, and human rights. It colors our views about the poor and oppressed, about men and women, about children and parents, about sexuality and sexual preference, about life and death, about nature, about power and greed, and even about racial and ethnic identity.

Gandhi once told an emotionally and mentally broken Hindu nationalist who had committed terrible acts against Muslims as revenge for the murder of his young son, "I know a way out of Hell."[3] I know a way out of Hell, also. Let us simply open our eyes and remember what all of the great spiritual teachers—Jeremiah, Jesus, Muhammad, Buddha, White Buffalo Calf Woman, Confucius, Isis, Krishna, Lao Tzu, Gandhi, and Mother Teresa—taught of tolerance, compassion, and love. This was

2. *Inside Islam: What a Billion Muslims Really Think* (Unity Productions, 2009). For example, in the 2009 Gallup Poll that covered most of the Islamic world, they discovered only 1% of all Muslims are militant, but that they receive the most media attention. Of Muslims covered by the media, 57% are militants. Hence, most of the Muslim world's true views and opinions are overshadowed by the militant minority.

3. Susanna Oommen Younger, "Gandhi: the Person and the Film," *Theology Today* 40:2 (July 1983): 172.

the God-given message they came to deliver. Have we listened? Have we believed that any one of them would have actually wanted us to go to war against a single brother and sister in their name or God's name? The answer is unequivocal. No!

Jesus said, "Love your enemies and pray for those who persecute you" (Matthew 5:44). Yet how many have died in the name of Jesus? Both Isaiah and Micah beseech us to do God's will for peace. "They shall beat their swords into plowshares, and their spears into pruning hooks; nation shall not lift up sword against nation, neither shall they learn war anymore" (Isaiah 2:4 and Micah 4:3). Muhammad's last sermon included the admonition that not only are all Muslims brothers, but:

> All of you are equal. All men, to whatever nation or tribe they may belong and whatever station in life they may hold, are equal. Even as the fingers of the two hands are equal, so are human beings equal to another.[4]

He adds that none can claim superiority over another person, including Arabs over non-Arabs and whites over blacks. Could he or any of these teachers be any clearer?

Universalism is the new religion of tolerance. It brings a message of hope and life. It is the Light of the World, the World of Light that we can be if we so choose, what many have called the Kingdom of God or the "Kin-dom of God." It is up to you and it is up to me. It is up to all of us to make better choices and truly follow the heart teachings of these many beautiful messengers of light, teachings mirrored in our own hearts. Let us begin.

New American Faces

Imagine a country whose paper money mirrors the changing population of its people. Let's imagine Jorge Washington staring up at us from a dollar bill, Ibrahim Lincoln's somber visage looking out from a five-dollar note, or Aleksi Hamilton's proud bearing residing on a ten-dollar denomination. This particular nation had already begun to recognize a long-neglected half of its population with Susan B. Anthony and Sacajawea dollar coins. Of course, that country is the United States. If it truly made these changes, they might more accurately reflect the changing face of America in the 21st century, rather than a hoary group of old white men from the

4. Quoted in Zahid Malik, "War and Peace," *Review of Religions* 88:5/6 (May/June 1993), http://www.alislam.org/library/links/war_peace.html.

18th and 19th centuries. Of course, we no longer need to imagine these changes. We had a president by the name of Barack Hussein Obama. He is an African American Christian of mixed racial parentage, carrying an African name, a Kenyan father, a Caucasian mother from Missouri, an African Muslim grandfather, and American grandparents who remind us of Auntie Em and Uncle Henry from *The Wizard of Oz*. It's quintessentially American. We have Washington, Jefferson, and Franklin bills. Depending on the long-term legacy of his presidency, why not someday an Obama bill? The times they are a' changin.'

As recently as 2003, it was widely reported that Hispanics are now the largest minority in the country.[5] Not only is the traditionally centrist population of White Anglo-Saxon Protestants (WASPs) the new minority, but by 2050, the Census Bureau tells us that non-Hispanic whites will only make up half of the population.[6] Moreover, 2000 Census Bureau statistics report that 11.5 percent of people living in the United States (32.5 million) are foreign-born[7], not including some estimated eleven million illegal immigrants[8]. However, the greatest surprise in our increasingly pluralistic, multicultural American stew is on the religious front. Pew Research Center finds that Americans do not fit into neat categories anymore.

> A new poll by the Pew Research Center's Forum on Religion and Public Life finds that large numbers of Americans engage in multiple religious practices, mixing elements of diverse traditions. Many say they attend worship services of more than one faith or denomination—even when they are not traveling or going to special events like weddings and funerals. Many also blend Christianity with Eastern or New Age beliefs such as reincarnation, astrology, and the presence of spiritual energy in physical objects.[9]

5. D'Vera Cohn, "Hispanics Declared Largest Minority," *Washington Post*, June 19 2003, sec. A, p. A:01.

6. U.S. Census Bureau, *Interim Projections of Age, Race, and Hispanic Origin* (Washington, D.C.: U.S. Census Bureau, Population Division, 2004), U.S. Government, 1, http://www.diversityresources.com/rc_sample/growth_uspop_hispanic.htm. (accessed February 12, 2006).

7. Dianne Schmidley, *The Foreign Born Population in the United States: March 2002* (Washington, D.C.: U.S. Census Bureau), U.S. Government, P20–539, 1, http://www.diversityresources.com/rc_sample/ForeignBornPop.pdf. (accessed February 12, 2006)

8. Robert Tanner, "Governors want Bush to tighten borders," *Miami Herald*, February 27 2006, sec. A, 3A.

9. Pew Forum on Religion and Public Life Survey, "Many Americans Mix Multiple Beliefs."

Diana Eck carries the point even further. She notes that, despite the rhetoric of the Moral Majority and the Christian Coalition over the past four decades, there is little awareness that the idea of "Christian America" does not mirror the new religious America—"the one Christians now share with Muslims, Buddhists, and Zoroastrians."[10] To completely unmask the Christian illusion, she accentuates the point:

> We are surprised to find that there are more Muslim Americans than Episcopalians, more Muslims than members of the Presbyterian Church USA, and as many Muslims as there are Jews—that is about six million. We are astonished to learn that Los Angeles is the most complex Buddhist City in the world, with a Buddhist population spanning the whole range of the Asian Buddhist world from Sri Lanka to Korea, along with a multitude of native-born American Buddhists. Nationwide, this whole spectrum of Buddhists may number about four million.[11]

Adding savory spice to that simmering religious stew is an entirely postmodern way of individualistic thinking that challenges all religions and institutions today. Two of my undergraduate religion students unconsciously summarized this sea change in perspective from the Modern to Postmodern Era[12] far better than I could have in a paper on "Defining the Role of Religion." The first, a twenty-year-old Caucasian woman who was raised Roman Catholic and is still devoted to her faith, wrote:

> It seems like almost every religion has its own special understanding of the world and our place in it, but not one fully agrees with the other. I would like to make my own decisions from now on as to what I believe to be true, what my values are, and according to what ideals I live my life . . . I don't think that people have to go to "church" every Sunday, but I do believe that people should *live* their religion. So, in other words, you don't have to attend your religious functions; you can do whatever you want, just live according to *your* word, and be sincere about that with yourself.[13]

10. Diana L. Eck, *A New Religious America* (San Francisco: Harper, 2001), 4.

11. Ibid, 2–3.

12. The Modern and Postmodern Eras are defined and discussed on pages 8–13.

13. Apryl Wall, "Defining the Role of Religion," *Religion: Analysis and Interpretation* (Miami: Florida International University, January 2006), 1/4. This is an unpublished undergraduate student paper.

The second student, a nineteen-year-old Hispanic woman, also a devout Roman Catholic, wrote:

> . . . I am a truly religious person, and, moreover, my religion is a substantial part of my life. In my personal point of view, religion is every part of who I am today. Furthermore, religion is a private matter in that it deals with individual beliefs, ideas, morality, and basically, faith. Religion is my personal outlook based on a combination of various aspects, as something that is inside of me, and therefore only I fully understand, as each individual can only understand his/her own "religion."[14]

Similar sentiments have echoed throughout my students' papers for several years now. No one is going to tell them what to do or what to believe anymore, and yet, many very much wish to remain within spiritual community. Being true to Buddhist form, with an expected twist of "no doctrine," the Dalai Lama once said:

> The most important thing is practice in daily life; then you can know gradually the true value of religion. Doctrine is not meant for mere knowledge, but for the improvement of our minds. In order to do that, it must be part of our life. If you put religious doctrine in a building and, when you leave the building, depart from the practices, you cannot gain its value.[15]

In these times, religion is becoming an individual experience of daily practical, personal revelation as much as it is a communal experience.

Message or Messenger

A final introductory thought revolves around questions I often ask my *World Religions* students: What is the real message of their churches, temples, and mosques? What were their religion's founders actually teaching and messaging? I usually receive the familiar doctrinal responses that reflect their personal religious background. Then, I ask them why it seems to be a human need to always place our great teachers on pedestals, just as we do our sports stars, rock stars, and Hollywood celebrities today. Yet,

14. Michelle Escobar, "Defining the Role of Religion," *Religion: Analysis and Interpretation* (Miami: Florida International University, January 2006), 2. This is an unpublished undergraduate student paper.

15. Dalai Lama, *A Policy of Kindness*, "A Talk with Western Buddhists," ed. Sidney Piburn (Ithaca: Snow Lion Publications, 1993), 843.

these intensely humble people wanted nothing of the sort. They were utterly disinterested in self-aggrandizement, power, politics, glory, fame, or wealth. Nonetheless, we attempt to make them more than human, super humans even, despite their protests to the contrary.

I finish my point by asking: If you are a Christian, what would you do if you learned beyond any doubt that Jesus was not born of a virgin birth and that he was a great prophet and Wisdom Teacher—and not the Son of God, any more than any of us are sons and daughters of God? If you are Muslim, what if you discovered, again beyond a shadow of a doubt, that two angels did not really come down when he was five and purify his heart from darkness by washing it with snow? And, if you are Buddhist, what if it was revealed beyond question that Siddhartha (the Buddha) was not really born speaking and walking with lotus blossoms growing in his footsteps? Would this shake your faith to the core? Would you find it hard to keep faith in your faith? Most of my students say it would not change their faith. Many of my students "get it." The message was always supposed to be about the message. The message wasn't supposed to be about the messenger. The messenger is not the message. All three religions proclaimed in their own profound way that the message is about love and community. What would Jesus, Muhammad, and Buddha feel today if they saw how their clear and straightforward call to loving action had been so misinterpreted and misplaced by the institutions that grew out of their teachings? They really would want to attend that Spiritual Masters Conference in Los Angeles and set the record straight.

CHAPTER 4

Escaping the Sheeple Herd

We are entering "postmodernity," an as yet ill-defined borderland in which central modern values like objectivity, analysis, and control will become less compelling. They are being superseded by postmodern values like mystery and wonder.

ANDY CROUCH

New Age

WE ARE UNEASILY STEPPING into a new age, although it is not the New Age of the spiritual pop culture contemporary society stereotypes like crystal shops, colorful candles, moon goddess dances, and Buddha statues. That is very much a part of the transition, but it is much more profound than that. It is a crossover from the Modern Age to the Postmodern Age. What we call the "Modern Era" surfaced some 500 years ago with The Age of Enlightenment and the resultant Industrial Revolution.[1] It was a powerful counterpunch to the iron fist of Holy Mother Church. For some 1500 years, the Church had demanded blind faith and unquestioning adherence to its doctrine and dogma. It had little stomach for the discoveries of the newly born sciences, many of which contradicted church teachings

1. Joseph Holland, "The Evolution of Modern Industrial-Capitalist Society and the Birth of the Postmodern Electronic-Ecological Era," in *The Association for the Sociology of Religion Annual Conference Held in Pittsburg, Pennsylvania, August 18, 1992*, (London: The Centre for the Study of Communications and Culture, 1992), 14–16, 31–33.

about nature and creation. For example, in 1610, after looking through his telescope many thousands of times, Galileo formulated the controversial notion that the Earth was not the center of the universe.[2] Cardinal Robert Bellarmine (1542–1621) marshaled the papal opposition to Galileo and the findings of his new telescope by reminding:

> . . . his tempted brothers that Saint Augustine himself had argued that the literal meaning of Scripture should always be taken as correct, unless the contrary was "strictly demonstrated." Since man's everyday experience "tells him plainly that the earth is standing still," and, from, the nature of the case, the rotation of the earth and its revolutions around the sun could not be "strictly demonstrated," the literal scriptures must be defended. King Solomon's observation that the sun "returns to its place" must mean precisely what he said.[3]

Prior to the Enlightenment, those who questioned the church's authority were most often executed as heretics. Galileo was one of the lucky ones. Because he was so well known, one of the greatest minds of the last millennium was not executed by the Inquisition but remained under house arrest for the rest of his life.

In response to this anti-scientific and authoritarian environment, a new movement of reason and science emerged. As Gavin Hyman suggests, Modernity "is the desire for an all-encompassing mastery of reality by rational and/or scientific means."[4] It was the Age of Empiricism (also known as the Scientific Revolution and the Age of Reason), which eschewed the non-rational and non-scientific. Under its tutelage, we witnessed the miracles of the Industrial Revolution and mass production, flight, global communication, evolving democracies, journeys to the moon, and harnessing the atom. However, as we progressed through the 20th century, things began to shift gradually. People began to view themselves and their world differently. As Jean-François Lyotard pointed out, the presumed absolute, sole legitimacy of knowledge and science was starting to wear thin.[5] Science and reason as "Supreme Authorities" were not selling so well. It had not prevented two devastating world wars, Hiroshima and the unblinking terror of a Nuclear Age, the irrational

2. Daniel Boorstein, *The Discoverers* (New York: Random House, 1983), 319–326.

3. Ibid, 323.

4. Gavin Hyman, *The Predicament of Postmodern Theology* (Louisville: Westminster John Knox Press, 2001), 11–19.

5. Ibid, 15.

Nazi madness of the Holocaust,[6] or 911. Countering views and alternative ways of thinking began to emerge. These were eventually labeled postmodern, although there is a hodgepodge of related terms, such as poststructural, deconstructionist, anti-foundationalist, post-metaphysics, and so on.[7] Just as modernity moved us from the feudal medieval to the modern scientific mind, postmodernity seems to be another of the inevitable evolutionary or revolutionary responses to a historical era or movement that has run its course.

Within the art world, the term "postmodern" was first coined in the 1930s by Spanish artist Federico de Onis. It became identified as a movement in the 1960s and 1970s, particularly within literature, philosophy, and architecture. Theorists, such as Lyotard, asserted we had moved from scientific to narrative knowledge.[8] A significant aspect of this postmodern movement was how it challenged Structuralism. As Finlayson and Valentine note:

> Structuralism assumes that everything has its place and fits together. Social change is simply a matter of readjustment through which societies and their orderings are reproduced . . . It is in the rejection of this a priori assumption of order that post-structuralist analysis (as well as the ethics and politics it implies) emerges.[9]

This poststructural movement contended that traditional philosophical, historical, and social science perspectives (Structuralism) were outdated. The traditional outlook of Structuralism is that language, myth, history, and other social structures are relatively stable and unchanging. In much of human history, this is certainly understandable since change happened very slowly. Until recently, little, if anything, changed in the average person's lifetime.

Then came the 20th century, where people saw more change occur than had been observed in all of human history up to that point. From the birth of human flight at Kitty Hawk to "the Eagle has landed" on

6. Theodor Adorno and Max Horkheimer belonged to the Frankfurt School of Critical Theory, which challenged the notion of Western rational thought since the Enlightenment. Their book, *Dialect of Enlightenment*, particularly focused on the Nazi horrors.

7. Alan Finlayson and Jeremy Valentine, "Introduction" in *Politics and Post-Structuralism: An Introduction* (Edinburgh: Edinburgh University Press, 2002), 2.

8. Hyman, 13–16.

9. Finlayson and Valentine, 11.

the moon—all in one lifetime. What Structuralism ignored is the simple fact that in any system, be it culture, territory, language, family, or government, the limits (boundaries) in the system are the actual defining point for and the core of the knowledge about that system. As James Williams summarizes this contention, ". . . any settled form of knowledge or moral good is made by its limits and cannot be defined independently of them."[10] This is not as complicated as it sounds. How could we determine a country without knowing its limits, its borders, and boundaries? How marriage is delimited is related to country, culture, and time in history, so in some places, monogamy is the only accepted form, and in others, polygamy is the norm. If marriage goes beyond the accepted limits, such as bigamy and child marriage in the United States, the marriage is not valid or legal. Yet, it does not always have a consistent parameter. In most states and cities in the United States, marriage by law could historically only be between a man and a woman—except for the growing number of states and towns where same-sex marriages were now legal. And, with the June 26, 2015 ruling by the Supreme Court, it is now the law of the land. In these and a multitude of other examples, it is impossible to remove the limits imposed by history, or culture, or geography, or population growth and shifts from the way a society, language, social norms, government, or marketplace evolve over time.

What is stable truth and knowledge in this system? If truth and knowledge were that stable and remained unrelated to historical and social context, then we might still be oral societies unheeding of the written word; most of the world might still be ruled by kings and queens; it might still be socially permissible for conquering armies to sack, loot and rape free of international outrage; and the question of gay marriage and transgender rights might never have even surfaced. Structuralism makes room for change in an additive way, allowing for changes in how a system is structured as more knowledge is amassed. But it misses the point that change is the core of any structure in question, and that core is defined by its limits.[11] It is an open-ended way of viewing where something begins and ends, what is possible and what is not possible in a particular society, group, or time period.

Boiling water does not gently transition to steam. Rather, at the level of the water molecules, there is a seething, roiling mix attempting to

10. James Williams, *Understanding Poststructuralism* (Chesham: Acumen Publishing, 2005), 2.

11. Ibid, 1–2.

remain relatively stable as liquid water in the face of higher energy (heat) pouring into the system. That energy creates so much movement that some of the molecules cannot maintain this stability. They become chaotic and unpredictable. The boundaries holding them together break down. It is at this tipping point between Stability and Chaos, the edge of chaos, that violent, disruptive change occurs. Voilà! We have steam. According to the new Complexity Theory in science, this border between stability and instability is where all change surfaces, whether it is the stock market, social revolutions, an argument, or a human cell dividing in mitosis.[12] This is a perfect metaphor for Poststructuralism. Consequently, poststructuralism rather defiantly champions the disruption of complacently held "settled truths" and considers disruption to be a form of positive advocacy for change in the face of social ills and rigid doctrines.[13] As we will denote later, this is also why Liberation Theology is at its core a postmodern and poststructuralist movement.

In theology, the movement engendered an intense, even fierce deconstructionist debate from the 1960s onward, beginning with Thomas Altizer's "Death of God Movement."[14] Deconstructionists began to question everything in modernity, taking an anti-worldview and savagely tearing down artistic, literary, philosophical, metaphysical, and theological conventions from the leaves and branches to the roots. It was an attempt to discern and dismantle the assumptions that laid behind these supposedly antiquated belief systems while frequently deriding those assumptions simultaneously.[15] According to Gavin Hyman, for Jacques Derrida and other postmodern deconstructionists:

> Postmodernism is a philosophy of difference. It universalizes difference and accentuates it so as to denounce naïve assumptions of unity, Universalism, and totality.[16]

12. M. Mitchell Waldrop, *Complexity: The Emerging Science at the Edge of Order and Chaos* (New York: Touchstone, 1992), 9–12.

13. Williams, 3–4.

14. Nancy Murphy and James W. McClendon, Jr., "Distinguishing Modern and Postmodern Theologies" in *Modern Theology* 5:3 (April 1989), 210; and Charles J. Sabatino, "The Death of God: A Symbol of Religious Humanism" *Horizons* 10:2 (Fall 1983), 289.

15. Frederick Ferre, *Knowing and Value: Toward a Constructive Postmodern Theology* with an introduction by David Ray Griffin (Albany: State University of New York Press, 1998), xvi and 270.

16. Anselm Kyongsuk Min, *The Solidarity of Others in a Divided World* (New York: T & T Clark International, 2004), 66.

Although much of early postmodern theology was deconstructionist, not all postmodern theologians dwelled under this tent. For example, Harvey Cox studied the Base Ecclesial Communities begun in Latin America and concluded that they are a genuine postmodern endeavor. These Base Communities are an outgrowth of Liberation Theology initiated in the 1960s after Vatican II's pastoral initiative. They gave poor and oppressed people a spiritual means to come together as an activist community and advocate for change, whether it was constructing a well for their village, petitioning their government for a medical clinic, or demanding the right to vote.[17] Unlike the backward-looking fundamentalist movement, the base communities movement is forward-looking, and it was the issue of community that led Cox to this conclusion. He believes they are creating a new style of "selfhood and community life." It is no coincidence that Cox also views Liberation Theology as a new and postmodern approach to reason and theology.[18]

Frederick Ferre advances a step further. While acknowledging the uneasy alliance with his deconstructionist postmodern bedfellows, he sets forth what he calls a postmodern constructive approach,[19] delineated by David Griffin here:

> It seeks to overcome the modern world view not by eliminating the possibilities of world views as such, but by constructing a postmodern worldview through a revision of modern premises and traditional concepts. This constructive or revisionary postmodernism involves a new unity of scientific, ethical, aesthetic, and religious intuitions. It rejects not science as such but only that scientism in which the data of the modern natural sciences are alone allowed to contribute to the construction of our world view.[20]

Rather than attempting to destroy and discard all that is modern, constructive postmodernism wishes to ensure that the great advances of Modernity are not lost while ushering them into a postmodern world with "postmodern persons, with a postmodern spirituality, on the one hand, and a postmodern society, ultimately a postmodern global order,

17. Andre Dawson, "The Origins and Character of the Base Ecclesial Community: A Brazilian Perspective" in *Liberation Theology*, ed. Christopher Rowland (Cambridge: University Press, 1999), 113–114, 118.

18. Murphy and McClendon, 208–209.

19. Ferre, 270.

20. Ibid, xvi.

on the other."[21] He believes this "postmodern constructive thought" will provide a foundation for the emancipatory movements of our time, such as ecology, peace, and feminism.[22]

From a more spiritually constructionist perspective, Joseph Holland views postmodernity as expressing:

> . . . the principle of holistic or communitarian creativity (or co-creativity)—a synthesis of the 'feminine' and 'masculine' dimensions of humanity's subjective depth and objective power, both participating in the mystery of Divine creativity."[23]

His is not the lone Christian constructionist voice. Brian McLaren's 2001 book *A New Kind of Christian* fostered the Emergent Church among conservative, evangelical Christians. Andy Crouch sums up the feelings of one of McLaren's central characters, Neo, as:

> We are entering "postmodernity," an as yet ill-defined borderland in which central modern values like objectivity, analysis, and control will become less compelling. They are being superseded by postmodern values like mystery and wonder. The controversial implication is that forms of Christianity that have thrived in modernity . . . are unlikely to survive the transition.[24]

McLaren has little patience for arguments "that pit absolutism versus relativism, and objectivism versus subjectivism." He believes they have little relevance for postmoderns,[25] and his is clearly a refreshing voice for postmodern constructionists who are likewise weary of this dreary, no-win debate.

Any way that you slice it, Universalism is plainly postmodern and post-structural, but it is not deconstructionist. It is a constructive postmodern spiritual venture with compelling connections to the values of "mystery and wonder." Rather than denigrating or rejecting traditional religions and churches from the modern mainstream, it constructs a new

21. Ferre, xvi-xvii.

22. Ibid., xvii.

23. Holland, "The Evolution of Modern Industrial-Capitalist Society . . . ," 14–16, 31–33.

24. Andy Crouch, "The Emergent Mystique," *Christianity Today* 48:11 (November 2004), 38–39.

25. From a Brian McLaren speech, "Issues of Truth and Power: the Gospel in a Post-Christian Culture," Billy Graham Center, summarized in "Emergent Evangelism," *Christianity Today* 48:11 (November 2004), 42.

way to view religion, spirituality, and self-in-community. It is adding to rather than taking from. It is inclusive rather than exclusive. And it is doing this within the heart of *koinonia,* a Greek word used in the New Testament. It is variously translated as participation, fellowship, unity, contribution, sharing, association, communion, close relationship, and communication.[26] Universalism only works as a spiritual *koinonia* community. It is a community of unique individuals in oneness who are aware of the interconnectedness of all things.

The Universalist Church

The terms "Universalist" and "Universal Church" are misunderstood by many and have taken on any number of conflicting meanings. Consequently, it is essential to define Universalism. Just by doing a Google search on the Internet or a book search on Amazon, upon entering the search terms "Universalism," "Universal Church," or "Universalist," one soon discovers that all of the references relate to the Quaker Society of Friends, the Unity Church,[27] or the 18th century Universalist Church of America, which later merged with the Unitarian Universalist Church in 1961.[28] One can quickly see the inherent problem here. These are all Christian denominations, although clearly on the margins of mainstream Christianity. For example, The Universalist Church of America, which founded Tufts University, was a Protestant denomination that came to believe in the controversial notion that salvation was universal; that all of humanity was saved by Jesus.[29] In recent years, the Unitarian Universalist Church has moved even deeper into Universalist waters, significantly beyond its Christian origins. Nonetheless, purely Universalist churches

26. Commission on Theology and Church Relations of the Lutheran Church: Missouri Synod, "Project Wittenberg: The Nature and Implications of the Concept of Fellowship," April 1981, http://www.iclnet.org/pub/resources/text/wittenberg/mosynod/web/fellow-2.html; and Robin Greenwood, "Ordering the Church for Working with God's Life in the World," Society for Promoting Christian Knowledge, 2002, http://ministry.ireland.anglican.org/articles/greenwood.pdf.

27. Unity Online, "Who We Are," (accessed March 20, 2008), http://www.unityonline.org/aboutunity/whoWeAre/index.html.

28. Unitarian Universalist, Association of Congregations, "History of Unitarian Universalism" (accessed March 20, 2008), http://www.unityonline.org/aboutunity/whoWeAre/index.html.

29. *The Columbia Encyclopedia*, "Universalist Church of America," Sixth Edition (2001–2008), http://www.bartleby.com/65/un/UnvrslCh.html.

are still separated from the more traditional Christian-based Universalist churches. For example, when I mention that I pastor a Universalist church, Christian ministers and theologians invariably ask if it is Unitarian or the Unity Church. Universalism that is not based within Judeo-Christian foundations is not a tradition that has gained widespread recognition in this country, so this book gains added impetus as it marks the birth and progression of a newer postmodern spiritual venture.

If there is a grandmother of Universalism beyond Christianity in the West, that would have to be Madame Helena P. Blavatsky (1831–1891). In New York in 1875, the famous Russian medium founded The Theosophical Society. The spiritual work of Madame Blavatsky and her European colleagues in Tibet and India introduced much of the Western World to Hindu, Yogic, Tibetan, and Buddhist mysticism. They also incorporated the teachings and beliefs of many Greek, Egyptian, and Christian esoteric philosophers.[30] This movement spawned many others, among them Rudolf Steiner's Anthroposophy,[31] Alice Bailey's Arcane School,[32] Guy Ballard's I AM Movement,[33] and John and Clare Prophet's Summit Lighthouse.[34] Even the Dalai Lama has had a warm relationship with The Theosophical Society since 1956.[35]

There is no question that a Universalist church will be influenced by these New Age prophets and utilize some of their philosophical and theological ideas. Two of these are the concepts of the "I AM," what we consider to be the highest aspect of God presence within us; and the Ascended Masters, great spiritual teachers who guide us from the higher realms, such as Jesus, Buddha, Mother Mary, Kuan Yin, White Buffalo Calf Woman, Hermes Trismegistus, Isis, and so on. Yet, as Madame Blavatsky

30. Eck, 181–82; and Helena P. Blavatsky, "What is Theosophy?" in *Theosophy Library Online*, http://www.theosophy.org/tlodocs/WhatIsTheosophy.htm.

31. *Steiner Books, Anthroposophic Press*, "About Rudolf Steiner," accessed January 2006, http://www.steinerbooks.org/aboutrudolf.html.

32. Lucis Trust, "About the Arcane School" (accessed March 20, 2008), http://www.lucistrust.org/en/arcane_school/introduction/about_the_arcane_school.

33 Religious Movements Project, "'I AM' Religious Activity." (Charlottesville: University of Virginia, 1997), 1, http://religiousmovements.lib.virginia.edu/nrms/iam.html.

34. Religious Movements Project, "Church Universal and Triumphant." (Charlottesville: University of Virginia, 1997), 1, http://religiousmovements.lib.virginia.edu/nrms/cut.html.

35. Dalai Lama Tenzin Gyatso, *The Opening of the Wisdom Eye* (Wheaton: Quest Books, 1966), vi.

reminds us, these were ancient teachings long pre-dating Theosophy.[36] So, it is only natural that a Universalist church builds upon many different traditions, including these. At the same time, a Universalist church is profoundly influenced by the core wisdom teachings of the central Eastern and Western religions, especially their founders and principal prophets, with an added deep appreciation of Native American spirituality.

Seen in this light, Universalism is unashamedly a syncretistic religion, although we might add that syncretism[37] is found in all faiths. It is a natural state of evolution that a religion is influenced by and blends with other religious traditions over time. How many examples do we need? The Neoplatonist (Greek) influence on Christian theology in the early church. Christmas and Easter practices (the Christmas Tree; Yule Log; Christmastime, formerly a Winter Solstice and Roman Celebration; Caroling; the Easter Bunny; Easter Eggs; and so on) which are entirely Native European Celtic and Greco-Roman pagan-based traditions. Christian services on "Sun Day," instead of the traditional Jewish Sabbath (Saturday), in order to adapt to the *Sol Invictus* practices of the large Roman population who became Christians in the early church. The co-opting of the *Hymn to Isis* by the early Christian Church and changing it to the *Hymn to Mary*. We can go on, but the point is made and demonstrates that syncretism is not just a New Age phenomenon.

To someone unfamiliar with Universalist traditions, then, they might be confused as to how the diverse individual strands of this theological weaving might ever come together. If we could borrow as metaphor a Native American totem animal,[38] *Iktomi*, the spider, we would note that, like her, Universalists are weaving an intricate web with many strands coming together in perfect sacred geometry and harmony. This book will follow the individual strands as they are woven together into a circular web pattern that illustrates the increasing interrelatedness and interlacing of theology and practice, of people and faith, of teaching and learning.

36. Blavatsky, "What is Theosophy?."

37. Syncretism is the influence of and blending with other religious traditions. It occurs through interactions with neighbors and trading partners, intermarriage across cultures and clans, conquest (conqueror and conquered both influence each other), and immigration.

38. Since all forms of life (animals, plants, minerals, elements, and celestial bodies) can be teachers and guides in Native American and shamanic tradition, a totem animal is a personal spiritual guide.

Here, then, is a clear, simple definition of Universalism: *God has spoken to and come to all the peoples of the earth in various human, earthly, and spiritual forms, through various means of revelation, and over many sacred pathways—all with an eye toward human growth and spiritual enlightenment.*

There is an old Tibetan Buddhist line we heartily endorse: "There are a million pathways to God." To Ramakrishna, the great 19th century Hindu saint, God seems to exist as a single reality behind all religions where all their truths become one.[39] Mahatma Gandhi summed it up neatly when confronted by an angry Hindu nationalist. "I am a Muslim, I am a Hindu, I am a Christian, I am a Jew—and so are all of you."[40] One of our church members added, "Universalism is relevant to anybody and everybody, anytime and every time, anywhere and everywhere."[41] So, if you ask why one would become a Universalist, I would simply answer, "Because God, the creator of all nations and the universe,[42] is a Universalist."

39. Lewis M. Hopfe and Mark R. Woodward, *Religions of the World* (Upper Saddle River: Prentice Hall, 2001), 102.

40. "Mahatma Gandhi: A Century of Peaceful Protest," *Mahatma Gandhi News Digest*, ed. Peter Ruhe, 11–17, September 2006, http://www.gandhiserve.org/news/mgnd/news200609110917.html.

41. Deborah McGinnis, "The Church of the Way of the Messiahs," interview by Thomas Norris, January 21, 2006.

42. For Isaiah knew this as well, when he said, "My house shall be called a house of prayer for all peoples." (Is: 56:7) There are numerous other references to God as the Creator of all nations and all things in the Hebrew Bible or Tanakh (Old Testament) and the New Testament, for example: Isaiah 40:28, 42:5; Job 38–41; the story of Jonah and his mission to the people of Nineveh, the Assyrian enemy of the Israelites; Psalm 148; John 1:3; Acts 10:34–35; Romans 1:20; Colossians 1:16; Hebrews 11:3; and Revelation 4:11, 10:6.

CHAPTER 5

Why be a Universalist? Because God is a Universalist.

And there are diversities of operations, but it is the same God which worketh all in all.

ST. PAUL, 1 CORINTHIANS 12:6

Even as the fingers of the two hands are equal, so are human beings equal to one another. No one has any right, nor any preference, to claim over another.

MUHAMMAD, *LAST SERMON*

Creative Tension Between Christian and Universalist

THERE IS A PLETHORA of literature on the new spiritual movements from Christian writers of all stripes. Although useful and sometimes insightful, much of this literature quickly betrays its bias through outright attacks from conservative evangelistic and fundamentalist groups.[1] They often lump them in with cults and disparagingly refer to them as NRMs

1. Erwin W. Lutzer, *Satan's Evangelistic Strategy for the New Age* (Wheaton: Victor Books, 1989), 24–25; Mitch Pacwa, *Catholics and the New Age* (Ann Arbor: Servant Publications, 1992), 191; and James J. LeBar, *Cults, Sects, and the New Age* (Huntington, Indiana: Our Sunday Visitor Publishing, 1989), 21.

(New Religious Movements),[2] to a somewhat more condescending attitude from relatively liberal sources.[3] Even the Vatican has weighed in on the topic, and despite its relatively accurate and thoughtful pontifical report, ends up cautioning Christians to beware:

> Some local New Age groups refer to their meetings as "prayer groups." Those people who are invited to such groups need to *look for the marks of genuine Christian spirituality*, and to be wary if there is any sort of initiation ceremony. Such groups take advantage of a person's lack of theological or spiritual formation to lure them gradually into what may in fact be a form of false worship.[4]

These Christian writers tend to minimize the sincere, genuine devotional, and spiritual experiences of these groups. It's as if that is an exclusively Christian territory, while they also generally perceive little that links these new postmodern spiritual happenings to Judeo-Christian traditions. As Carol Becker points out, this occurs because there is the human tendency "to put ourselves in the center of the universe and others on the fringe." She calls this an egocentric, geocentric, even "Christocentric" perspective that undermines an objective viewing of other religious experiences.[5] Consequently, newer spiritual movements have generally not been taken seriously by mainstream religions and denominations. Yet, many of these mainstream Christian churches have incorporated or "rediscovered" the spiritual practices and traditions of many of these groups, such as meditation, candlelight services, angelology, hands-on healing, and light symbology. We might add that some Christian groups are quietly ignoring their own history of interest in metaphysics, such as the prominent clergy called the Protestant Experimentalists in the early 20th century. They delved scientifically into telepathy, psychic healing,

2. Lorne L. Dawson, "Who Joins Religious Movements and Why: Twenty Years of Research and What We Have Learned" in *Cults and New Religious Movements*. ed. Lorne L. Dawson (Oxford: Blackwell, 2001), 116–119.

3. Harmon Hartzel Bro, "New Age Spirituality: A Critical Appraisal" in *New Age Spirituality*, ed. Duncan S. Ferguson (Louisville: Westminster John Knox Press, 1993), 194–95.

4. Pontifical Council for Culture and Pontifical Council of Interreligious Dialog, *Jesus Christ, The Bearer of the Water of Life: A Christian Reflection on the 'New Age'* (Vatican City: The Vatican), accessed January 2006, http://www.vatican.va/roman_curia/pontifical_councils/interelg/documents/rc_pc_interelg_doc_20030203_new-age_en.html.

5. Carol E. Becker, "In Any Age: Can We Hear God?," in *New Age Spirituality*, ed. Duncan S. Ferguson (Louisville: Westminster/John Knox Press, 1993), 22.

and other psychic energy research.[6] On top of this, there is a considerable amount of ignorance about postmodern spiritual movements, such as Universalism. For example, it seems to be a common conviction that they are new movements, an outgrowth of the drug-addled 1960s.[7] However, as we have seen, their modern roots delve deeply into the mid-19th century—with ancient roots reaching back further, perhaps beyond even the Old and New Testaments.[8] Fortunately, theologians and religious studies scholars are beginning to take notice, as evidenced by the September 2007 *Journal of the American Academy of Religion*, which devoted a large portion of the issue to American metaphysics. According to Catherine Albanese, it is the third religious force in American history, living alongside the other two, mainstream denominational Christianity and evangelicalism, where "numbers of Americans by the mid- and late-19th century had embraced it.[9] Finally, I might note that each of the founders of many of the great religions, including Buddha, Jesus, and Muhammad, were also viewed with great suspicion by the religious authorities of their time. Even though they were reformers, they were perceived to be cult leaders, revolutionaries, and heretics, even apostates. Their traditionalist opponents minimized the devout sincerity of their work and message and frequently attacked them as frauds and false prophets

The New Dialog

As this book first took form, I expressed the hope that it would lay the groundwork for inspired dialog and mutual tolerance. That it would be a passionate, shared message from Jesus and his Universalist sisters and brothers to the Christian community.[10] As a Universalist, I would now amend that passage to include all peoples and traditions. It is our

6. Pamela E. Klassen, "Radio Mind: Protestant Experimentalists on the Frontiers of Healing" *Journal of the American Academy of Religion* 77:3 (September 2007): 652, 672–675.

7. Steven J. Sutcliffe, *Children of the New Age* (New York: Routledge, 2003), 27–28.

8. Morton Kelsey, "The Former Age and the New Age: The Perennial Quest for the Spiritual Life" in *New Age Spirituality*, ed. Duncan S. Ferguson (Louisville: Westminster John Knox Press, 1993), 52–54.

9. Catherine L. Albanese, "Introduction: Awash in a Sea of Metaphysics" *Journal of the American Academy of Religion* 75:3 (September 2007): 582–583.

10. Thomas Norris, "Sociological Methodologies: The New Age and Christianity" (Miami: Florida Center for Theological Studies, 2003), 2.

conviction that one crucial message of Universalism supports Jesus' central message, what he called the greatest commandment: "You shall love the Lord your God with all of your heart, and with all your soul, and with all your mind, and with all your strength." Then, he added, "You shall love your neighbor as yourself. There is no greater commandment than these" (Mark 12:30–31).

In this light, as Universalists, we express love and gratitude for God as the Divine Creator; love and gratitude for Creation as the divine gift; love and gratitude for each other as the wondrous children of God; and love and gratitude for ourselves as a beautiful son or daughter of God. Another way to put it is that we honor and bear witness to the miracle of the Creator and Creation. It is in the way we express our love for the Creator, self, and others in the community of Creation (*koinonia*[11] or communal brotherhood and sisterhood). It is in the way we live our lives (*martyria*,[12] or witnessing to and living the message of the Kingdom of God). It is in the way we act toward the Creator and Creation through service and justice to the Created (*diakonia*,[13] or service and social justice).[14] The beauty is that this is not just a Christian message or Jesus' message alone. We have come across similar messages of love and enlightenment among many of the great teachers of the Divine that have come to Planet Earth. For example, in the 6th century BCE, Confucius averred in his principle of reciprocity, *shu*, "What you do not wish others should do unto you, do not do unto them."[15] Muhammad likewise noted:

> Do not say, that if people do good to us, we will do good to them; and if people oppress us, we will oppress them; but determine, that if people do you good, you will do good to them; and if they oppress you, you will not oppress them.[16]

11. Commission on Theology and Church Relations of the Lutheran Church—Missouri Synod.

12. Vernard Eller, *The Most Revealing Book of the Bible* (Grand Rapids: Wm. B. Eerdmans, 1974), 1, http://www.hccentral.com/eller7/index.html.

13. Myra Blyth and Wendy S. Robins, *No Boundaries to Compassion? An Exploration of Women, Gender and Diakonia* (Geneva: World Council of Churches Program Unit on Sharing and Service, 1998), http://www.wcc-coe.org/wcc/what/regional/compas.html.

14. These three Greek words from the Christian New Testament are considered to be the foundation pillars for much of Christian theological thought and action.

15. Confucius, *The Wisdom of Confucius*, trans. Lin Yutang (New York: Modern Library, 1966), 110.

16. Abdullah Al-Mamun Al-Suhrawardy, "Of the Duty of Believers, 118" in *The Wisdom of Muhammad* (New York: Citadel Press, 2001), 64.

Similarly, Rabbi Hillel, in the 1st century CE, declared, "What is hateful to you, do not do to your fellow creature. That is the whole law; the rest is commentary."[17] Of course, the Golden Rule sounds familiar, just as it was similarly quoted from the Torah (Leviticus 17:18) by Rabbi Jesus. "In everything, do to others as you would have them do to you; for this is the law and the prophets" (Matthew 7:12). These and many other deep-seated universal truths are the alpha and omega of Universalist theology.

Consequently, some of the light this book hopes to shed will substantiate that there are clear and strong links between Judeo-Christian and Islamic principles of tolerance and justice and Universalism. Since little has been written from the Universalist side, this book will point out the connections while also defining, outlining, and delineating how Universalism fits within the ranks of legitimate 21st century religious expression. It is time to make the first sketch and fill in the blank spaces of ignorance, speculation, and ideological suspicion. I am not so naïve as to imagine that Christians, Jews, Muslims, and people of other faiths will now overwhelmingly embrace Universalist principles once this book answers some of their fundamental questions. Nonetheless, as noted earlier, I hope that it will lay the groundwork for inspired dialog and mutual tolerance.

Mitakuye Oyasin (All Our Relations)

It would be a typically Eurocentric blindness to ignore the rest of the world beyond Christianity, Judaism, and Islam. However, since Universalism owes so much to these wonderful other traditions, I will not make that mistake. One way to couch this is to determine where the common ground is, or as we put it, where the bridges are to understanding between religions, cultures, and indigenous traditions.

As the book progresses through the following chapters, you will see the development of a Universalist theology that embraces all religions and cultures. If each religion represents a brick in the foundation of a spiritual house, then a number of bricks will correspond to the foundations of Judaism, Christianity, and Islam. Likewise, as many bricks will be formed

17. Hillel, *Talmud, b. Sabb.31a*; quoted in Robert A. Guleich, "The Golden Rule" *The Oxford Companion to the Bible*, ed. Bruce M. Metzger and Michael D. Coogan (New York: Oxford University Press, 1993), 257.

from Hinduism, Buddhism, Jainism, Sikhism, Confucianism, Taoism, and other Asian spiritual traditions. Similarly, Zoroastrian, Baha'i, Sufi, and Ancient Mystery Religions from Egypt, Persia, and Greece will not be ignored. At the same time, the bricks that all of these later religions were originally built on are indispensable to the final structure, including the Shamanic and indigenous traditions (Native American, Native Australian, Native African, Native European, Native Asian, Native Islander, and Arctic Peoples), Neopagan (Celtic, Wiccan, and Druidic traditions), and Goddess religions,[18] as well as Ancient Mystery Schools.[19] In the end, this structure becomes the House of Humankind; we could also call it the "House of God." If this spiritual home is missing any of its foundational bricks, then the whole structure is weakened, for the Creator embraces all of its Creations. None are excluded; all are part of the One. We often say God is the Many and the One, and the One and the Many.

To emphasize the importance of finding the bridges, let us take ecology as one example of a venomous challenge facing the whole world. We must give thanks to our Shamanic, Native, and Neopagan friends who, through their Earth Religions, have brought us back to the consciousness of Mother Earth and Lady Gaia. This consciousness necessitates harmony

18. Mary Jo Weaver, "Who is the Goddess and Where Does She Get Us?" in *Journal of Feminist Studies in Religion* 5:1 (Spring 1989), 49; and Rosemary Radford Reuther, "Feminism and Religious Faith" in *Feminism and the Religious Experience* 3:2 (Winter 1986), 1. To quote Mary Jo Weaver, "Neopaganism is a generic term for a loosely connected group of practitioners who believe that their religious tradition is older than any of the major world religions. As such, neopaganism includes contemporary revivals of witchcraft and Goddess religion as well as Druids, believers in old Celtic religion, and others." I would add that it now relates to Wicca and other pagan and shamanic religions, and not only those of European origin. Rosemary Radford Reuther also reminds us that the word, pagan, originally meant "religions of the people of the countryside."

19. Rosemary Radford Reuther, "Feminism and Religious Faith" in *Feminism and the Religious Experience* 3:2 (Winter 1986), 2; Marvin W. Meyer, *The Ancient Mysteries* (San Francisco: Harper and Row, 1987), 157–59, 199–201; and Manly P. Hall, *The Secret Teachings of All Ages* (Los Angeles: Philosophical Research Society, 1988), XXI. The Ancient Mystery Schools refer to the various esoteric traditions from a number of cultures, including: Greece's Hermetic Schools (Hermes Trismegistus, the God of Wisdom); the Egyptian Mysteries of Isis, Osiris and their son, Horus (including the Cult of Isis, which influenced the Mary traditions, since both were the loving Queens of Heaven); the Greco-Roman Mysteries of Mithras, which had an influence on Christian beliefs and rituals; the Eleusinian Mysteries; Zoroastrian and Magi Mysteries from Persia; and so on. There were Mystery Schools in Asia as well, with ancient teachings and traditions, such as the Yin-Yang. They were competitors of and influenced many later religious traditions from Christianity to Hinduism.

and balance in nature and respect for all living things. It brings the language of Earthwise, Greenwise, natural living, clean air, clean waters, natural medicines, and health foods to the forefront of contemporary life. These initiatives represent a revival of humanity's earliest and greatest natural wisdom—that all aspects of nature are essential to the survival of humankind and all life on Planet Earth. All is community. The relationship between ecology and the Earth Religions is only one of many bridges we will find among the various world religions that may help us find a way out of hell. It can be a path to healing and resolution for the other great challenges of our time: poverty, war, oppression, and injustice.

In *The New Dialog* section above, we began with the phrase *Mitakuye Oyasin.* It is from the Lakota people of the Midwest and translates to "All Our Relations" or "We are all related," which is used in prayer ceremony as a benediction or closing phrase. To emphasize something, they will also add *Ho*! or *Aho*!, which is an emphatic "Yes!" So, I can best end this chapter on Universalism by saying, "Aho! Mitakuye Oyasin."

PART II

The Theology

In this section, we will venture through a series of chapters that cover the little-traveled pathways and byways of a Universalist theology. It explores the nature of all things spiritual: On the Nature of God; On the Nature of Revelation; On the Nature of Humankind; On the Nature of Good, Evil, and Suffering; On the Nature of Illusion; On the Nature of Love and Community; On the Nature of Liberation; and On the Nature of Purpose. It cannot flesh out this theology, however, without relying on the backbone of this work, a series of twenty-seven spiritual principles. We use as an example throughout the book called *A Universalist Spiritual Manifesto* (Appendix A), revealed within the auspices of the Universalist Church, *The Church of the Way of the Messiahs* (Appendix B).[1] From here, we will move beyond ideas and theory in Part III. In *The Praxis (Living Practice)*, we tackle how to put Universalism into real-world, down-to-earth practice in our daily lives, in the marketplace, and in our world vision. Again, we will be using *The Church of the Way of the Messiahs* as our Universalist model, as it has a lot in common with many postmodern spiritual ventures.

1. A brief history of the church will provide context and background for this *Statement*, which can be found in Appendix B. For purposes of self disclosure, I am the founder and senior minister of The Church of the Way of the Messiahs.

CHAPTER 6

Just Who is this God Guy or Gal Anyway?

(On the Nature of God)

I should like to speak of God not on the borders of life, but at its center, not in weakness, but in strength, not in man's suffering and death, but in his life and prosperity.

DIETRICH BONHOEFFER

The Many and the One, The One and the Many

As a Universalist theological premise, let us begin with but one example of a Universalist Church, South Florida's *The Church of the Way of the Messiahs*. Its very name advances a revolutionary message; all humans are Messiahs-in-potential, all Christs-in-possibility, all Buddhas-in-time. Like all Universalist groups, it has incorporated many seemingly disparate theological strands from various eastern, western and native traditions into its faith system. Yet, upon close examination, they are not so disparate. Common themes and spiritual patterns soon emerge. This is clearly laid out in the church's 1997 revelatory document, *A Universalist Spiritual Manifesto*, particularly in the tenth principle:

> 10. We recognize and affirm the limitless beauty and truth of the Divine Creation Spirit, the Holy Spirit that reveals itself through the many religions and peoples of faith throughout history and throughout the world. We acknowledge that a Divine Creation

> Spirit of all nations, of all peoples, of all creatures appears in many forms of Revelation through Divinely-guided Teachers, oral and written scriptures, and individual inspiration among all the peoples of the world. We call these revelations, inspirations, and teachings the loving, universal, divine truths of Great Spirit that shine through time, culture, personality, history, and geography.[1]

From this, it is clear that God has not come only through one human being or through one religious tradition. For example, as much as Universalists love, admire, and honor Jesus, they would not necessarily disagree with Christian theologian William Sloane Coffin. He stated in effect that God may be defined by Jesus but not confined to Jesus.[2] The more one investigates various spiritual heritages, teachings, and scriptures, the more one comes away with the distinct feeling that God has been speaking with one voice through many voices. Despite the cultural, literary, historical, and geographical differences between these spiritual voices, there is an essential truth underlying all religions. This is not a new message. Karen Armstrong points out that Islam not only has a long history of tolerance of other religions,[3] but even carries a Universalist flavor:

> The religion of al-Llah that Muhammad would shortly begin to preach in Mecca had begun not on Mount Hira but on the day of Creation. God had made Adam his *kalipha* or vice-regent on earth and after that time He had sent one prophet after another to every people on the face of the earth. The message had always been the same, so all religions were essentially one. The Qu'ran never claimed to cancel out previous revelations, but in principle one cult, one tradition, one scripture was as good as another.[4]

Muhammad himself told overzealous followers more than once, "Say not that I am better than Moses." And, another time, "Let none of you say that I am better than Jonah." He knew the revelation from Gabriel quite well, which says, "We make no distinction between any of His messengers"[5] (Qu'ran, Surah II, 285). All of the Qu'ran's prophets and

1. The Church of the Way of the Messiahs, *A Universalist Spiritual Manifesto*, ed. Thomas Norris (Miami: The Church of the Way of the Messiahs, 1997), 6–7.

2. Marcus J. Borg, *The Heart of Christianity: Rediscovering a Life of Faith* (New York: Harper Collins, 2003), 89.

3. Karen Armstrong, *Muhammad* (San Francisco: Harper, 1992), 87–88.

4. Ibid, 87.

5. Martin Lings, *Muhammad: His Life Based on the Earliest Sources* (Rochester,

messengers (including Jesus and Mary) are very special ones called to God's work, but none is greater than the other in God's eyes.

Closer to home, in 1893, the Hindu Swami Vivekananda addressed the World Parliament of Religions in Chicago. He brought that staid body to its feet with his compelling, fresh advocacy of Universalism learned at the feet of his teacher, Ramakrishna (1836–1886), the great Hindu saint and religious reformer mentioned earlier.[6] Lewis Hopfe and Mark Woodward report of Ramakrishna, once a priest of Kali:

> He later became convinced that behind all religions was a single reality that might be called God. His religious experience with Christians and Muslims, as well as Hindus, convinced him that truth was essentially one.[7]

Pursuing this idea that critical theological truths are essentially one, Universalist theology also has an interesting take on the nature of the Supreme Being. As odd as it may seem to a Christian, Jewish, or Islamic theologian, Universalists may perceive God from both a monotheistic and pantheistic perspective. The pantheism of Hinduism and most ancient and contemporary indigenous, shamanic peoples around the world view the Creator and Creation as one. God is experienced throughout all of nature, and all of nature is alive. God dwells within and through everything. Thus, for us, there is one God and this God is part of all things. The modern Christian Panentheistic Theology[8] of Charles Hartshorne, Matthew Fox,[9] and Jurgen Moltmann has come achingly close to embracing this same principle of pantheism. Alan Gragg provides Hartshorne's definition of panentheism.

> . . . that literally everything exists in God and that God, like the universe, has no external environment. All actualities are actual in God, and all potentialities are potential in God. He is the Whole in every categorical sense, all actuality in one individual actuality, and all possibility in one individual potentiality.

VT: Inner Traditions International, 1983), 102.

6. Christoper Isherwood, *Ramakrishnaand His Disciples* (Hollywood: Vedanta Press, 1965), 320–321.

7. Hopfe and Woodward, 102.

8. Note the slight difference in spelling between panentheism and pantheism. It is almost like these Christian theologians could not take the last step and acknowledge how pantheistic their ideas were.

9. C. Alan Anderson and Deborah G. Whitehouse, *New Thought: A Practical American Spirituality* (New York: Crossroad Publishing, 2003), 89.

> Panentheism thus differs from traditional theism by asserting that all the world is entirely inside God instead of outside him . . .[10]

Richard Bauckham expands upon this as he notes Jurgen Moltmann's growing stress on the immanence of God in creation, as his eschatological panentheism (the hope that God will indwell all things in the new creation) has been increasingly accompanied by a stress on the co-inherence of God and the world already. As the Spirit, God is already present in his creation, both in suffering the transience and evil of the world and in anticipating the eschatological rebirth of all things.[11]

This is a God who is both transcendent (High God) and immanent (down-to-earth God),[12] holy individual, and wholly community. It is not particularly necessary to explain this seeming paradox, for it is simply one of the many mysteries of God. This can be seen through the first, fifth, and seventh principles in *A Universalist Spiritual Manifesto*:

> 1. There is one Divine Creation Spirit of All That Is, Seen and Unseen, Known and Unknown, Understood and Not Understood.
>
> 5. The Divine Creation Spirit is the One and the Many, the Many and the One. The Divine Creatress-Creator is female and male, infinitely large and infinitely small, Spirit and Substance, Light and Dark, beyond understanding and wonderfully simple, Manifest and Unmanifest, Mind and Heart. The Great Spirit is All That Is.
>
> 7. Along with all our relations, we are constantly in Oneness with Great Spirit, knowingly or unknowingly, in lightness or in darkness, in the physical or in the spiritual, as we are all the divine manifestation of Great Spirit, and in All That We Are, we are the Many and the One, the One and the Many.[13]

Ninian Smart might observe this within his experiential and emotional dimension of religion. Universalist theology seems to combine two

10. Alan Gragg, "Charles Hartshorne" in *Makers of the Modern Theological Mind*, ed. Bob E. Patterson (Waco, TX: Word Books, 1973), accessed June 2005, religion-online.org.

11. Richard Bauckham, "Jurgen Moltmann," in *The Modern Theologians*, ed. David F. Ford (Cambridge: Blackwell Publishers, 1997), 221.

12. The transcendent aspect of God is the High God in the sky; pure, holy (separate), and far above us and creation. The immanent aspect of God is the down-to-earth, intimate, up close and personal God.

13. *A Universalist Spiritual Manifesto*, 3 and 5.

poles of religious experience. At one pole, there is Rudolf Otto's sense of the numinous; God as Other. This outside Holy Other is a mystery beyond comprehension. At the other end is the contemplative, meditative experience where there is no outside Other, only an inner truth or non-other.[14] Clearly, Universalism is an integrationist theology. Consequently, within this expansive universe of meaning, one is at liberty to experience the presence of God as Mother and Father, as communion and community,[15] as partner and friend,[16] as outer Other and as inner Self. If God is the Many within the Oneness (the diversity within the unity), then why can't God be experienced this intimately and personally?

God as Friend and Lover?

More and more, God is emerging as a personal experience in the postmodern arena.[17] It is not just church teachings and scripture that help us define our theological identity, but also our biography, our life experiences. Where we are born, when we are born, who raises us, and what community or society we live in will have more influence on our views of our God, ourselves, and our world than almost anything else.[18] In other words, our religious affiliations and beliefs are almost solely a result of geographical, historical, and cultural context. Recognizing the sociological (family and societal), geographical, historical, and anthropological (cultural) influences on our development, it will make a world of religious and theological difference if you are born in Jakarta, Rome, Cairo, Calcutta, Llasa, Buenos Aires, Stockholm, Tokyo, Johannesburg, Shanghai, or Detroit. It will make a world of religious and theological difference if you are born in 2 million BCE, 1450 BCE, 300 BCE, 300 CE,

14. Smart, 167.

15. As Dietrich Bonhoeffer suggests in his *Sanctorum Communio*, quoted in *Dietrich Bonhoeffer: Witness to Jesus Christ*, ed. John de Gruchy (Minneapolis: Fortress Press, 1991), 49–50, and 60.

16. Linda Moody, *Women Encounter God* (Maryknoll: Orbis Books, 1996), 30.

17. Smart, 194.

18. Edward Antonio, "Black Theology" in *The Cambridge Companion to Liberation Theology*, ed. Christopher Rowland (Cambridge: Cambridge University Press, 1999), 67–68. For example, Antonio discusses James Cone's refusal to concede the absolute existence of universal truths and revelation. Theological perspectives, instead, are based upon the historical context and experience of the person formulating a position on the divine. Your theology will be quite different from the slavemaster if you are the slave, and vice versa.

1450 CE, 1900 CE, or 2021 CE. With this in mind, then, let us look at a few ways God can be experienced.

As Elaine Pagels tells us, the early Gnostic Christians started their prayers to both the Divine Mother and Father.[19] One can almost sense the comfort received in their prayers to a nurturing set of protective, loving parents in a hostile world of Roman occupation and persecution. Fast forward 2,000 years, and we discover Christian Womanist and Mujerista Liberation theologians for whom God is personalized to their own life experiences as African American, Amerindian/*mestiza*, and Latina Women, both as individuals and within their particular communities.[20] With this in mind, Stephanie Mitchem shifts the theological playing field by noting that Black women understand God "as a partner in life rather than a distant observer."[21] She asks,

> Where is God in the experiences of black women? By what name should this God be called? What does it mean to live a life of faith? How should black women respond to God's call?[22]

God as a Black woman in Harlem or African woman slave? God as a Latina woman in the slums of Peru or Los Angeles? God as *mestiza* woman in Puerto Rico? Why not? How long have we had to accept the narrow, European and North American definitions of God as fact and reality? God as an old white grandfather on a throne. Jesus as a pale, slight, light-haired northern European. God is far more expansive than anything we could envision, so perhaps our hopes, our dreams, and our imagination are the best places to begin. A limitless Creatress-Creator requires limitless vision.

So, carrying our mandate of expansive definition even further, Sallie McFague, a feminist liberation theologian and Christian minister, suggests the idea of God as friend—and even as lover.

> God as lover is the one who loves the world not with the fingertips but totally and passionately, taking pleasure in its variety and richness, finding it attractive and valuable, delighting in

19. Pagels, 49.

20. Mitchem, 22–23; and Ada Maria Isasi Diaz, *Mujerista Theology* (Maryknoll, NY: Orbis Books, 1996), 71–72, 77–79.

21. Ibid., 48.

22. Ibid., 23.

its fulfillment. God as lover is the moving power of love in the universe, the desire for unity with all the beloved.[23]

According to Shahram Shiva, this same sentiment resounded long ago through the great 13th century Sufi founder and poet Rumi, whose spiritual transformation made him an "enraptured lover of God."[24] Julian of Norwich, the remarkable English Christian mystic from the 14th century, spoke of her God in enraptured terms as well. In one vision, she calls Him "my Maker, Lover, and Keeper."[25] Later, she observes His joy in a soul returning to Him. "He says sweetly, "My darling, I am glad you have come to Me. In all this misery I have ever been one with you. Now you see My loving, and we are made one in bliss."[26]

Within these expanded definitions of God, God is creator; God is creation; God is guide; God is comforting, healing, nurturing, birthing mother;[27] God is liberator; God is Lover; God is the Holy Shekinah Spirit, She Who Dwells Within;[28] God is All That Is; God is part of you; and God is part of me.

As an aside, within this definition, one can hardly not be an environmentalist, for this indwelling nature of God in all things is a foundation of Christian Green Theology. Even the Vatican and the Southern Baptist Convention in 2008 finally weighed in on the Christian duty to protect the environment and prevent global warming.[29] Mother Earth, all her creatures, and all God's creations are meant to be honored and protected on

23. Sallie McFague, *Models of God: Theology for an Ecological New Age* (Philadelphia: Fortress Press, 1987), x and 133.

24. Jalal Al-Din Rumi and Shahram Shiva, *Hush Don't Say Anything to God: Passionate Poems of Rumi,* trans. Shahram Shiva (Fremont, CA: Jain Publishing, 1999), accessed March 2005, http://www.geocities.com/ostercy/rumi.htm.

25. Dame Julian of Norwich, *The Revelation of Divine Love in Sixteen Showings,* trans. M. L. del Mastro (Liguori, MI: Liguori/Triumph, 1994), 67.

26. Ibid, 120.

27. Johanna W.H. van Wijk-Bos, *Reimagining God* (Louisville: Westminster John Knox Press, 1995), 55, 59, 64, and 70.

28. Elizabeth A. Johnson, *She Who Is* (New York: Crossroad, 1996), 86; and Pagels, 52–53.

29. CNN.com, "Vatican lists new sinful behaviors," March 12, 2008, http://www.cnn.com/2008/LIVING/wayoflife/03/10/vatican.updates.sins.ap/; and *Dallas Morning News*, "Southern Baptists change stance, say stopping global warming a biblical duty" in Local News/Religion, March 9, 2008, http://www.dallasnews.com/sharedcontent/dws/dn/religion/stories/031008dnnatsouthernbaptists.31bd4ca.html.

behalf of God, for God is within them as well.[30] Thus, there is no limit to this God. The great rabbinical Jewish sages partially comprehended this.

> They conceived the idea of a God who, as it were, is able, at will, to expand and contract, to concentrate Himself into a small space, or to fill all space *and more*, and who . . . remains always, in His final and ultimate essence, eternally one and the same. They were helped in the development of this idea . . . by their doctrine of the Shechinah, or the Indwelling of God.[31]

Great Mystery

To be fair, and at the same time further stir up the brew, I must also add that Universalist theology is both theistic and non-theistic.[32] If this seems confusing, it can be pointed out that one translation for *Wakan-tanka*, the name of God in the Lakota language, is "Great Mystery."[33] The Lakota believe it is the height of absurdity to attempt to anthropomorphize the Creator of All That Is, which is also All That Is, for the Supreme Being is beyond human understanding.[34] This is not unlike the Muslim distaste for idle doctrinal speculation (*zanna*) about the ineffable nature of God and theological matters. It is considered merely "human projection and wish fulfillment."[35] Principle 24 echoes this conviction, which underscores our oneness and our need to be in oneness.

30. John B. Cobb, Jr., "The Role of Theology of Nature in the Church" in *Liberating Life: Contemporary Approaches in Ecological Theology*, eds. Charles Birch, William Eaken and Jay B. McDaniel (Maryknoll: Orbis Books, 1990), accessed July 2005, religion-online.org. John B. Cobb, Jr. and other Christian theologians affirmed from the 1970s onward.

31. G. G. Montefiore and H. Lowe, *A Rabbinic Anthology* (New York: Schocken Books, 1974), 15.

32. A theistic religion, as expressed by Christians, Jews, Muslims and Greco-Romans, is one that believes in a god or gods/goddesses as beings. A non-theistic religion, such as Buddhism, Taoism, and Jainism, do not believe in a Supreme Creator Being, but instead see the divine as a universal force and use terms like The Way, The Changeless Unity, Absolute Reality, and so on.

33. James R. Walker, "Walker's Outline of Oglala Mythology" in *Lakota Belief and Ritual*, ed. Raymond J. Demalie and Elaine A. Jahmer (Lincoln: University of Nebraska Press, 1991), 51.

34. Walker, 70–74; and Barrett Eaglebear, Lakota Sundancer, "Lectures on the oral teachings of the Lakota Elders" in many workshops and seminars, 1990–2004, Miami and Sunrise, Florida.

35. Armstrong, *Muhammad*, 98, 100.

> 24. It creates imbalance and disharmony to over-analyze and over-interpret the Divine Creation Spirit or Great Spirit's works. An equally wonderful name for the Divine Creation Spirit is "Great Mystery," a mystery far beyond our limited vision in the physical plane. Staying only in the limited human mind, without the love and inspiration and reason of Divine Mind and Holy Spirit, has created much suffering throughout history in war and division. Divisiveness, separation, judgmentalism, nationalism, and theological hairsplitting were not the teachings of the divinely guided teachers who came to assist us. In splitting theological hairs over the "correct" beliefs, laws, and rituals, that is, in following what was thought to be the letter of the law, we have sorely missed the spirit of the whole thing. There is no justification for war against, hatred for, or separation from any of our Brothers and Sisters, and no divinely guided teacher would justify such.[36]

For this reason, Universalist theology can be as comfortable with the Hindu concept of Brahman as Ultimate Reality—the sexless, eternal, infinite, unfathomable, and unknowable force of creation that is beyond time and space and is a part of all things[37]—as it can be with the *Tao*, The Way, which is the creation energy flow of all things,[38] as well as the Buddhist *Dharma*, Absolute Truth.[39] In their way, each describes the energy flow of the universe as an intelligent, organized foundation of everything. However, this is not in terms of an intellectualized human concept of a Divine Being. John Dominic Crossan puts an interesting spin on this topic as he notes that God is Order for Confucians, a Force for Taoists, a State of Mind for Buddhists, and a Being in Western religions.[40] Maimonides, the eminent Jewish Sage, although an Aristotelian theist of sorts,[41] sums it up thusly: ". . . the human mind cannot comprehend God. Only God

36. *A Universalist Spiritual Manifesto*, 12.

37. Hopfe and Woodward, 82.

38. Lao-Tzu, *Te-TaoChing*, trans. Robert G. Henricks (New York: Ballantine, 1989), xviii-xix.

39. Masao Abe, "Buddhism" in *Our Religions*, ed. Arvind Sharma (San Francisco: Harper, 1993), 76; and Robert Linssen, *Living Zen* (New York: Grove Weidenfeld, 1958), 68.

40. John Dominic Crossan, "Past and Future" in the Chautauqua Institute Great Lecture Series, September 16, 2001, Chautauqua, New York.

41. Ehud Z. Benor, "Meaning and Reference in Maimonides' Negative Theology," *Harvard Theological Review* 88:3 (July 1995), *Library and Information Resource Net.*

can know Himself. The only form of comprehension of God we can have is to realize how futile it is to try to comprehend Him."[42]

Hidden Foundations

Normally, we might have ended this section here, but throughout this exploration of the House of God, there has been a partially hidden foundation stone. Sadly, it has been covered by centuries of mossy propaganda and disinformation debris. To complete our discussion of the Creator and to remain faithful to our Universalist heritage and history, we can no longer ignore Her. Riane Eisler, Monica Sjoo, Barbara Mor, and other archeological revisionists have discovered significant scientific support and historical information to argue an interesting conclusion. *God was female for almost all of the last 200,000 years of human life on earth.*[43]

> [The] cave sanctuaries, figurines, burials, and rites all seem to have been related to a belief that the same source from which human life springs is also the source of all vegetable and animal life—the great Goddess or Giver of All we still find in later periods of Western civilization. They also suggest that our early ancestors recognized that we and our natural environment are integrally linked parts of the great mystery of life and death and that all nature must therefore be treated with respect.[44]

If this is the case, then we can no longer overlook the Cosmic Mother, the divine feminine that governed so much of our planetary religious history. Furthermore, we remember that it has not been entirely forgotten in the Judeo-Christian tradition. *Sophia* (a Greek feminine noun) is the Wisdom aspect of God. Her origins begin with the Hebrew word *Chokmah*, a feminine noun and later translated in the Latin Bible as *Sapientia*, a Latin feminine noun.[45] There is more material on her than anyone else in the Old Testament scriptures except God, Moses, Job, and David.[46] She

42. Maimonides, "Guide for the Perplexed," I, 59, quoted in Mary Pat Fisher, *Living Religions: Eastern Traditions* (Upper Saddle River: Prentice Hall, 2003), 25.

43. Monica Sjoo and Barbara Mor, *The Great Cosmic Mother*, (San Francisco: Harper and Row, 1987), 46, 49; and Riane Eisler, *The Chalice and the Blade* (San Francisco: Harper Collins, 1987), 3–6.

44. Eisler, 3.

45. Elizabeth Johnson, *She Who Is* (New York: Crossroad, 1996), 86–87.

46. Susan Cole, Marian Ronan, and Hal Taussig, *Wisdom's Feast: Sophia in Study and Celebration* (Lanham, MD: Sheed and Ward, 1997).

is found in Proverbs, the Book of Job, the Wisdom of Solomon, and the Book of Sirach (or *Ecclesiasticus*), and she carries a distinctly feminine voice.[47] In Proverbs 8:27–31, Sophia tells us:

> When God set the heavens in place, I was present.
> When God drew a ring on the surface of the deep,
> When God fixed the clouds above,
> When God fixed the vast wells of the deep,
> When God assigned the sea its limits—
> And the waters will not invade the land,
> When God established the foundations of the earth,
> I was by God's side, a master craftswoman,
> Delighting God day after day,
> Ever at play by God's side,
> At play everywhere in God's domain,
> Delighting to be with the children of humanity.

Likewise, in the *Talmud*, Rabbi Judah, a great Jewish Sage, refers to the Holy *Shekinah* (a Hebrew feminine noun), the indwelling Spirit of God, as a mother who follows the children of Israel, "her children," into captivity.[48] In other Talmudic discussions pertaining to the tradition of covering the head, the majority view eventually accepted that it was "impertinent to allow the *Shekinah*, the female manifestation of God, to see their bare heads below Her."[49] In the mystical Jewish *Kaballah* Movement, the *Shekinah* is "the crowned bride of God."[50] The Jewish *Shekinah* later morphed into the Christian notion of the Holy Spirit,[51] a nurturing Advocate, Healer, and Comforter (John 14:16–26 and Acts 9:31). She is even perceived as an indwelling spirit by the Apostle Paul (Romans 8:8). Finally, Julian of Norwich goes so far as to call Jesus "our heavenly Mother, Jesus," for his all-encompassing love is likened to a mother for her child.[52]

Although it is worthwhile to mention these surviving remnants of the Goddess, it is not possible to do justice to the collapse of the matriarchal

47. Johnson, 86–87.

48. Montefiore and Loewe, citing Lamentation Rabbah 1:33, 1:6, 518.

49. George Robinson, *Essential Judaism* (New York: Pocket Books, 2000), 28.

50. Leah Novick, "Encountering the Shechinah, the Jewish Goddess" in *The Goddess Reawakening*, ed. Shirley Nicholson (Wheaton: Theosophical Publishing House, 1989), 206.

51. Michael Lodahl, *Shekinah Spirit: Divine Presence in Jewish and Christian Religion* (New York: Paulist Press, 1992), 56.

52. Julian of Norwich, 171.

world some 7,000 years ago. Like dominos, they fell under the onslaught of the nomadic, patriarchal tribal groups with their conquering male war gods.[53] At a minimum, that is a complete academic field of inquiry unto itself. However, Universalist theology carries an imperative to honor and comprehend the role of the divine feminine. It is part and parcel of Universalist worship. It affords an excellent opportunity for planetary healing and for once again bringing equilibrium to the Yin and the Yang, the feminine and the masculine. Jennifer and Roger Woolger so eloquently describe this paradise lost.

> Seen from the larger perspective of world religion, the cultures of Western civilization are like the children of a family that has suffered a terrible divorce. The children now live only with the father and are forbidden to mention the mother's name or remember those warm and happy times they once spent in her embrace. With only a father to guide us, despite his love, we have become hardened, relentlessly heroic, and grimly puritanical in our effort to forget the lost security and sensual trust in the earth the Mother once gave us. Long ago, we dimly sense, there was a primordial unity, when an Earth Mother and a Spirit Father enjoyed happy and harmonious union. But that paradise is lost, and in our estrangement we have been forced to swallow the embittered propaganda of a guilty, yet all-powerful Father. The Mother herself is disempowered: her cults scattered, divided, unattended, persecuted.[54]

It is long past time to bind Her wounds, His wounds, and our wounds. It is time for a renewed inspiration and revelation of All That Is.

53. Eisler, 43–44.

54. Jennifer Barker Woolger and Roger J. Woolger, *The Goddess Within* (New York: Fawcett Columbine, 1989), 16.

CHAPTER 7

Ask God.com

(On the Nature of Revelation)

The Kingdom is spread out over the whole world and people do not see it.

JESUS, *THE GOSPEL OF THOMAS*

Whoever undertakes to set himself up as judge in the field of truth and knowledge is shipwrecked by the laughter of the gods.

ALBERT EINSTEIN

Darwin or Genesis?

GOD AS PARTNER, PARENT, and friend is a revealing God. This is not a God of close-kept secrets, although the limitless immensity and vastness of creation, and the creation process itself, certainly is a mystery to our limited understanding. Nonetheless, our sciences keep forging ahead in learning more and more of the mystery. And, as Messiahs-in-potential and the standard-bearers of the sacred, much is revealed to all of us at all times. To paraphrase Jesus, we suggest if we have but "the eyes to see and the ears to hear" (Matthew 13:11–15).

Throughout Christian history, and even to this day, there has been an ongoing battle between science and religion. Most recently, we have witnessed the largely unsuccessful attempts by the Christian Right to oppose the teaching of Evolution Theory. They have imposed "Creationist Theory" and it's subtly veiled and relabeled "Intelligent Design Theory" on American public school science curricula across the country. Most scientists argue this is inappropriate because Creationism is not a scientific theory. Instead, they reflect religious beliefs, which have no place in our public schools.[1] Normally, Universalist theology would happily embrace both science and religion as equally fascinating pathways to God. However, in this case, we support the scientists and the U.S. Constitution. Principle 27 heals this old split between science and religion. They are no longer competitors in knowledge but partners in exploration.

> 27. There is room for both science and spirituality, since both are creations of Great Spirit. Science attempts to explain the Mystery, and faith attempts to experience the Mystery. In the end, they will be one.

Revelation-in-Action

From the spiritual end, it seems that the Creator is always sending humanity revelatory messages. These arrive either in the form of great teachers and prophets or sometimes as *avatars*.[2] These are incarnations of God such as Jesus, Krishna, and White Buffalo Calf Woman. They may also appear as personal revelations that could be called "spiritual intuition" or "divine inspiration." Sadly, as a species, we often seem hell-bent on killing the messenger or ignoring the message. Happily, much of the message still manages to squeeze through and is available to anyone who chooses to search, see, and listen. Keeping this in mind, Universalists assert that all humans are equally capable of direct connection to the divine, although all are not equally adept. Like all learning, it not only requires openness but practice and patience. What often surprises beginners in this newfound process of prayer, meditation, and connection, is that the messages somehow feel familiar. They have been receiving them all along; they just didn't know it. Throughout the Qu'ran, Muhammad frequently pointed

1. John Roach, "Does 'Intelligent Design' Threaten the Definition of Science?," *National Geographic News*, April 27, 2005, 1–2, http://news.nationalgeographic.com/news/2005/04/0427_050427_intelligent_design.html.

2. In the Hindu traditions, an *avatar* is an incarnation of God, that is, God coming into human form. Hence, Hindus would consider all of these teachers to be *avatars*.

out that it was a "Reminder" of things that they already knew and that had already been revealed in earlier times.[3]

One observation about revelation is that it is not a passive process. It is Revelation-in-Action. Thankfully, revelation does not always nearly kill the messenger, despite the intensely overwhelming experiences of the Divine Presence by Muhammad, Isaiah, Moses, and countless other prophets over the ages. Although it does not have to be a life-threatening experience, it is, of course, a highly interactive, life-transforming experience. Interactions with Spirit are rarely dull or routine. For example, I find that when I am being asked by Spirit to take a new step or explore a new area of my spirituality or spiritual work, I am bombarded with information, signs, and messages about the particular topic. I finally throw my hands up in defeat after something occurs that completely strips away any remaining doubt, and off I go on a new path of discovery and adventure.

You might find it surprising that I did not always believe in reincarnation. Why should I? Like you, I was raised in Western science and religion. However, after being bombarded with information, signs, and messages from all directions, and a direct past life experience that was too real to be ignored, I gave in and let go of years of left-brain Western science and programming. It just felt right. You may find Spirit brings a similar process to your life from time to time. Nonetheless, sometimes the process is much quieter. Our Native American friends remind us that Great Spirit speaks to us in every blade of grass. The signs of revelation are all around you in books, movies, people, nature, self, and life. Learning to read the signs of daily life is just as important as a major life-changing epiphany. The first keeps us in the flow, and the second unearths the flow.

Many wonder, well, how exactly does God speak to us? As noted above, sometimes, it is a bombardment of messages, signs, and symbols from all directions. Sometimes it is a vision or voice in the midst of a deep meditation. Sometimes it is in an intuitive feeling, even a hunch. Sometimes it is the still, quiet voice that so many of us have ignored for so long, not exactly knowing what it is.

I was in a meeting several years ago with some local clergy. One gentleman, a prominent Jesuit priest, proudly discussed in some detail how his parishes were bringing in many new people through challenging weekend encounter retreats. He felt that the standard Sunday Masses brought in just the usual "captive audience," members who were there

3. Armstrong, *Muhammad*, 95.

because they were following the rules of being good Catholics. On the other hand, the retreats seemed to genuinely bring people closer to God. They provided a safe space where God could speak with them. Then he added, almost as an afterthought, "Of course, God has never spoken to me." This was stated with such a deep longing and aching sadness that it hurt my heart.

Cate, with all her passion and enthusiasm, sometimes jumps in where angels fear to tread. This was one of those moments. She immediately replied, "Why don't you come to one of our Sacred Circles? God speaks to all of us there every week." There was dead silence around the table. How do you help a man of God, a highly educated and successful priest, who knows not God's voice? I wondered what blocked him from seeing and hearing God all around him. Even Cate's statement was a message from Spirit. I felt a profound sadness for him and sensed his deep soul longing for connection.

Since the messages come through in so many ways and through so many people, Universalists find no contradiction in pursuing the teachings of Ascended Masters such as Jesus, Buddha, Muhammad, Lao Tzu, White Buffalo Calf Woman, Kuan Yin, Mahavir, Freya, Moses, Quetzalcoatl, Isis, Kuthumi, and so on. The timeless truths these great beings bring to humanity ripple down through the ages and swell above the tide barriers of orthodox religion. Thus, Universalists are just as comfortable chanting under the heavenly vault of a starlit sky on the side of a mountain; purifying themselves in the womb of Mother Earth in a Native American *Inipi* (Sweat Lodge) Purification Ceremony; listening to the various holy men and women deliver their measure of truth in temple, mosque, church or cathedral; or meditating in forest and cave with the winds and currents of Mother Earth streaming around and through us as we become one with the divine. Until one has experienced it, one cannot comprehend the incredible, unconditional love created in raptly listening to all of us and all of creation singing countless melodies with innumerable harmonies in untold voices, all coming miraculously together in one epic aria. All barriers seem to melt away, and one then wonders why we have the seeming human need to construct so many obstacles in opposition to the message of oneness.

Mysticism is Alive and Well on Mother Earth

It is important to note that, in Universalism, personal revelation is indispensable to an individual's spiritual growth and community worship. Many feel a direct link with some of these Ascended Masters, angelic hosts, celestial beings, and spiritual teachers. They offer guidance to them in their daily lives and spiritual work. It is not unusual for a Universalist to work directly through prayer, meditation, and reading with Buddha, Jesus, Mary, Kuan Yin, St. Francis of Assisi, White Buffalo Calf Woman, Archangel Michael, Krishna, or other less well-known guides who are not in the body but are in spirit. Sometimes, it feels like one actually embodies the teachings and energies of a particular Ascended Master or spiritual guide. It is part of the discovery of his or her spiritual path. In addition to the well-known names of the great masters, there are many Native American, Native African, Native Asian, Aborigine, Pacific Islander, and Native European guides who have also come to spiritual seekers. Sometimes these are living people, but more often, they are guides in spirit.

This is clearly a form of mystical union with God, and there is no question that Universalism carries within its soul a deep mystical tradition. Harvey Egan defines mysticism as involving "an experience of God that is somehow direct, immediate, intuitive, and beyond the normal workings of the senses and intellect."[4] This is not terribly unlike aspects of *Bhakti Yoga* in which disciples devote themselves entirely to the study and love of a *Mahatma* (Great One). They attempt to emulate the Great One in hopes of releasing the ego and becoming more pure, loving, and divine themselves. It is the Yoga of the heart and loving devotion.[5] From this perspective, a Mahatma, be it Krishna, Muhammad, Jesus, Buddha, Mother Theresa, Gandhi, or even John Lennon and Bob Marley, is just another aspect or face of God. Thus, in connecting with a chosen Great One, one is connecting with God. Eventually, the practitioner becomes one with this Great One, and as Kirpal Singh relates,

> The process of bhakti gradually widens the outlook of a bhakta until he sees the light of his chosen idol pervading everywhere in and around him, and he begins to feel himself expanding

4. Harvey D. Egan, *An Anthology of Christian Mysticism* (Collegeville: Liturgical Press, 1996), xxiii.

5. Kirpal Singh, *The Crown of Life: A Study in Yoga* (Bowling Green: Sawan Kirpal Publications, 1980), 106–109; and Fisher, 61–62.

> with love, till he embraces the entire creation of God. This is the climax to which love brings him.[6]

Mysticism is not just a Hindu, Buddhist, or Asian tradition. Even many Christians have noted the considerable influence within Christianity of Julian of Norwich, Hildegard von Bingen, St. Francis of Assisi, St. Clare, St. John of the Cross, and Thomas Merton, to name only a few. Nor can the proponents of Jewish mysticism ignore over the past two millennia the impact of Rabbi Akiva, Bahya ben Joseph Ibn Paquda, Moses Cordovero, Isaac Luria (the Ari), and Israel ben Eleazer (Baal Shem Tov) among the ranks of great mystics.[7] And a strong case can certainly be made that Muhammad was a mystical prophet with his revelatory visions from the Angel Gabriel culminating in the Qu'ran. The Sufi Muslim mystics certainly consider Muhammad to be Sufi. Turning to Jesus himself, Marcus Borg notes that among the many fascinating things that he was, primarily he was "a Jewish mystic."[8] Bruce Chilton goes even further, asserting that His healing miracles demonstrated that the Holy Spirit worked through Him. This proclaimed Him a *Chasid,* those

> rabbis who were shown to have obtained divine mercy not only for themselves, but more strikingly, for others. These rabbis cured sickness and relieved drought through prayer; that was the mark of divine compassion working through them. *Chasidim* were ancient Judaism's shamans, faith healers, witch doctors, and sorcerers.[9]

Chilton adds that Jesus, the shamanic rabbi, also was a teacher of the ancient rabbinic mystical and meditative traditions of the divine chariot or throne of God, the *Merkaba.* These are some of the core meditative and mystical teachings of our Universalist Church.

To summarize, then, a centerpiece of Universalist theology is its mystical traditions and practices and one's individual and communal

6. Singh, 108.

7. Perle Epstein, *Kaballah* (Boston: Shambhala, 1978), 3, 4–5, 14, and 17–18.

8. Marcus Borg, *The Heart of Christianity: Rediscovering a Life of Faith* (New York: Harper Collins, 2003), 89. Note that this is a major theme with Matthew Fox in *The Coming of the Cosmic Christ* (San Francisco: Harper and Row, 1988), 67. For a fuller treatment of mysticism in general, I refer you to the first two parts of Fox's book: "A Dream—Your Mother is Dying—A Crucifixion Story for Our Times" and "Mysticism—A Resurrection Story for Our Times," 11–74.

9. Bruce Chilton, *Rabbi Jesus: An Intimate Biography* (New York: Doubleday, 2000), 109.

mystical connection to the divine. For Universalists, this is part of God's method of revelation and our experience of oneness with the Creator. And we are not such a small minority after all. Nearly half of the American public (49%) says "they have had a religious or mystical experience defined as 'a moment of sudden religious insight or awakening.'"[10] This is heartening, in light of what Matthew Fox, the revolutionary Roman Catholic theologian, reports. Despite all the advances and awakening of the Enlightenment (also called the Age of Science, the Age of Reason, and the Modern Age) over the past 500 years, this left brain, patriarchal, age of rational mind would effectively "drive out mysticism, intuition, imagination, and above all cosmology . . ."[11] In this case, cosmology is the study of the universe from a philosophical, theological, and metaphysical perspective, which is the non-scientific end of cosmology. Hence, as a Modern people (and even among seminary and rabbinical students[12]), we will have heard little of the ancient Jewish and Christian mystical traditions or the mystical foundations underlying every known ancient, indigenous, and contemporary religion.

The revelation of God as Universal Revealer is illustrated in Principle 10 (discussed earlier) and as Universal Message in Principles 13, 14, and 26 below. They affirm the many messengers of God, their message of unity and oneness, and their respect for sacred ceremony and ritual.

> 13. We honor and acknowledge the Great Christed-Buddhic-Yogic-Messianic Teachers, Avatars, and Masters, Messengers of Light and Love for all who have come to us, the Awakening Daughters and Sons of Great Spirit.
>
> 14. We honor the great spiritual teachers and guides, not in-the-body who support and assist us in our growth as individuals, families, communities, nations, and world.
>
> 26. All rituals, ceremonies, and places of worship, which honor life and the Divine Creation Spirit, and bring us into Great Spirit's presence, are worthwhile and respected. Whether simple or ornate, whether in temple, synagogue, church, sweat lodge, cave, or sacred mountain, they will be known by the divine revelation, inspiration, love, healing, and peace that they bring. Rituals, ceremonies, and places of worship are simply a means to

10. "Many Americans Mix Multiple Beliefs," *Pew Forum on Religion and Public Life Survey.*

11. Fox, 77.

12. Ibid, 42.

> focus our attention and to gather divine energies into our presence more directly and consciously. They are only meaningful if the celebrant moves beyond the action or place and allows them to be experiences felt from the level of the heart and soul.[13]

In the end, it would appear that all these great prophets and teachers would have worked in unison just fine. How strange to imagine that Jesus, Buddha, Muhammad, Miriam (Mary), White Buffalo Calf Woman, and the others would not have anything to say to each other if they met on the road. Can one even imagine that Jesus and Buddha, or Jesus and Muhammad, or Jesus and White Buffalo Calf Woman—these teachers of love and non-violence—would have ever raised a hand against the other or moved to the other side of the street for fear of being tainted and being led astray? Rather, they would have embraced and held wonderful and lively discussions. They would have immediately recognized that they were all emissaries of the Way and the Truth—brothers and sisters in the Light.

13. *A Universalist Spiritual Manifesto*, 8 and 13.

CHAPTER 8

Ye Are Gods!

(On the Nature of Humankind)

I say, "You are gods; you are all children of the Most High."

PSALMS 82:6

Jesus answered, "Is it not written in your law, 'I said, you are gods?'"

JOHN 10:34

You don't really understand human nature unless you know why a child on a merry-go-round will wave at his parents every time around and why his parents will always wave back.

WILLIAM TAMMEUS, JOURNALIST

He who knows others is wise. He who knows himself is enlightened.

LAO TZU

There is no heresy or no philosophy which is so abhorrent to the church as a human being.

JAMES JOYCE

Let us consider that we are all insane. It will explain us to each other; it will unriddle many riddles . . .

MARK TWAIN

Body and Soul

So, WHERE DOES THAT leave us, the human side of the divine equation? Who are we? What are we? Why are we? How are we? These are the age-old philosophical questions of all time, and we will probably be asking them for all time. In the meantime, I have amassed some suggestions.

In Principle 4 below, Universalists would agree with Pierre Teilhard de Chardin (1881–1955), the great Jesuit priest, who declared, "You are not a human being in search of a spiritual experience. You are a spiritual being immersed in a human experience."[1] Similarly, our Native American friends insisted that the European priests had it all wrong when they claimed we humans are a body with a soul. The Native American elders replied that, on the contrary, we are a soul that happens to have a body. Europeans emphasized the physical body and the material world, while Native Americans looked to the spiritual world as their reality. As the elders would comment, this world is the "dream." The Native Americans also liken the body to a robe. When it wears out, we discard the old robe and put on another. This is a common Native American view of reincarnation.[2] Again, as Principle 4 states:

> 4. Along with all our relations, we humans are Spirit, One with the Divine Creation Spirit, manifesting in this plane through the vehicle of the physical body.[3]

In Principle 8, we take a strong Universalist stand on behalf of the universal love of the Creator for all. As pantheists, Universalists affirm that God is part of all Creation—all things and all beings, including us (Principles 4–7). Why would the Creator reject a part of Itself? No one son or daughter of God or group of sons and daughters are more special, important, or unique than any other. This certainly builds the case

1. Pierre Teilhard de Chardin, Think Exist, accessed in March 2006, http://en.thinkexist.com/quotation/you_are_not_a_human_being_in_search_of_a/257982.html.

2. Eaglebear Lectures; and Walker, 26.

3. *A Universalist Spiritual Manifesto*, 4.

for tolerance and acceptance of the multitude of ways we can express ourselves as human beings: male and female; child and adult; black, white, red, brown, and yellow; gay and straight; young and old; whole or disabled; citizen of a nation or citizen of Planet Earth; Christian and non-Christian; Jew and non-Jew; Muslim and non-Muslim; Hindu and non-Hindu; and so on. It states:

> 8. We are all Sons and Daughters of the Divine Creatress-Creator with all the love and inheritance of such when we so choose. It is the height of arrogance to believe that a Divine Creation Spirit of All That Is, a Creatress-Creator of unconditional love and unlimited wisdom, would not love all creation, or would come to only one community or people, or favor one group over another, or one sex over another, or one person over another. We are all favored Sons and Daughters, equally and yet uniquely loved by Great Spirit, which is the beauty and mystery of the divine paradox of the Many and the One.[4]

Yet, if we are building to any crescendo in this theology of the House of Humankind, it is probably set out most definitively in Principle 17. It is at the very heart of Universalist theology—and a significant departure from traditional Christian assumptions:

> 17. We humans are all Christed-Buddhic-Yogic Beings and Messiahs and can begin to express this as we are awakened to our true nature. We are all ministers, priests, priestesses, gurus, lamas, shamans, imams, medicine men and women, and rabbis of love, faith, and truth. We will serve Great Spirit's creation of love in all pathways of life, each according to our talents and interests and calling.[5]

The Christ and Buddha Within

Martin Luther, the great Protestant Reformer, called it the priesthood of all believers. We are all ministers of God in our own way.[6] We expand on this point and call it the Christ Within. We take to heart the words of Angelus Silesius (1624–1677), the 17th century German poet

4. *A Universalist Spiritual Manifesto*, 5–6.

5. *Ibid.*, 9.

6. Heinrich Boehmer, *Road to Reformation*, trans. John W. Doberstein (Philadelphia: Muhlenberg Press, 1946), 332–333, 336.

and mystic. "Were Christ born a thousand times in Bethlehem, and not in thee, thou art lost eternally."[7] The Christ Within concept has enjoyed a broad conceptual base from the Quakers to the spiritual philosopher, Rudolf Steiner, to Christian non-denominational, evangelical churches such as Alabama's Fellowship West ("The well that springs up within us."),[8] and to the New Thought churches, like the previously mentioned Unity Church. Rudolf Steiner (1861–1925), the founder of Anthroposophy, envisioned the Christ Within as a primordial cosmic force. It allows humans to evolve to a higher God consciousness as they connect to this "Christ Impulse" within themselves and find their "Christ Light."[9] This concept can be clearly envisioned through the figure of the man, Jesus of Nazareth, who literally embodied the Christ Within. Marcus Borg tells us he is the heart of God, the God made flesh, and shows us "what a life full of God looks like."[10]

Where we differ with many of our Christian brothers and sisters is in their belief that Jesus is the only son of God. Within the Universalist persuasion, we are all capable of this godliness, this Christed consciousness. There are many teachers, healers, and prophets in all faiths who have taken on this Christed consciousness. We will see in chapter 11, in the section *On the Nature of Divine Purpose*, that when filled with this original creation God Spark, each of us has a Higher Purpose. There will be a day when we will awaken to that godly purpose and path. It may be as powerful as being a great parent or as encompassing as leading a community to a more harmonious and loving future. Consequently, it goes far beyond the man, Jesus of Nazareth, and is not confined to his worldly self or Christianity. Perhaps, a more expansive way to put it is to call it the God Within, or in different traditions, the Buddha Within, the Messiah Within, the Shaman Within, or the Goddess Within.

In 13th century Japan, *Nichiren,* a fisherman's son, became a great Buddhist leader. Despite being persecuted for his convictions, *Nichiren* introduced the "bodhisattva ideal" and the concept of the Buddha

7. "Angelus Silesius aka Johannes Scheffler," *The Columbia Encyclopedia* (New York: Columbia University Press, 2001), http://www.bartleby.com/65/an/AngelusS.html.

8. *Fellowship West*, accessed March 2005, http://www.fellowshipnet.com/2within.html.

9. Rudolf Steiner, "The Birth of Christ Within Us," Berlin Lecture, December 27, 1914, http://wn.rsarchive.org/Lectures/19141227a01.html.

10. Borg, 88, 97–98.

potential in each person.[11] In Buddhism, it is believed that we are already Buddhas. We just don't know it yet. Each of us bears a Buddha Within, affirming that all human beings can achieve enlightenment. There is a time (perhaps in the not-so-distant future) when each of us will choose this path. As Daisetz Teitaro Suzuki explains:

> O my good and intelligent brethren, common mortals are Buddhas, and all the passions and desires are born of Wisdom [or enlightenment, *bodhi*]. As long as your thoughts are confused you are common mortals, but at the very moment you are enlightened, you are Buddhas.[12]

In a similar vein, Robert Linssen correlates the Christian and Buddhist experience.

> Certain common ground exists between Buddhism in general, Zen in particular and Christianity, with regard to the frequently expressed notions of 'Body of Truth' or 'Body of Buddha (*Dharmakaya*) of the Buddhist and the 'Glorious Body' or Body of Christ' of the Gospels . . . According to Zen, all beings and all things are the 'Body of Truth,' but we can only perceive it by freeing our mind of its habitual method of dualistic perception.[13]

The Ahimsa Way

As we have come closer to answering the questions of who are we, what are we, why are we, and how are we, we close this section on the nature of humankind with Principle 19. It presses us to consider our oneness with all of our brothers and sisters (not only human). It begins the theological mapping of a higher purpose of harmony and doing no harm. In Jainism, they call this bedrock principle of nonviolence *ahimsa*. Coupled with their pantheistic belief that everything has a soul consciousness and that every soul is equal, then *ahimsa* applies to everything in the universe (plants, people, animals, Mother Earth, etc.). *Ahimsa* strongly influenced

11. Mary Pat Fisher, "Buddhism," in *Living Religions* (Upper Saddle River: Prentice Hall, 2008), 163.

12. Daisetz Teitaro Suzuki, *Studies in Zen*, ed. Christmas Humphreys (New York: Dell, 1955), 32.

13. Robert Linssen, *Living Zen*, trans. Diana Abrahams-Curiel (New York: Grove Weidenfeld, 1958), 217.

both Gandhi and Dr. Martin Luther King, Jr. in their development of nonviolent civil resistance.[14] As Principle 19 states:

> 19. All life is to be honored. All life has purpose and meaning for itself and the Divine Creation Spirit. Through the eyes of love and Great Spirit, there is no justifiable harm or injury done to another being, whether physical, emotional, mental, or spiritual. When we are in the heart of love and Creation, we no longer bring that disharmony into our lives or the world. We no longer perceive or accept separateness, nor believe that any human is higher than any other being in the eyes of Great Spirit. We know with all of our being that we are in Oneness with all beings and all creations, for we are all in Oneness with the Divine.[15]

As you begin to see by now, Universalism is inclusive. It rejects exclusion and exclusivity. What saddens Universalists about many religious people is their belief that their way is the best and only way to salvation or enlightenment. For example, it is beyond us how the former Neoconservative Pope Benedict XVI, living in a postmodern world, could so undermine all the work of Pope John XXIII, Pope Paul VI, and Pope John Paul II, his immediate predecessors. He brought back the outdated, dogmatic, medieval beliefs that the Roman Catholic Church is the only unflawed and correct path to salvation.[16] So much for Ecumenism, although the new Pope Francis I seems bent on returning the Church to its inclusive foundations. In Christianity and Islam particularly, Pope Benedict's mindset demeaned their founders. When you study the words and teachings of Jesus and Muhammad, you are struck by the fact that they were feminists for their time and that they embraced all as children of God. Consequently, whether it is our Christian friends who insist you can only achieve salvation through Jesus Christ, our Islamic friends who look down upon the other "People of the Book" (Jews and Christians), or our Orthodox Jewish *Kaballah* friends who speak of a Jewish soul (and that the path to divinity is only through a Jewish soul),[17] we are saddened

14. Sister Samani Charitra Prajna, Lecture on "Jainism and Nonviolence," at Florida International University, October 17, 2006; and Fisher, 124.

15. *A Universalist Statement of Principles*, 10.

16. Phil Stewart, "Vatican Reaffirms Catholic Primacy," *The Washington Post*, 11 July 2007, sec. A: 11.

17. Rabbi Arthur Seltzer, "The Kaballah and Reincarnation," speech delivered to Temple Beth David, December 11, 2005, Miami, FL.

by the gulf created between brother and sister—among God's children—by such narrow, parochial attitudes.

CHAPTER 9

Pandora's Box

(On the Nature of Good, Evil, Sin, and Suffering)

I form light and create darkness. I make weal and create woe; I the Lord do all these things.

ISAIAH 45:7

What really raises one's indignation against suffering is not suffering intrinsically, but the senselessness of suffering.

FRIEDRICH NIETZSCHE

Evil is unspectacular and always human, and shares our bed and eats at our table.

W. H. AUDEN

There is not a righteous man on earth who does what is right and never sins.

ECCLESIASTES 7:20

All through history, there have been tyrants and murderers, and for a time they can seem invincible, but in the end they always fall, always.

MAHATMA GANDHI

After Prometheus had stolen fire from heaven and bestowed it upon mortals, Zeus determined to counteract this blessing. He accordingly commissioned Hephaestus to fashion a woman out of earth, upon whom the gods bestowed their choicest gifts. Hephaestus gave her a human voice, Aphrodite's beauty and powers of seduction, Hermes' cunning and the art of flattery. Zeus gave her a jar, the so-called "Pandora's box," containing all kinds of misery and evil, and sent her, thus equipped, to Epimetheus, who, forgetting the warning of his brother Prometheus to accept no present from Zeus, made her his wife. Pandora afterwards opened the jar, from which all manner of evils flew out over the earth. Hope alone remained at the bottom, the lid having been shut down before she escaped.

PANDORA'S BOX, GREEK MYTH

Lives of Han (Suffering)

THROUGHOUT HISTORY, MUCH OF theological deliberation has been preoccupied with the dualism of good (light) versus evil (dark), human happiness versus suffering, and, for Christians, sin versus righteousness. The Buddhists establish a good case for this preoccupation as the young Siddhartha was confronted with the immensity of human pain and suffering all around him. He announced that he was choosing the mendicant's path to liberate humanity from suffering.[1] Thus, one name for the Buddha was "The Compassionate One."[2] As the Dalai Lama avows, "Our highest duty, as human beings, is to search out a means whereby beings may be freed from all kinds of sufferings or unsatisfactory experiences (*dukkha*)."[3]

Within Korean Christianity, there is the *Minjung* Liberation Movement. It advocates liberation from suffering (*Han*) for the *Minjung*, "the nameless people without a voice."[4] Ahn Byung-Mu sees a direct correla-

1. Sherab Chodzin Kohn, *The Awakened One: A Life of the Buddha* (Boston: Shambhala, 1994), 34–35.

2. Piyadassi Thera, "The Buddha: His Life and Teachings," Buddha Dharma Education Association, BuddhaNet, accessed June 2005.

3. Tenzin Gyatso, *The Opening of the Wisdom Eye*, 14.

4. Choo Chai-Yong, "A Brief Sketch of a Korean Christian History from the

tion between the *Minjung* and the Jewish *ochlos* in the Gospel of Mark. They were the people who gathered around Jesus, the so-called sinners, the outcasts, the alienated, those who had been "marginalized and abandoned" by their society. In the Hebrew Bible, they are the *am ha'aretz*. They are the *Minjung* of Galilee.[5] Whether they were the villagers and city dwellers Buddha taught in ancient India, or Moses liberated from Egypt, or Jesus spoke to in the wilderness, or Christians recognized in historical Korea, these marginalized souls, who to this day still encompass the majority of the world's population, all suffered under the burden of *Han*. *Han* is the individual and collective experience of the *Minjung*. It is a wellspring of lamentation and an unresolved bitterness of suffering.[6] A. Sung Park provides a Christian perspective as he explains:

> Sin is the wrongdoing of people toward God and their neighbors. Han is the pain experienced by the victimized neighbors. Sin is the unjust action of the oppressors; Han the passive experience of their victims. Sin is of the oppressor; Han of the victims.[7]

In Universalism, we also recognize and grieve for the immensity of human pain and suffering that surrounds us in a world still overrun by the Four Horseman of the Apocalypse: Death, Disease, War, and Famine. Moreover, when we later delve into the nature of purpose, we believe it is the responsibility of an active faith to reach out to *Han*-laden humanity and work toward a renewed world of Life, Health, Peace, and Plenty. However, Universalists approach this activism and the issues of good, evil, sin, and suffering a bit differently than many Westerners. Borrowing from Buddhist, Hindu, Taoist, Korean Christian, and Native American traditions, we look beyond or above the dualism apparent at this worldly level of experience and existence.

There is a solid case to be made that if one takes one step above the dualism of light-dark and good-evil, one shall only see the balance of

---

Minjung Perspective," in *Minjung Theology*, ed. Commission on Theological Concerns of the Christian Conference of Asia (Maryknoll: Orbis Books, 1981), 74.

5. Ahn Byung-Mu, "Jesus and the Minjung in the Gospel of Mark, "in *Voices from the Margin*, ed. R. S. Sugirtharajah (Maryknoll: Orbis, 1995): 88–90, 100–102; and Suh Nam-Dong, "Historical References for a Theology of Minjung," in *Minjung Theology*, ed. Commission on Theological Concerns of the Christian Conference of Asia (Maryknoll: Orbis Books, 1981): 159.

6. A. Sung Park, "Theology of Han (the Abyss of Pain)," Quarterly Review 9 (Spring 1989): 48.

7 Ibid, 50–51.

polarities and everything in between. From an Asian perspective, Yung Young Lee points out that Western philosophy has remained under the tyranny of "conflicting dualism." It derived from Aristotelian logic and the concept of the "excluded middle." There are no alternatives in this type of thinking. It is always "either/or" thinking. In contrast, much of Oriental thinking is cyclical and inclusive, as epitomized by the Yin-Yang symbol. Yin-Yang thinking is "complementary dualism," in which the middle is included. It is the joining of opposites to make the whole. This is "both/and" thinking. In the Yin-Yang way, "what makes things good is the harmony and balance of opposites"[8] or as the old song goes, "You can't have one without the other." (See Figure 1 below.)

Figure 1: Yin-Yang Unity Principle and the Harmony of Opposites

From this perspective, then, there is no actual evil, only lessons and growth to a higher good. In Isaiah 45:7, the prophet tells us of God, "I form light and create darkness, I make weal and create woe; I the Lord do all these things." All things are included in the Creator's beingness and Creation, including evil, suffering, and darkness—but not without purpose. In fact, it is the purpose that makes it sufferable and comprehensible. It gives us answers as to why there may be injustice, evil, disharmony, and suffering in the world. Principles 2 and 3 accentuate this non-dualistic view.

> 2. All that is of and from this Great Spirit is, in essence, good and perfect, even if we do not always understand the higher purpose of things that appear dark, shadowy, evil, or unjust. There is

8. Yung Young Lee, *The Trinity in Asian Perspective* (Nashville: Abingdon Press, 1996), 31–33.

divine purpose in All That Is, and no lesson is imposed upon us without our free choice, permission, and participation, even if we are not always conscious of the choice at this physical level of consciousness.

3. We humans are gifted with free will by Great Spirit, and by our choices in this world, we find joy or suffering, lightness or darkness, peace or turmoil in our lives. Then, as we awaken further, we begin to understand our free will choices and the reasons for the lessons, difficult or gentle, we have drawn to ourselves.[9]

Clearly, there is an implicit message that all of the Creator's creations are good. Consequently, Universalists believe in the intrinsic goodness of humanity because the spark of the Creator-Creatress lies within each and every creation. Gandhi maintained, "I have seen children successfully surmount the effects of an evil inheritance. That is due to purity being an inherent attribute of the soul."[10] Free will beings may choose for a time to move away from life energies (creation activities) and towards death energies (entropy; the disruption of vibrant, energetic creation activities). In Hinduism, this is seen as part of the natural cycle of creation (through the god/goddess Brahma/Sarasvati), moving to preservation and equilibrium (through the god/goddess Vishnu/Lakshmi), and later dissolution or destruction (through the god/goddess Shiva/Devi).[11] Nothing is permanent, and the old must give way before the new (creation) can emerge, similarly affirmed by the Buddhist Doctrine of Nonpermanence.[12]

Dead Zones

Before we travel further down the highway of good and evil, let us take a brief detour onto the avenue of *Han* and Nonpermanence. In the Buddhist Law of Nonpermanence, change is the only constant in the universe. Nothing stays the same, so, in effect, much of what we worry over and brood about is an illusion (*maya*). Even suffering is not permanent, as this hopeful axiom states, "This, too, shall pass." At the same time, suffering can exert a mighty hold over so many.

9. *A Universalist Spiritual Manifesto*, 3.

10. *Satyagrha*, www.salsa.net/peace/satyagraha/quotes.

11. Hopfe and Woodward, 92–94.

12. Theodore M. Ludwig, *The Sacred Paths of the East* Upper Saddle River: Prentice Hall, 2001), 107

Here we visit the land of the "dead zones" and the "walking dead."[13] What inhibits the natural cycle of creation-stabilization-dissolution-new creation, depicted in one tradition as the Hindu Trinity Gods (Brahma, the Creator, Vishnu the Preserver, and Shiva the Destroyer)? Is it possible to think of evil, sin, and suffering as anything that hinders the fullness of life and creation energies, anything that is anti-life? Alice Miller was clear on this when she observed that depression is not the absence of gaiety but the absence of vitality.[14] For much of my career, I have worked with the victims of anti-life energies—abused children, rape victims, battered women—and their abusers. In these cases, we don't need the fantasy of horrible Dementors from the Harry Potter novels. The victims of these real-life Dementors felt like their abusers were literally draining the life energy out of them, whether at the insistent, prying hands of a molester, or from the brutal fists of a drunken husband or father, or at the point of a knife to the throat. Moment by moment, year by year, drop by drop, the life was being squeezed out of them until many reported that they became numb and consciously or unconsciously shut down their feelings. Life no longer seems promising, hopeful, joyful, or present. For those feeling suicidal—when life no longer seems worth living—the first thing to depart is hope. When we lose hope, we lose a sense of future. When we lose a sense of future, we lose a sense of purpose. Without a sense of purpose, we are just going through the motions—one way to be the walking dead. Many of these victims have experienced suicidal urges lasting moments or years.

There are others caught in different sticky webs of anti-life energies—alcoholics, drug addicts, sex addicts, relationship addicts, food addicts, and workaholics. If anyone has worked with or known people with these addictive disorders, when the disorder has had control of the person's life for any length of time, there is a definite decrease in life energies. Some look and sound like the living dead. Many are so stuck that all they can think of is their next "fix"—their urges reign supreme. Hence, there is great joy in watching an addict come back to life. Yet, there is pain in watching the process as well, for it entails a fair amount of suffering. There is the physical and emotional detoxing; the feeling of all the emotions you have suppressed for years; the confronting of tremendous feelings of failure,

13. My thanks to Francine Lipnicki, a member of The Church of the Way of the Messiahs, for her passionate discussion and input on the concepts of the "dead zone" and the "walking dead."

14. Alice Miller, *The Drama of the Gifted Child* (New York: Basic Books, 1981), 57.

facing social stigma and judgment; and the disaster of those you have hurt riding in your wake never far behind. It does not matter if the addiction is to crystal meth, marijuana, alcohol, internet porn, an abusive husband, an alcoholic wife, or the next work project in an exhausting work schedule. All are meant to help the person run away from their pain. Some kill more quickly than others, but all are soul-killing over time. A person in counseling once said that the heart of an addiction is a dead place, a dead zone, and that is so true. Within the deadness, the addict or alcoholic is trying desperately to feel something, to bombard themselves with sensation and stimuli. However, the addictive substances or people they choose eventually only heighten the deadness.

Once I asked the wife of a workaholic to write a letter to her husband about how his workaholism affected her and their children. It was an incredible tale of emotional abandonment and loss. One could not tell from the letter whether she was the wife of a heroin addict, an alcoholic, or a workaholic.The deadness and emotional distance were the same. When she read the letter to her husband, he sobbed—but he did not change. He was not ready to face his pain, and as a consequence, lost his wife and children to divorce.

Another dead zone, literally, is war. At this time, we are seeing the effects of men and women returning after three, four, or five year-long tours in the war zones of Iraq and Afghanistan. The terrible increase in the divorce rate, domestic violence, mental health and addiction problems, suicide, children's feelings of abandonment as a parent leaves for a war zone, and Post-Traumatic Stress Disorder (PTSD) cases is a grim witness to the life-killing energies of war. We saw the same thing in my generation during the Vietnam War. When will we learn?

Finally, what about the youngest victims of dead zones? What does a child experience living in a war zone? A young Croatian woman I know could not play outside as a child for fear of Serbian warplanes dropping bombs. She tearfully described the environment in her junior high school as "crazy." Everyone, teachers and students alike, was frightened and angry after years of war, and the violence, bullying, misconduct, and lack of discipline in the school was a measure of the war's impact. A Salvadorian friend talks about the bodies she had to step over as a ten year-old on her way to school. It was nearly a daily occurrence during the civil war in El Salvador. Her family finally had to send her to the United States because she was so terrified a bomb would explode in her home, as had happened to some of the homes in her neighborhood. She is now a successful banker, but still has nightmares.

A young Columbian woman once calmly described to me her months of rape and abuse at the hands of Columbian guerillas. Clearly, her sense of trust in men and humanity had been severely scarred. She never cried about the experience after she was rescued. She felt she was no longer able to cry, despite the haunted grief in her eyes.

Finally, just after 9/11, I was working as a hospital chaplain on a pediatric ward at Baptist Hospital in Miami, Florida. For weeks, I had to reassure terrified children, from preschoolers to early teens, that a terrorist plane was not going to crash into the hospital, their homes, or their schools. All they heard on television and from the adults around them was that the terrorists could attack anytime and anywhere. Children take these things literally. We saw the same thing after Hurricane Andrew in 1992, when many children anxiously awaited the return of the one-eyed giant, Andrew, to once again destroy their homes and neighborhoods. Every windy rainstorm terrified them.

Return to Hope

The essential message of Universalism is the restoration of hope and purpose, and, consequently, the restoration of a future—for individuals, families, communities, nations, and the world. This is why we spend a fair amount of thought and intent on Liberation Theology. We wish to liberate all of us from the anti-life energies and open us to all of life. Naturally, these anti-life energies and pathways incur painful lessons. However, in the end, we believe we will be drawn back to our center, the God-breath spark of life, which the Hindus call "Brahman" (Ultimate Reality).[15] Moreover, these painful lessons are freely chosen for a purpose; the purpose of growth, healing, understanding, and renewal. For example, in Buddhism, there is no angry, judging God at death. In both Buddhism and modern Hinduism, *karma* and reincarnation (*samsara*) are not punishments, but lessons for growth and learning to release *dukkha* (unhealthy desires and attachments).[16] For instance, how can we understand

15. Hopfe and Woodward , 91–92.

16. Edward Conze, ed. and trans., *Buddhist Scriptures* (New York: Penguin Books, 1959), 229–230; and Swami Yogatmananda, "Reincarnation," (Miami: Florida International University Center for Spirituality, December 5, 2005).

the misuse of power if we have not misused power and equally been the victim of the misuse of power? Likewise, how can we comprehend suffering if we have not caused suffering as well as undergone suffering? It is living the human dilemma from all sides. This understanding leads to compassion for others as well as ourselves. "Love your neighbor as yourself" (Matthew 22:39). Eventually, this compassion leads to a higher calling of service. Principle 22 brings us to a higher understanding of the "duality" of good and evil and foreshadows our later section *On the Nature of Illusion*.

> 22. Evil is an illusion. In the higher planes, what has occurred here, in the physical plane, is seen and understood entirely differently. It is not duality, but Oneness. As part of our work here, all humans will choose to do evil for some time until the lessons are learned, as roles are played on both sides as the oppressor and the oppressed, the power hungry and disempowered, and the abuser and the victim. Depending upon the soul's motivation and awareness, each choice of darkness or evil slowly or quickly leads to spiritual growth and the lifetimes where the commitment to the Light and to Love and Harmony become stronger. Remembering all that we have been and accepting responsibility for all that we have done, both in the Light and in the Darkness, leads to the redemption of the Self and the return to Oneness.[17]

Obviously, this is a distinct departure from much of traditional Christianity, where humans have been viewed intrinsically as lost sinners and under the dominion of Satan. Traditional, conservative Christianity has resided in the prison of believing that we are creatures of sin: ruled by it, conquered by it, dying to it. There is little room for self. It's all about God. What a strange view of God as the ultimate, narcissistic egoist who needs our unceasing worship and praise. It's as if the Creator-Creatress doesn't have more important things to do than be bathed in self-adulation and our adulation. What strange egoism on our part to think that we are so important to God that He or She cannot live without us and our praise.

As Universalists, we believe that God gave each of us talents and gifts to be used. If we are captive in sin, it is by our own free will choice. And, if we free ourselves from that jail, it is by our own free will choice. Similar to Confucius and the Buddha, we believe each of us has the capacity somewhere within to achieve greatness. This is the greatness of

17. *A Universalist Spiritual Manifesto*, 12.

service to others (which is serving God), the greatness of humility, the greatness of majestic and beautiful works, the greatness of compassion and love. We may not evidence this as much as we would like in our daily lives or see as much of it as we would like on the planet, but it is there. It is a rare human that has not done one kind or generous thing in his or her life. And, if they have not, perhaps we must question his or her basic humanity. There are so many small stories out there of quiet courage, quiet compassion, quiet comfort, and quiet community. They are the hallmarks of humanity as well. It is not just the incessant headlines of defeat, failure, and despair in the local news.

We are more than creatures of sin. We are creatures of free will. We are creatures of choice. We are creatures of hope. Our divine parents have hardly given up on us simply because they take the long view. Individuals, families, communities, and whole societies, even our world, are in a process of evolutionary growth and learning. It is a long education to heal and clean out the distortions in our thinking. Do you see the glass as half empty or half full? It depends on which perspective will determine your view of humanity and our future. Will we always be mired in sin and only be saved by some supernatural champion (God, Jesus, whomever) because we cannot do it by ourselves? Or will we grow and learn from the great teachers and messengers God sent us to help us have faith in ourselves, in each other, and the Creator? It is a team effort. And, yes, God could live quite comfortably without us. Yet, She or He chooses not to out of love, hope, and faith that his or her creations can and will eventually "get it." It would be a lonely universe without God, but it would be an equally lonely universe without God's creations. And God's creations apparently exist on a vast scale beyond our imagining, far exceeding these few billions of humans on our little planet.

As you can see, then, Universalists do not subscribe to this concept of original sin. However, since the Age of Enlightenment in the 17th century, we are not entirely alone in this. Many Christian theologians have also questioned the idea that sin has been sexually and genetically transmitted to all humans from generation to generation because of and since the fall of Adam and Eve.[18] Universalists tend to lean much closer to the views of the controversial Roman Catholic priest, Matthew Fox.

18. Hans Kung, *On Being a Christian*, trans. Edward Quinn (Garden City, NY: Image Books, 1984), 454; and Marjorie Suchocki, "Original Sin Revisited," *Process Studies*/20, no. 4 (Winter 1991), *Religion Online*, accessed June 2005, religion-online.org.

> I also object to original sin as the starting point of religion because of the tremendous psychic damage it has done. People are already terribly vulnerable to self-doubt and guilt, especially members of minority groups—women, blacks, Native Americans, homosexuals. The whole ideology of original sin increases one's alienation and feeds the sado-masochistic energies in the culture–the sense that one is not worthy. If you start with the notion that you are born a blotch on existence, you will never be empowered to do something about the brokenness of life. In creation spirituality, we begin with the idea that each of us is born a unique expression of divinity, an image of God.[19]

Moving toward the Far East, we, likewise, do not perceive life as a nearly endless karmic curse, lifetime after lifetime, as classical Hinduism might.[20] We align more with Native American, Buddhist, modern Hindu, and Confucian thought, whereby humans can be seen as evolving toward a higher beingness. Paramahansa Yogananda, the great Hindu saint who died in California in 1954, is very practical about it.

> The condemnation so often encountered in religious work does quite as much harm as good. The way to help people out of their ignorance is to inspire them with a longing for understanding. To scold them for their ignorance would be like scolding a blind man for his inability to see.[21]

Hence, there has been no fall from grace, at least not as Christianity has historically perceived it. Furthermore, we take a less Pauline interpretation of Jesus' mission. The Apostle Paul hardly spoke of the life and teachings of Jesus,[22] but mainly emphasized the crucified and resurrected Jesus Christ.[23] A typical Pauline proclamation is in Romans 5:15. "For if the many died through the one man's trespass [Adam], much more surely have the grace of God and the free gift in the grace of the one man, Jesus Christ, abounded for the many." Most of Christian theology

19. Matthew Fox, "Original Blessing, Not Original Sin—Matthew Fox and Creation Spirituality," interview by Sam Keen, *Psychology Today* (June 1989); in *FindArticles* [database on-line]; accessed June 13, 2005.

20. Ludwig, 40, 61–62.

21. Paramahansa Yogananda, as remembered by Swami Kriyananda, *The Essence of the Bhagavad Gita* (Nevada City: Crystal Clarity Publishers, 2006), 164.

22. David Wenham, *Follower of Jesus or Founder of Christianity?* (Grand Rapids: William B. Eerdmans Publishing, 1995), 3.

23. Kung, 399.

centers around this theme, "that Christ died for our sins" (I Corinthians 15:3). However, Christian theologian Marcus Borg suggests this is an 11th century conceptual misreading of the meaning and the historical context of Jesus' death. Rather than a literal interpretation, Borg saw it as a subversive anti-Temple and anti-institutional metaphor. One no longer needed to go through the Temple priesthood and the Temple sacrificial system in order to receive God's grace and forgiveness.[24]

In essence, then, Universalists do not tend to believe that Jesus came to do all the work for us. He did not take on all of our sins and die for us so we can return to a state of grace. Rather, we see the Jesus, who teaches by word and example how to overcome our own sins and return to a state of grace. I would never ask Jesus or anyone to take on my sins. Why would I want to burden them with the weighty bricks of my life's mistakes? Why deprive myself of the courage, strength, and lessons learned as I overcome my sins? Only I can work through and learn from my sins. Sometimes they have been my greatest spiritual teachers. My wife calls sins "energetic mistakes." What do you do with a mistake? You correct it. Thus, as good postmodernists, we tend to be individualistic and acknowledge that our growth and enlightenment is no one's responsibility but our own, not even God's or Jesus'. As Tina Turner sang so soulfully in *Beyond Thunderdome*, wondering if we need another hero,[25] we ask the same thing. In our case, we are not looking for another savior. As one Universalist church member emphasized, "If you need to be saved from something, this implies something is wrong with you."[26]

As we have rejected the concept of original sin and instead suggest that there is original goodness in human beings, the Christian concept of salvation just does not work for us. Where others need salvation, we think of these sins and problems as "energetic mistakes" or "blessons,"[27] the teaching blessings and lessons of life that help us grow. Again, the member commented, "We are working our process. Let the child skin their knee and learn from it."[28] It is the God Within and the Christ With-

24. Borg, 94–95.

25. Referring to her 1985 hit song from the soundtrack of *Mad Max: Beyond Thunderdome.*

26. Scott Gerard, interview by Thomas Norris, February 25, 2006, The Church of the Way of the Messiahs, Miami, FL.

27. Gary Smith, "Sacred MerkabaTechniques," in a series of lectures and workshops in Florida, California, and Oregon, 1997–2002.

28. Gerard interview.

in that heals and accepts the Satan Within (our Shadow). It is the Buddha Within that leads to enlightenment. It is the grace of their teaching and the example of their goodness and righteousness that is the grace of God. So explains Principle 12:

> 12. We understand that the "fall of humanity from Grace" was a free will choice for teaching and learning purposes, experienced as individuals, as families, and as a community of peoples in our towns, provinces and states, nations, and world. This choice manifested through the physical plane will teach us much of all creation, both the Light and the Dark, and that through this "fall," that is, the acceptance of the shadow teachers of suffering, pain, ignorance, fear, and the illusion of death, we will learn from our experiences and grow in our understanding in order to return to the higher states of Spirit, Joy, and Grace; to the Oneness that we knew in the Beginning and which has always resided within us.[29]

As Principle 15 asserts, even the Dark Side has an essential role to play in the play. Swami Kriyanada remembered that his guru, Yogananda, would suggest that there is no real dark or light side when he said,

> God it is, in reality, who acts even when the parts He plays are those of the villains. Satan himself is—when the whole tale is told—an instrument of God. As my Guru put it, "The villain is needed in a play to make you love the hero."[30]

Carl Jung, mystical psychologist of archetypes and explorer of Asian spiritual traditions, always believed the darkness in the Shadow Self was the wellspring of our deepest emotions, creativity, and impulses. It is our artistic and archetypal connection to symbols and myth. It is an essential, if uncomfortable, presence in our being and must come to balance with the light of our consciousness.[31] As Laurens van der Post, his dear friend, summarized:

> All at once it was clear that man could only be well and sane when the quarrel between him and his shadow, between the primitive and the civilized, between the Jacob and the Esau in

29. *A Universalist Spiritual Manifesto*, 7

30. Yogananda, 123.

31. Carl Jung, *Pysche and Symbol*, ed. Violet S. de Laszlo (New York: Doubleday, 1958). This theme is shaped throughout his chapters on "The Shadow," "The Animus and Anima," "The Self," and "Christ a Symbol of the Self," 7–60.

himself, was dissolved and the two reconciled and together enter the presence of the master pattern as Jung's imagination had already done. Only there and then did he become something Jung called whole.[32]

Jung goes so far as to implicate the chaos and divisiveness in the world as emanating from this unresolved split within ourselves:

> Today humanity, as never before, is split into two apparently irreconcilable halves. The psychological rule says that when an inner situation is not made conscious, it happens outside, as fate. That is to say, when the individual remains undivided and does not become aware of his inner contradictions, the world must perforce act out the conflict and be torn into opposite halves.[33]

How many ways is this split acted out in our world? There is the War of the Sexes as seen by the inherent tension in Jung's anima (feminine) and animus (masculine) principles, and the God-Goddess split mentioned earlier by Roger and Jennifer Woolger. We cannot forget the War of Heterosexism between straight and gay. The War of Religions—Jewish vs Muslim, Roman Catholic vs Protestant, Hindu vs Muslim, Sunni vs Shia, and so on. The War of the Classes—rich and poor, haves and have-nots, the 1 percent and the 99 percent. Genocide—Native Americans, The Holocaust (*Shoah*), Cambodia, Bosnia and Kosovo, Rwanda, and Darfur. The ancient War between Generations. And on. And on. And on.

Native American teachings speak of the forked stick or the Flowering Forked Tree in their sacred stories and ceremonies. The fork represents duality; the mirrors within us of our own reflections of light and shadow, good and evil, male and female, young and old, and so on. It appears that the fork separates and divides, but in reality, it still comes from the same tree of harmony and wholeness.[34] Such are we. In her sharing of Native American teachings, Jamie Sams speaks of the importance of our Shadow Teachers, our Shadow Selves.

> When the shadow is denied, it gains strength and will one day wake up with life-force of its own and eat the beauty inside you. Teach others to use the shadow parts of themselves as examples

32. Lauren van der Post, "Jung's Understanding of the Meaning of the Shadow," *Jung and the Story of Our Time* (1975), accessed June 2005, http://www.ratical.org/many_worlds/LvdP/Jung.html.

33. Jung, 60.

34. Hyemeyohsts Storm, *Seven Arrows* (New York: Ballantine, 1972), 14–20.

> of the worthy opponent who can stir the growth of beauty inside the Self.[35]

Jung could not have agreed more, as does Principle 15.

> 15. Those that serve darkness, whether in body or spirit, are adversaries and shadow teachers, often of great power and influence until we begin to see through them. Yet, even the darkest beings, as creations of Great Spirit, carry the divine spark at their center. As energy and part of Great Spirit's creation, the divine spark cannot be extinguished. Also, we have played all the roles of Light and Dark, good and evil. We have been "them." There is no elitism in this higher awareness. There are no Elect, or we are all Elect. One sign of a less-awakened soul is pride and a "holier than thou" belief. Eventually, and they have all time, all will remember who they truly are. Perhaps Lucifer, unconditionally Beloved Son of the Creatress-Creator, shall simply be the last Prodigal Son to trudge home.[36]

The Christian figure of Satan as evil incarnate is not shared by Judaism, where *ha'satan*, the adversary, is even a member of God's court and, in a sense, the royal tester of humanity (Job 1:6). In Islam, *Shaitan* is a more trivial figure, and his tragic "fall" is not an absolute sin. Similar to the sentiment in Principle 15 above, the Qu'ran envisions that Satan will also be forgiven on the Last Day.[37]

This mention of Satan leads us directly to the concept of hell, which cannot be ignored in any discussion of good, evil, sin, and suffering. It is not a concept we joyfully embrace, as Principle 25 below succinctly denotes. It is also a fine way in which to introduce the next chapter on the nature of illusion.

> 25. Hell is a human-made creation. An all-loving, all-forgiving Creatress-Creator would have no need to punish its own beloved creations. We do a fine job of punishing ourselves all by ourselves.[38]

Truly, we have seen people who manage to bring a piece of the Kingdom of God into their lives. Despite the vicissitudes and perils of life on

35. Jamie Sams, *Sacred Path Cards: The Discovery of Self through Native Teachings* (San Francisco: Harper, 1990), 295.

36. *A Universalist Spiritual Manifesto*, 9

37. Armstrong, *Muhammad*, 114.

38. *A Universalist Spiritual Manifesto*, 13.

this planet, they hold hell at bay and enjoy a bit of heavenly waters in their lives. It is not that they have perfect, unmarred lives. It is simply that they have learned to co-create a better flow, a more positive mindset, and a way of turning hardships into lessons and victories rather than tragedies and defeats. Contrarily, we have seen people who have transported their lives to a living hell. It takes a lot to change their mindset, as some of the guiding principles of being in hell include being stuck, closed, angry, and afraid. It is not a prescription for healthy change and growth and requires significant effort to overcome the illusion. Perhaps the Buddha's very practical approach to ethics is useful here. There are "skillful actions" which avoid harmful consequences for self and others, and there are "unskillful actions" that lead to some form of harm to self or others. Skillful actions are creative and insightful and they are not clouded by illusion or delusion. "Skillful means" or *upaya* "encourages imaginatively applying wisdom to whatever circumstances one is in to assist in easing suffering or cultivating insight."[39] One could say a good life is filled with skillful action and a bad life is filled with unskillful action. Heaven is filled with skillful action and hell is filled with unskillful action. Through many lives of learning, growth, and soul evolution, it is our choice which path we are ready to follow.

39. Nystrom et al, "Buddhism" in *Exploring World Religions* (Unpublished manuscript from Oxford University Press, 2009), 26–27.

CHAPTER 10

Seeing Through a Glass Darkly

(On the Nature of Illusion)

Be in the world, not of the world.

JESUS, JOHN 17

Reality is merely an illusion, albeit a very persistent one.

ALBERT EINSTEIN

There are as many pillows of illusion as flakes in a snow-storm. We wake from one dream into another dream.

RALPH WALDO EMERSON

Veils and More Veils

THERE ARE A NUMBER of religious traditions that deem this earthly life and this material world as only one level of existence in the "Grand Play." Parting the veils of illusion (*Maya*) that keep us from seeing the grand scheme is the chief theme in Hinduism and, later in a modified form, in Buddhism. Rather than seeing *Maya* as a negative, Universalists view it as a means to accomplish the work of the soul—the tests and lessons of life that lead to growth and, eventually, enlightenment. When that breakthrough is accomplished, one may more closely perceive and experience Brahman or *Dharma*, Ultimate Truth.[1]

Similarly, in Islam, there is the sense of an ultimate reality beyond this mortal plane, which even inspired their scientific curiosity. Unlike medieval Christendom, Muslims were urged to use their intelligence and look for the signs and messages of *Allah* that abide everywhere in creation.[2] One interesting outcome of this endorsement to look both inward and outward in search of God—to pierce the veils of illusion—was the development of Muslim research into the "lost" classics of Greece and Egypt and simultaneously delving into the natural sciences. Bakir Tarabishy and Karen Armstrong both note that the medieval Europeans had to turn to Muslim scholars and scientists for the curriculum, scholarship, and translated classical works essential to their first universities. This is a fact generally unrecognized among Westerners.[3] The Europeans had lost everything during the Dark Ages (5th to 11th centuries CE) due to the Church's aversion to knowledge, science, and books at the time. Anything not found in the Bible or sanctioned by Mother Church was disavowed. Armstrong further reports that the Qu'ran itself is a vehicle of this higher reality.

> By approaching the Koran in the right way, Muslims claim that they do experience a sense of transcendence, of an ultimate reality and power that lie behind the transient and fleeting phenomena of the mundane world.[4]

Thomas Merton, Roman Catholic contemplative monk and Christian mystic, long held a fascination with Buddhism and Eastern religions. He felt that discovering their mysteries was perfectly in line with the spirit of the Second Vatican Council in the early 1960s.[5] As part of this discovery, he comments on the teachings of Thich Nhat Hanh, the Vietnamese monk and scholar.

1. Ludwig, 61–62, 102–103.

2. Karen Armstrong, *A History of God* (New York: Alfred A. Knopf, 1994), 143; and Ahmad Bakir Tarabishy, "Why Have Muslim Scholars Been Undervalued Throughout Western History?," *Islam for Today* (June 2005), 1, http://www.islamfortoday.com/scholars.htm.

3. Armstrong, *Muhammad*, 29; and Tarabishy.

4. Armstrong, *A History of God*, 144.

5. Thomas Merton, *Mystics and Zen Masters* (New York: Delta, 1967), vii-ix.

> The problem of human suffering is insoluble as long as men are prevented by their collective and individual illusions from getting directly to grips with suffering in its very roots within themselves. To set up party, race, nation, or even official religion as absolutes is to erect barriers of illusion that stand between man and himself and prevent him from facing his own reality in its naked existential factuality . . . The aim of Buddhism is then the creation of an entirely new consciousness which is free to deal with life barehanded and without pretenses. Piercing the illusions in ourselves which divide us from others, it must enable man to attain unity and solidarity with his brother through openness and compassion, endowed with secret resources of creativity. This love can transform the world.[6]

Thus, we are swinging back temporarily to our section on good, evil, sin, and suffering. But here we are trying to dig beneath the dry surface and expose the heart of the illusion, or the heart of illusion.

As Philip Kapleau reminds us, this is a very Buddhist way to approach the issue. The Buddha, The Compassionate One, was not philosophical about suffering, for he clearly saw "the agonies of existence." He came first and foremost to bring us relief.[7] As the Buddha himself said, "One thing only do I teach; Suffering—its causes and the way to overcome them."[8] This does not mean that Buddhists do not appreciate the illusion of suffering, that it is created by us, but that is precisely the point. For a Buddhist, humans must free themselves from the illusory causes of suffering. These are the desires and attachments (*dukkhas*) of the world which we often take too seriously, and which bring us harm (greed, envy, lust for power, fear of loss, and such). Once freed, only then can we be truly happy.[9] Hence, Principle 21 affirms the paradox between the illusion and the reality of suffering. Despite it being an illusion, it is nonetheless a compelling one in this world, and we can do nothing less than take a compassionate stance on behalf of all who suffer.

> 21. Suffering is an illusion. With enough clearing of the illusionary material we have accumulated over many lifetimes, and as our Higher Awareness increases, suffering can be released as

6. Merton, 286–287.

7. Philip Kapleau, *The Wheel of Life and Death* (New York: Anchor Books, 1990), 109.

8. Gautama Buddha, quoted in *The Wheel of Life and Death*, 109.

9. Kapleau, 110–11.

> we remember our Co-Creatress-Creator status and the gift of creating our own lessons, destiny, and path. When each tragedy becomes a lesson, even a triumph, the pain is lessened and truly transformed. At the same time, the pain and suffering experienced at this level of existence is very "real" to us, so genuine compassion for the less fortunate and the oppressed is part of unconditional, non-judgmental love. Whatever the fancy, metaphysical explanations, there is no room for intellectual and philosophical distancing from the profound grief and pain of the Holocaust; of the abuse of children; of the genocidal wars against the Native Peoples around the world; of the effects of famine, poverty, and disease; of the oppression of women; of the effects of war; and the other harsh lessons of humanity. Even as the Buddha came to free the world from suffering; Christ opened his heart to the thief, the prostitute, and the leper; and White Buffalo Calf Woman came to awaken her people to goodness and to Spirit, so we carry a responsibility to follow in their footsteps of compassion and understanding.[10]

Excluding acts of nature, such as natural disasters or death from old age, there appears to be an inherent link between suffering and evil. In down-to-earth terms, suffering is frequently created through unenlightened, dark, and/or evil choices made by self or others against self or others. Returning to the Buddhist concept of *dukkha* (cravings and over-attachments), it is easy to see how we create suffering for ourselves and others through our unenlightened actions. Would one Jew have been exterminated in a concentration camp if individual Nazis and their collective ethic were not motivated by egoistic greed, lust for power, and pride? Would Saddam Hussein have been a brutal dictator against his own Iraqi people if he had not been ruled by that same *dukkha*? Would Colonial white Europeans have enslaved or attempted genocide against many native peoples around the world if they had not been ruled by those same desires and attachments? Would the governments of the world place far more resources into war than the cure for cancer or the end of poverty if they were not governed by these materialistic, fear-based principles? Would one child victim suffer if their physical, emotional, or sexual abuser were not driven by these same dark impulses? Finally, could one Jew, Christian, or Muslim have ever killed in the name of their God, anytime in history, if they truly understood the message of love and compassion delivered by their founders?

10. *A Universalist Spiritual Manifesto*, 11.

It is blindingly simple. People who are not too attached to the things and ways of the world are less affected by the harsh realities of the world. A Hindu, Buddhist, Sikh, or Sufi would heartily agree with Jesus' implicit message to his followers in John 17, "Be in the world, but not of the world." Such people just do not get tangled up in the Mexican *novela*, the soap opera of life. This is a form of emotional, mental, and spiritual stability and security. Stable, secure people do not maim, murder, torture, abuse, belittle, humiliate, or attempt to control others, consciously or unconsciously. Thus, dark or evil acts are the illusory product of a lack of light upon the subject, that is, enlightenment. It has little to do with intelligence and intellect, for evil doers can be mental geniuses. It has everything to do with wisdom and heart—the essential human capabilities of empathy, understanding, and compassion. Hannah Arendt found these so singularly lacking in her study of the Nazi leaders, particularly Adolf Eichmann, that it led to the telling title of her 1963 work, *Eichmann in Jerusalem: A Report on the Banality of Evil.*[11] In stark contrast to that banal evil, the Gospel of Luke 23:34 reports that Jesus could, at the last agonizing moments of his crucifixion, utter in all truth: "Father, forgive them; for they do not know what they are doing." He knew that if they truly understood what they were doing—if they could just see the spiritual big picture—they would not be executing anyone, much less innocent messengers of God. This mercy and compassion would apply equally to Nazi totalitarians as well as Roman dictators in the realm of Jesus. As the messenger of Resurrection, Jesus would have added (and not as the Terminator), "I'll be back." Of course, when we speak of the grandest illusion of all, death, we could all say that. Principle 20 reminds us that this particular illusion, when viewed in a metaphysical manner, is simply "the pause that refreshes." It is a time of rest and re-creation and an opportunity for accelerated spiritual growth.

> 20. Death is an illusion. The release of our physical vehicle is simply a transition from one form of existence to another. It may be chosen as a moment of great joy as we directly reunite with our Creatress-Creator; are finally freed to explore other planes of existence and select our next lessons and steps of spiritual growth. No

11. Jerome Kohn, "Evil: The Crime Against Humanity," *Hannah Arendt Papers of the Library of Congress*, accessed March 2008, http://memory.loc.gov/ammem/arendthtml/essayc1.html.

> physical death occurs without the higher self's permission, and there is a higher purpose in even the most tragic deaths.[12]

It is difficult for the Western mind to understand how a child's death on the operating table, or from a car bomb on a Baghdad street, or in an airplane crashing into the World Trade Center on 911, can hold a higher purpose and is nothing less than a tragedy. Surely, when I interned as a hospital chaplain, I was deeply shaken by the deaths of these young innocents and felt utterly helpless as I attempted to console their inconsolable loved ones. In one instance, I came to the operating room where a three year-old girl had just died. She had a virus that attacked her heart and ended her young life, despite the surgeon's desperate attempts to save her. As I entered the room, a young, blonde woman fell into my arms, sobbing. I assumed it was the child's mother. It was the surgeon. This type of loss affects everyone involved.

Nevertheless, over the past twenty-eight years, I have conducted hundreds of past life regressions on people from all faiths and walks of life. It appears all of us have played all the archetypal roles—innocent child and mad bomber, saint and sinner, Madonna and whore, slave and slave master, liberator and oppressor, and so on.[13] In addition to the archetypal roles, we have lived life from all vantage points: black, white, red and yellow; male and female; gay and straight; healthy and ill; disabled and whole; happy and sad; and so on. In each case, no matter how dreadful or fantastic the quality of an individual life, there was an essential soul lesson being learned. Beyond the illusion of the three-penny opera in each lifetime, there is the wider view of the evolutionary soul ever-growing, ever-changing, ever-learning.

Again and Again

It is not the purpose of this book to debate the merits of reincarnation, only to proclaim its place within Universalist theology. Not all Universalists may even believe in it, but it is not something they rule out. Western civilization is uncomfortable with reincarnation, although there

12. *A Universalist Spiritual Manifesto*, 11.

13. Roger Woolger, *Other Lives, Other Selves* (New York: Bantam, 1988). We owe so much to Roger Woolger's early and insightful book that presented his clinical research on the existence of dark past lives (evil, meaningless or unfulfilling), as well as our more productive past lives.

are substantial Jewish and Christian antecedents for it. For example, it was probably a Pharisaic belief and the *Hasidic* Jews, *Kaballah* Jews, and some Orthodox Jews believe in it to this day.[14] Additionally, the Christian Church Father, Origen (185–254 CE), was an adherent of reincarnation.[15] In one of his treatises on John the Baptist, Origen explains the common belief that John may have been Elijah, which even Jesus affirmed in Mark 9:13 and Matthew 11: 13–14.

> This will be the explanation of those who find in our passage a support for their doctrine of transcorporation, as if the soul clothed itself in a fresh body and did not quite remember its former lives. These thinkers will also point out that some of the Jews assented to this doctrine when they spoke about the Saviour as if He was one of the old prophets, and had risen not from the tomb but from His birth.[16]

To sum up, we will note that not only is reincarnation (or the transmigration of souls) the belief of many religions around the world, including the Celtic Druids found throughout Europe with their belief in the Otherworld[17] and a number of Native American tribes, but, as noted, has historical precedents within Christianity and Judaism as well. Moreover, it is not a "New Age" subject of interest born only of the late 20th century. The research of Courtney Bender and other scholars illustrated how it had been an active interest in North American metaphysical groups since the latter half of the 19th century.[18] There are also legitimate Western theologians, such as Geddes MacGregor, Professor Emeritus at the University of Southern California,[19] who have addressed the subject, as well

14) Woolger, 72–73; and Elizabeth Clare Prophet, *Reincarnation: the Missing Link in Christianity* (Corwin Springs, MT: Summit University Press, 1997), 52, 57.

15. Prophet, 174–175.

16. Origen, "Commentary on the Gospel of John (Book VI)," *Ante-Nicene Fathers*, vol. 9, *Gospel of Peter, Diatessaron, Testament of Abraham, Epistles of Clement, Origen and Miscellaneous Works*, ed. Allan Menzies (American Edition, 1896–97), http://www.newadvent.org/fathers/101506.htm.

17. Peter Beresford Ellis, *The Druids* (Grand Rapids: Wm. B. Eerdmans Publishing, 1994), 176–177.

18. Courtney Bender, "American Reincarnations: What the Many Lives of Past Lives Tell Us about Contemporary Spiritual Practice," *Journal of the American Academy of Religion* 75:3 (September 2007), 592–593.

19. Geddes MacGregor wrote that there are grounds for bridges between reincarnation and Christianity in *Reincarnation in Christianity: A New Vision of Rebirth in Christian Thought* (Wheaton, IL: Quest Books, 1989).

as several scientists and universities. Among them are the University of Virginia's Department of Psychiatry (since 1961) and the University of Sydney, which have researched this phenomenon for many years with astonishing results.[20]

Nor is the dialog confined to the scientific community and among non-Christians. Rosemary Radford Reuther, the great Christian feminist minister and theologian, sounds positively New Age as she ponders death and reincarnation. According to her, we return to a cosmic, everlasting "Matrix of energy-matter out of which new centers of individual beings arise." She calls it a "ground of being" or "ground of personhood" and adds, "The component parts of the matter-energy that coalesced to make up our individuated organisms are not lost. Rather, they change their form and become food for new beings which arise from our bones."[21] This adventurous statement, reaching well beyond her Christian roots, is part of the courage she has routinely demonstrated throughout her long, illustrious career. So, apparently many Westerners are also opening up to this notion, as the Gallup Organization reported in 2001 that some 25 percent of Americans (across all age and education groups) believe in reincarnation.[22] In 2009, the Pew Research Center described similar findings, with 24 percent of the public and 22 percent of Christians believing in reincarnation.[23]

20. Peter Ramster, *In Search of Lives Past* (Somerset: Somerset Films and Pub, 1992); Ian Stevenson, *Children Who Remember Previous Lives: A Question of Reincarnation* (Jefferson, NC: McFarland and Company, 2000); and Jim B. Tucker, *Life Before Life: A Scientific Investigation of Children's Memories of Previous Lives* (New York: St. Martins Press, 2005). For example, Psychologist Dr. Peter Ramster (University of Sydney), and Drs. Ian Stevenson and Jim Tucker (University of Virginia) have conducted extensive research on reincarnation for many years and have discovered surprising scientific support for the phenomenon.

21. Rosemary Radford Reuther, "Eschatology and Feminism," ed. Susan Brooks Thistlewaite and Mary Potter Engel, *Lift Every Voice* (Maryknoll: Orbis Books, 1998), 140–41.

22. George Gallup, "Americans' Belief in Psychic and Paranormal Phenomena is Up Over the Last Decade," *Gallup News*, June 8, 2001, http://home.sandiego.edu/~baber/logic/gallu.html.

23. Pew Forum on Religion and Public Life Survey, "Many Americans Mix Multiple Beliefs," Pew Research Surveys, December 9, 2009, http://pewforum.org/docs/?DocID=490.

We Are What We Think

Have you ever heard someone complain (perhaps your teenager), "I didn't ask to be born." Spiritually, we would answer, "Yes you did, even if you do not know it at the earthly level." However, this is an unusually plaintive cry when a person has experienced great suffering and cannot understand why it seems to go on and on. Why is this happening to me? Why am I a victim? That is just not the time to go into lengthy discussions of *karma*, or spiritual tests, or how they are co-creating their reality. All of that may be true, but it certainly is insensitive to the legitimate feelings of the person undergoing the suffering and their need for compassion. Can you imagine telling a rape victim that they brought the lesson to themselves? How many of us have endured a divorce, or the death of a loved one, or the end of a relationship, only to hear someone with apparently decent intent say tritely, "Time heals all wounds." Fortunately, most of us are able to curb the urge at that moment to fling the speaker off the nearest cliff, for these banal and unthinking comments are far too common. A deeper look into the issue of "reality" is needed here.

One clue is given in the popular spiritual documentary, *The Secret*, which asserts from just about every possible angle that we truly are the creators (or creatures) of our own destiny.[24] This is a very hard concept for the Western mind to accept with our two millennia of Judeo-Christian programming that the universe is entirely in God's hands. As the old song from the 1950s went, "He's Got the Whole World in His Hands." As such, we are creatures only of God and the whims of the gods. Yet, the Buddha came from a very different vantage point. In *The Dhammapada* (Wisdom of the Buddha), the "Twin Verses" begin:

> The mind is the basis for everything.
> Everything is created by my mind, and is ruled by my mind.
> When I speak or act with impure thoughts, suffering follows me
> As the wheel of the cart follows the hoof of the ox.
> The mind is the basis for everything.
> Everything is created by my mind, and is ruled by my mind.
> When I speak or act with a clear awareness, happiness stays with me.
> Like my own shadow, it is unshakeable.
> "I was wronged! I was hurt! I was defeated! I was robbed!"
> If I cultivate such thought, I will not be free from hatred.
> "I was wronged! I was hurt! I was defeated! I was robbed!"

24. *The Secret* (Prime Time Productions, 2006).

If I turn away from such thoughts, I may find peace.
In this world, hatred has never been defeated by hatred.
Only love can overcome hatred.
This is an ancient and eternal law.[25]

I spent many years feeling like a victim, and as a child, I had been sexually victimized many times. I stayed stuck in the memories, the hurt, the pain, and the anger well into my late thirties. I kept recreating victimizing events, whether it was losing a job "unfairly" or a feeling that I would never dig myself out of a financial hole or the end of yet another relationship. It took many years of confronting these old wounds and healing before I began to realize how my victim mentality was keeping me in a victim state. Learning to love me and not just loving others was my first pathway out of that particular hell. The second pathway out was working with victims of child abuse and family violence throughout my career. I help them release the victimization and old wounds as well, so they, too, can get on with their lives. The third pathway out was finding the courage to face the frightening idea that, in some lifetime, we have all been the Nazi and the Jew, the abuser and the victim. That indeed leads to a nonjudgmental road of forgiveness—not easy to find, but well worth the search.

The Way Out

In concluding our section on death, victimization, and illusion, we cannot ignore that other grand illusion mentioned earlier in Principle 25: a place of purported eternal torment and damnation. What is a Universalist supposed to do with that? We remember once again what Gandhi suggested to the wild-eyed, grieving Hindu father standing before him, edging toward horrified insanity because he had murdered a Muslim child in an act of vengeance. "I know a way out of hell."[26] Principle 18 shows the way out of hell; it is the way of God, and it is the way of love.

> 18. By following the example of unconditional love through complete forgiveness of self and others, we heal our karmic patterns of darkness, suffering, blindness, ignorance, and fear, especially

25. Gautama Buddha, *The Dhammapada*, trans. Wikisource, accessed February 2015, http://en.wikisource.org/wiki/Dhammapada_%28Wikisource%29.

26. Susanna Oommen Younger, "Gandhi: the Person and the Film," *Theology Today* 40:2 (July 1983), 172.

> through the courage of Self-exploration and Self-discovery. Life is not about being perfect, although Great Spirit sees us in our perfection at all times. Mother Life is about experience, knowledge, growth, and love. By facing our Shadow Teachers and Shadow Selves with love and acceptance, and through genuine remorse for wrongs committed or imbalances created towards self or others, now and in any lifetime, we heal and grow.[27]

We have done it. We have experienced it. It works! Following Jesus' lead, to love our neighbors as ourselves, what could be more loving than forgiveness—for our neighbors, ourselves, even our enemies? This love and forgiveness undertaking is a path out of hell and leads to freedom from the fear and deceptive power of death. It is the way to the Christ and Buddha consciousness. It is liberation in its deepest meaning. It is living this precious gift of life to the fullest measure. It is the anti-illusion breakthrough of the breath of life. It is becoming one with God, for love, forgiveness, and life seem to be the very pulsating heart-mind of God and God's universal message.

27. *A Universalist Spiritual Manifesto*, 12.

CHAPTER 11

All We Need is Love

(On the Nature of Love and Community)

Compassion is my religion.

LAMA KHEMSAR

Love is patient, love is kind. It does not envy, it does not boast, it is not proud. It is not rude, it is not self-seeking, it is not easily angered, it keeps no record of wrongs. Love does not delight in evil but rejoices with the truth. It always protects, always trusts, always hopes, always perseveres. Love never fails . . . And now these three remain: faith, hope and love. But the greatest of these is love.

ST. PAUL I CORINTHIANS 13: 4–8, 13

Religious Seekers and Universalists Today

For a Universalist, love, forgiveness, and life are also the pulsating heart-mind of their faith, and this ancient, universal message could not come at a more crucial time. It would hardly be unfair to characterize the postmodern era as a time of feeling cast adrift: as societies, communities, families, and individuals.[1] With all the promise of the 21st

1. Graham Ward, "Postmodern Theology," *The Modern Theologians*, ed. David F. Ford (Oxford: Blackwell Publishers, 1997), 585–587.

century, there is still so much upheaval and division, so much swift, radical change, and so little to cling to. It has left many floating alone on a vast and stormy ocean of indifference and estrangement. Joseph Holland comments upon the uneasy transformation taking place in the West and its profound effects.

> This passage from modern to postmodern culture is an extremely dangerous one, because the West in general and America in particular is promoting globally a technological path which threatens the ecology of all life on planet earth. At the same time, America is promoting a profound erosion of our social ecology, seen especially in the decline of community, the crisis of family, and the triumph of individualism.[2]

In the face of this erosion of community, the challenge to all communities of faith has always been how to bring us together. How do we transform the human experience into more than a bitter vale of tears or loneliness—what sociologist Wade Clark Roof names "wholeness-hunger." How do we make us whole again, as a world, as a people, and as souls?[3] We are a world once again precariously poised on a precipice of peril or promise. And, as always, it is not just about the external threats of annihilation and suffering but also reaches into the very core of what it means to be human.

There are some in the world who are not seeking for a deeper meaning to human existence, but there are also many who are. According to Roof, and contrary to popular belief, "Surveys show that large sectors of the American population today are interested in deepening their spirituality."[4] And this spiritual search appears to be a worldwide phenomenon affecting every continent.[5] For example, there has been a "re-

2. Holland, "The Postmodern Transformation of Religious Life: Prophetic-Mystical Lay Communities of Ecological, Societal and Spiritual Regeneration," *The Annual Assembly of the Conference of Major Superiors of Men*, August 8, 1990, ed. Conference of Major Superiors of Men (Miami: St. Thomas University, 1990), 4.

3. Wade Clark Roof, *Spiritual Marketplace* (Princeton: Princeton University Press, 1999), 62–63.

4. Roof, 9 and 81.

5. James A. Beckford, "New Religious Movements and Globalization," *New Religious Movements in the 21st Century*, eds. Phillip Charles Lucas and Thomas Robbins (New York: Taylor and Francis, 2004), 254–257. Globalization occurs even in the spread of postmodern religious movements, as noted by the great number of articles in various theological and social analysis journals about New Age and related spiritual ventures in Central and South America, Europe, Asia, and the former Eastern and

ligious boom" in Japan over the past twenty years, much of it noticeably focused on new postmodern spiritual seekings. The same can be said in Eastern Europe and Latin America.

Like many of our postmodern and New Age neighbors, those drawn to postmodern spirituality and to postmodern spiritual centers and churches have been churched before. Of course, there are some who are discovering their faith or their need for spiritual community for the first time. Yet, in our experience, many who come to Universalism were raised in Christian and Jewish families of all persuasions (Roman Catholic, Protestant, Orthodox, Reformed, Liberal, and Conservative). Additionally, there has been a smattering from Muslim, Hindu, Buddhist, Wiccan, Santeria, and Rastafarian backgrounds.[6] Over the years, the Christian and Jewish members have turned away from or supplemented their original faiths for various reasons, including boredom; rebellion against family, tradition, or unbending dogma; exploration of new faiths; dropping away after moving away from the family; the perceived rigidity of organized religion; the busyness of the secular world; too many unanswered questions by conventional churches; and so on. Yet, instead of staying away for good, many are touched by a profound inner pull, a yearning for a spiritual life. In response, they often search far and wide until they find the spiritual community that best aligns with their hopes and needs.

This quest has not always been easy, especially with few societal or religious markers to light the way. The postmodern spiritual community has had to make its own way in its own markedly individualistic manner. Yet, many soon discovered it was not uncomfortable for them to be trailblazers. It seems to be part of their unconventional, even maverick personalities, coupled with their mystical belief in a direct connection to God. They feel this is Spirit's guidance leading them on these new voyages. Universalists seem to be questioners and seekers of truth who do not assume, as some mainline religions assert, that all of God's truth has already been revealed. For many of them, God is an ongoing revelation and doesn't come exclusively through a priesthood, a sainthood, or an institution. In retrospect, this is a form of *gnosis* (insightful, intuitive

---

Soviet Bloc. In Russia, for example, their influence is strong enough that there is significant resistance to them by entrenched governmental and church hierarchies.

6. Thomas Norris, *On the Nature of Universalism: The New Religion of Tolerance* (Miami: Published doctoral dissertation, Florida Center for Theological Studies, 2006): 59.

knowledge).[7] Hence, there are the unflattering comparisons from some Christians to the old, supposedly heretical, Gnostic Christians of the early Christian Church who were very devout Christians.[8]

The Search is for Love and Community

For those who are seeking, some are finding it through the traditional, well-plowed fields of organized religion, and some are questing in virgin meadows. Today's Universalism begins with this last group of seekers, but most certainly does not end there. It hopes and dreams for a world where all religions and communities honor and respect each other as people of faith. Another word for this Universalist search is love, as Principle 23 affirms:

> 23. As unconditional love, Great Spirit is All-forgiving. The God of fear and judgment is a human-made creation and an earlier step in our evolution of spiritual understanding. It is easier to believe in that God than the far more difficult task of accepting responsibility for our own actions and the hells we can create in our own lives all by ourselves. Great Spirit is not an interfering parent. Interestingly, the hardest task is forgiving ourselves as we begin to remember and awaken, for we are still under the programming and illusion that we are bad, that the God of fear and judgment finds us unworthy and unsightly.[9]

This principle accentuates the postmodern transition that is taking place in our view of God, Other, and Self, and especially our role and responsibility in the healing of these three elements of All That Is. It is not just up to God, for we trust that we are evolving into a more responsible partner in the co-creation of our destiny as a people and as a world. However, following in God's unconditionally loving footsteps is no easy task.

Islam provides one enlightened possibility for accomplishing this. Muslims are quick to point out that their highest duty is to express their gratitude for Allah's great bounty and graciousness as the life-giver. They do this by emulating his example, by developing compassion, graciousness, kindness, and generosity within themselves for "all God's

7 Elaine Pagels, *The Gnostic Gospels* (New York: Vintage Books, 1979), xix.

8. One such comparison is included in the aforementioned Vatican Report on "Jesus Christ, The Bearer of the Water of Life: A Christian Reflection on the 'New Age.'"

9. *A Universalist Spiritual Manifesto*, 10.

creatures."[10] Similarly, Principle 16 offers up our greatest role model, the Creator-Creatress:

> 16. The Divine Creatress-Creator is the essence of all-encompassing and unconditional love for all of Creation and for all beings. This is our model and ideal for our own participation in the world and in creation. Once Self-remembered and Self-realized, we are likewise the essence of this same love, for we have been told and shown that the greatest commandment is love.[11]

In an individualistic, materialistic Western society, this may seem more and more problematic. God and religion are no longer "an unquestioned fundamental fact of life," as they were until the Enlightenment of the 17th century.[12] Nevertheless, there are signs of a counterbalancing trend around the world in a renewed search for broader spiritual meaning. Universalists represent one small example of this trend but probably reflect the concerns of many more traditional and non-traditional seekers as well.

Spiritual Psychobabble and Belongingness

A primary frustration among many Universalists lies in a perceived disconnection from their spiritual roots. Although it is safe to say that the individualistic and inward approach they adopt to poke about their spiritual beliefs is common to this postmodern age,[13] it has come at a price. From the perspective of traditional religion, the New Age and related postmodern religious trends, with their notions of a "spiritual quest" and the buzzword of "spirituality," have been accused of being so much "psychobabble."[14] What an ironic shift this reflects. Sister Ada Maria Asasi Diaz remembers that the word "spirituality" was often only used by the priests and nuns in her convent as a traditional means to set themselves apart from lay people.[15] Now using this same terminology, but with a world of difference in meaning, nontraditional groups are

10. Armstrong, *Muhammad*, 97.
11. *A Universalist Spiritual Manifesto*, 9.
12. Fisher, 13.
13. Roof, 57–58.
14. Ibid, 295–296.
15. Ada Maria Isasi Diaz, *Mujerista Theology* (Maryknoll, NY: Orbis Books, 1996), 31.

perceived merely as "spiritual lite," airy-fairy dilettantes with no discernible spiritual foundation. In contrast, Roof and other social researchers have found that these seekers are not generally religious, but they are certainly profoundly spiritual.[16] Moreover, in addition to the rejection of their beliefs by the traditional churches, and most certainly the conservative churches,[17] many members of our Universalist Church have had to put up with disparaging comments from family and peers. For them, then, there has not just been the loss of spiritual tradition, but also of spiritual community. Perhaps that is why the idea of spiritual family and community is so important to them; a place where they can be accepted as they are and for whom they are. This has been a key element of our Universalist Church's mission and this book—how to address this spiritual disconnection. One way we have answered that is to proclaim that Universalists have the "Good News," too. We are all brothers and sisters!

As they talk about what a Universalist Church means to them, one of the comments frequently heard from our congregants is how they feel they have finally found a loving home. They often feel closer to the spiritual family in the church than to their own families of origin. Of course, as noted earlier, a sense of belongingness is essential to the survival of any group or organization. This fellowship (or sistership) is supposed to be especially central in churches. Yet, we have often heard from our Universalist sisters and brothers that the reason they turned away from the traditional churches, temples, and mosques of their upbringing was this very lack of a sense of belongingness. They did not consistently feel warmth and love within its walls or between its members. The churches were either too large, too impersonal, too doctrinal, or too removed from the real problems and issues they confronted in their homes and offices or on the street every day. Other Universalists, including me, have had generally positive, engaging, and warm experiences in the churches, temples, and mosques of our youth. Yet, even though there was a sense of belongingness in our churches, we eventually realized that we were looking for something more.

In Christianity, this belongingness, as we noted earlier, is called *koinonia*. For Universalists, these are not just ideals and talk, but our consistent sacred experience within the church. It is not just our theology, but our praxis (living practice). It is our daily actions and interactions as a

16. Roof, 58.

17. Ibid, 288–289.

spiritual family. This is best expressed when the church group is smaller, more intimate and personal; not terribly rigid or doctrinal, but rather open and expansive; and working with and through the real issues of the day and contemporary life. Someday, we hope to expand *koinonia* to mean the family of the whole world—that we are all brothers and sisters.

In a related vein is the concept of the lay-centered community, very much a *koinonia* community. The word "lay" is derived from another Greek New Testament word, "laos," or "people of God."[18] A Universalist Church is a lay-centered community, very similar to the earlier-noted ecclesial base community in Liberation Theology. Again, to paraphrase Martin Luther, it encompasses the priesthood (and priestesshood) of all believers.[19] Smart also notes that "Part of Luther's revolution was to emphasize inwardness again. What was important was faith (not ritual works)." By making the experiential and emotional dimension of faith the most important, it deemphasized ritual and the priesthood.[20] Not only are rituals minimal in a Universalist setting, but the traditional Roman Catholic and Protestant forms of separate lay and clergy stations in the work of the church[21] will not succeed in a Universalist Church. All life roles, from the business community to community service to family life to politics to teaching to health services to church management and so on, represent a potential ministry of service and light. Within a Universalist Church, all members are responsible for the direction of the church, and any ministerial leadership is of the facilitator-teacher-coordinator-administrator kind only. Within a Universalist group, all are equally responsible to live their spirituality in the home and office and on the street. Further enhancing this sense of *koinonia* are its origins within a community of great diversity that meets in a community space, often the home. In this, we sense a direct historical connection to the early church and synagogue, something Holland notes is common to modern lay-centered communities.

> By embracing women and men, marrieds and singles, and children, the new form is returning to the model of the early

18. Eugene La Verdiere, *The Beginning of the Gospel: Introducing the Gospel According to Mark*, Vol. 2 (Collegeville, MN: Liturgical Press, 1999), 226; and Byung-Mu, 98–100; and Holland, 7.

19. Boehmer, 332–333.

20. Smart, 266.

21. Holland, "The Postmodern Transformation of Religious Life: Prophetic-Mystical Lay Communities . . . ," 30.

> church, that is rerooting its energy in the spiritual power of the foundational *laos*.[22]

Like the early church, and unlike modern monastic, clergy, and apostolic communities, these lay-centered communities "insist on their lay character and the sacred roots of their 'secular' life."[23]

Up to this point, we have covered issues surrounding God, creation, humanity, revelation, good and evil, love, and community. Now we move to the raison d'etre for the existence of a Universalist paradigm and the higher purpose its adherents serve. First, we begin with the concept of liberation.

22. Holland, 30.

23. Ibid.

CHAPTER 12

The Freedom Express

(On the Nature of Liberation)

There can be no love without justice. Love "surpasses" justice, but at the same time, it finds its verification in justice.[1]

POPE JOHN PAUL II

Of all the preposterous assumptions of humanity, nothing exceeds the criticisms made of the habits of the poor by the well-housed, well-warmed, and well-fed.

HERMAN MELVILLE

Since there will never cease to be some in need on the earth, I therefore command you, "Open your hand to the poor and needy neighbor in your land."

MOSES, DEUTERONOMY 15:11

The healthy man does not torture others. Generally, it is the tortured who turn into torturers.

CARL JUNG

1. Pope John Paul II, "General Audience on Justice" (Vatican City: Libreria Editrice Vaticana), The Vatican, November 8, 1978.

Four Years of Intolerance

When this book was being written, Donald Trump was just a blip on the horizon, a New York City real estate mogul known for his unbounded ego, bombast, failed casinos, celebrity marriages, and numerous bankruptcies. Then, he became president. He ushered in an era that is antithetical to the very definition of Universalism. We saw how intolerance strengthened the forces of chaos and division. He did not create these forces, but he championed them and encouraged many Americans to listen to their darker angels. Muslims, Mexicans, "shithole countries," Confederate generals, immigrants, transexuals, journalists, government workers, women, gun laws, people of color, Socialists, and Democrats all became watchwords for intolerance. Enemies were created who were not enemies—just people and noble ideals. The dark underbelly of America was exposed: racism, sexism, heterosexism, religocentrism, and ethnocentrism. Spiritually, I thank Donald Trump for that. It is now out in the open. Now we can see what we are dealing with and what needs to be healed.

Many books have been and will be written on this strange period in American history and politics. This book is not one of them. I simply point out that the past four years of the Trump Era are not the path to making "a more perfect union" or bringing humanity into oneness. As you read this chapter on freedom and liberation, you hear a plea to listen to our better angels. You will understand that the voices of intolerance are the voices of fear and insecurity. They do not represent the voices of Jesus, Buddha, Muhammad, Krishna, White Buffalo Calf Woman, Isis, or any of the great teachers who have graced us with their love and wisdom. They are not the voices of heart and spirit. They are not the voice of a loving, beneficent, merciful God.

Liberation Theology

The question is, "Liberate who and from what?" A corollary question is, "When and where?" In traditional Christian theology, through Church Fathers such as Paul and Augustine, the real goal of salvation has been the liberation from sin and the temptations of the world. In this way, you could enjoy a heavenly afterlife in the Kingdom of God. It was clear that the City of God (sacred, heavenly realm) was the only one that really mattered compared to the City of Man (sinful, earthly realm). Within this context, many traditional Christians even viewed poverty and suffering as something noble, relating the plight of the poor to Jesus' suffering on the cross.[2] For the Buddhist, it has traditionally meant the liberation from suffering through individual spiritual means, The Middle Way or The Buddha Noble Eightfold Path.[3] This is a wonderful path to self-realization. Indeed, no one can deny the spiritual impact Buddhists such as the Dalai Lama and Thich Nhat Hanh have had on bringing the world's attention to Buddhism, its inner beauties, and even its activism against war and aggression. Yet, many chafe at the slow manner in which the change in suffering seems to occur—one enlightened human at a time. These impatient advocates might answer the initial "liberate who and from what" question by noting the vast numbers of oppressed peoples suffering injustice and worldly harm around the world, every day and in every country. Furthermore, these advocates might opt for more direct intervention approaches, so they would also answer the corollary question by declaring the "where" is here (in the physical world) and the "when" is now.

For them, this is not a matter of quietly waiting for spiritual liberation through meditation and detachment, or in an afterlife meeting with God, or in a rapturous reunion with Christ, or after numerous reincarnations and an eventual soul evolution toward enlightenment. They believe this loving God can, has, and will continue to act within history using Great Spirit's best advocates for change and liberation: US.[4] Jews, Christians, and Muslims (and certainly Universalists) can find little in their various theologies that support a doctrine favoring the center (the dominant cultural group in any society) over the margin (the marginalized people in any society). As we see later in this chapter, the prophets, Jesus and Muhammad, explicitly and repeatedly spoke out on behalf of the marginalized (the poor, the oppressed, and the social outcasts). In the 1960s, Father Gustavo Gutierrez melded the concern for the victims of oppression with a theology of liberation.

> This is a theology which does not stop with reflecting upon the world, but rather tries to be part of the process through which

2. Ricardo Planas, *Liberation Theology: The Political Expression of Religion* (Kansas City: Sheed and Ward, 1986), 19–22, 27–28.

3. The Noble Eightfold Path of the Buddha is a path to spiritual transformation and enlightenment: Right Thought, Right Intent, Right Speech, Right Action, Right Livelihood, Right Effort, Right Mind, and Right Concentration. According to Buddhism, anyone who follows this path will eventually attain enlightenment.

4. Diaz, 73.

> the world is transformed. It is a theology which is open—in the protest against trampled human dignity, in the struggle against the plunder of the vast majority of the people, in liberating love, and in the building of a new, just, and fraternal society—to the gift of the Kingdom of God.[5]

This was a bold, new, radical theological adventure that was part Restless Sixties, part postmodern phenomenon, and part ecclesiastical passion finding expression in stolid Vatican City, of all places.

With the advent of the Vatican II Council (convened in 1962 by Pope John XXIII and completed by Pope Paul VI in 1965), there emerged an energetic and stirring new sense of the Roman Church and its role in social change. Sadly, since then, there has been significant retrenchment, a move toward conservatism under John Paul II and most especially Benedict XVI. Although the jury is still out on the promising, progressive actions of the new Pope Francis I, he did take the name of St. Francis of Assisi, patron of the poor and oppressed, and the birds and the beasts. Despite the efforts of the conservatives, the profound legacy of Vatican II cannot be wholly eradicated. Liberation Theology is one of its many offspring.[6] The Council also aligned with many children, although not all arising solely from Roman Catholic or Vatican II genes. These include Latin American Liberation Theology,[7] Feminist Theology,[8] Black Liberation Theology,[9] Womanist Theology,[10] *Mujerista* Theology,[11] and the afore-mentioned *Minjung* Theology.[12] As an outgrowth and affirmation of Vatican II, then, Liberation Theology focused a much-needed and long overdue lens on the peoples of the world who had been excluded; the people of the margin. It was not a

5. Gustavo Gutierrez, *A Theology of Liberation,* excerpted from *Readings in Christian Ethics*, ed. J. Philip Wogaman and Douglas M. Strong (Louisville: Westminster John Knox Press, 1996), 343.

6. Juan Luis Segundo, *Liberation of Theology* (Maryknoll, NY: Orbis, 1999), 126–127; and Gustavo Gutierrez, 341–342.

7. Gutierrez, 344.

8. Johnson, 22.

9. James H. Cone, *A Black Theology of Liberation*, excerpted from *Readings in Christian Ethics,* ed. J. Philip Wogaman and Douglas M. Strong (Louisville: Westminster John Knox Press, 1996), 358–359.

10. Delores Williams, *Sisters in the Wilderness: The Challenge of Womanist God-Talk* (Maryknoll, NY: Orbis, 1995), 178.

11. Diaz, 73.

12. Chang-Nack Kim, "Korean Minjung Theology: An Overview," *Register* 85:2 (Chicago Theological Seminary, Spring 1995), 5.

theology of the ivory tower, but a theology of praxis (action in practice); of solidarity with the poor and oppressed.

Sister Ada Maria Isasi Diaz, feminist and *Mujerista*[13] theologian, reframes Gutierrez's liberation "gift of the Kingdom of God" as the "unfolding of the kin-dom of God." She makes no bones about what makes a good Christian. Within *Mujerista* theology, being a Christian who works for liberation and justice is being a good Christian.[14] This echoes Martin Luther King, Jr. in his 1963 clarion call for support, justice, and love to the complacent Christian churches in his "Letter from Birmingham City Jail."[15] Although Universalists are not Christian-bound, they would also affirm in parallel terms that a godly person is one who labors to liberate all women, men, and children from oppression and injustice. We would even add all oppressed beings, including the plant, animal, and elemental "kin-doms" of Mother Earth. In this, we are deliberately expanding the liberation question of whom to include.

While Liberation Theology primarily began as a Christian-based movement, it naturally has ecumenical, pluralistic, and universalistic elements in its work with marginal peoples, regardless of race, sex, and religion. At this time, there are Liberation Theologians within Islam,[16] and the pan-Asian feminist movements are forming many cross-cultural, cross-religious linkages.[17] Rosemary Radford Reuther, the eminent feminist Christian theologian, has also distinctly called for a dialog between Christian, Jewish, Muslim, Buddhist, and Neopagan women.[18]

13. Mujerista is defined as poor and oppressed women who are Latina (Hispanic), *mulatez* (mixed African-Caucasian), or *mestizaje* (mixed Amerindian-Caucasian).

14. Diaz, 33, 73.

15. Martin Luther King, Jr., "Letter from Birmingham City Jail," *Readings in Christian Ethics*, ed. J. Philip Wogaman and Douglas M. Strong (Louisville: Westminster John Knox Press, 1996), 355–356.

16 Riffat Hassan, "Challenging the Stereotypes of Fundamentalism: An Islamic Feminist Perspective," *The Muslim World*, Vol. 9:1 (Spring 2001), 55. Riffat Hassan has been developing Islamic feminist theology since 1974.

17 Kwok Pui-Lan "Speaking from the Margins," Appropriation and Reciprocity in Womanist/Mujerista/Feminist Work, *Feminist Theological Ethics*, ed. Lois K. Daly (Louisville: Westminster John Knox Press, 1994), 97–99. Chinese Christian Theologian Kwok Pui-Lan is an emerging voice in this Pan-Asian feminist network.

18. Rosemary Radford Reuther, "Eschatology and Feminism," in *Lift Every Voice*, ed. Susan Brooks Thistlewaite and Mary Potter Engel (Maryknoll: Orbis Books, 1998), 130.

Green Theology

Liberation now covers all beings and aspects of creation who are abused and neglected by humanity. Correspondingly, theologian Angelos Vallianatos is not just speaking of Green Theology or Ecology Theology when he reminds us that we are "co-creators with God" and we "are the artists of creation." He goes on to assert,

> Every human being is co-responsible for the continuation of life, as every human is bound to the world, without which he or she cannot survive. Everyone who feels the destruction and misuse of the world has a duty to express this agony in the name of the ones that cannot or do not wish to do so.[19]

Why is this so? Vallianatos demonstrates a strong panentheistic leaning as he proclaims:

> Theology must show that all people—rich and poor, masters and servants, free and slave—have the same possibility to work out their salvation by understanding that they can encounter God, by recognizing themselves in God's image, by recognizing God's image in their neighbours.[20]

Naturally, he includes all God's creatures as our neighbors, and they are the ones who cannot speak out on their own behalf. Moreover, as Principle 6 below elucidates, every creation has a purpose, and all of creation is needed for creation to work in harmony and wholeness.

> 6. All creations of Great Spirit have their own consciousness of self and purpose. Though it may differ from ours, their consciousness is nonetheless quite real and essential to the workings of the Whole. Thus, Mother Earth, all nature, and the heavens above are guides and messengers of the Divine if we have but eyes to see and ears to hear.[21]

So there is no misunderstanding, we must clearly delineate that, in this theology, an atom, a stone, a human cell, a carrot, and a tiger all have a consciousness of self and purpose, although it may differ markedly from ours. All creations are animated—*anima* (spirit), alive—which is why this

19. Angelos Vallianatos "Creation, koinonia, sustainability and climate change: The Churches and Climate Change," *The Ecumenical Review* (World Council of Churches, April 1997), FindArticles, *findarticles.com.*

20. Ibid.

21. *A Universalist Spiritual Manifesto*, 5.

indigenous belief was labeled Animism by 19th-century social scientists Sir Edward Tylor and Bishop R.H. Codrington.[22] In this shamanistic,[23] pantheistic theology, there are no elite or chosen in creation, or more accurately, all are chosen. The Melanesians entitled this life force and soul consciousness in all things *mana*.[24] Jeffrey Masson and Susan McCarthy have presented extensive scientific evidence that animals lead emotional lives and need to be respected as such.[25] Correspondingly, Sue Savage-Rumbaugh has discovered that our closest primate cousins, the Bonobo apes, know and show forgiveness. It is a fundamental value within Bonobo culture.[26] St. Francis of Assisi, patron saint of the birds and the beasts, would hardly have been surprised by these findings. He regularly spoke to the animals, like the good Christian shaman that he was, and believed that animals had souls. The Franciscans tell how he was a peacemaker even with the wild animals. They relate an old story of how he spoke with a fierce, murderous wolf, which listened to him and agreed to end its killing ways. The wolf became a beloved local guardian and, upon its death, was even buried on hallowed ground in the church cemetery.[27] Some seven centuries later, Pope John Paul II affirmed Francis' vision when he proclaimed in 1990, "The animals possess a soul and men must love and feel solidarity with our smaller brethren."[28]

This only underscores Principles 8 and 19, cited earlier, in which the equality of beingness and tolerance for all is the nucleus of Universalism. Any position other than that must be resisted as unloving and unjust, or we are not truly loving and honoring all our sisters, brothers, and cousins in life. This is a *koinonia* of life in intimate communion and partnership with creation, creator, and created.

22. Hopfe and Woodward, 15 and 19.

23. Arnold Mindell, *The Shaman's Body* (San Francisco: Harper, 1993), 41–44.

24. Hopfe and Woodward, 15.

25. Jeffrey Moussaieff Masson and Susan McCarthy, *When Elephants Weep* (New York: Delacorte Press, 1995), 226.

26. Sue Savage-Rumbaugh, "Bonobos Know and Show Forgiveness," *Science and Theology News* 6:1 (September 2005), 9.

27. Order of Franciscans, "Franciscan Spirituality: An Invitation to Peacemaking From the Life of St. Francis—Reconciliation," http://www.franciscanfriarstor.com/stfrancis/stf_blessing_of_animals.htm.

28. Pope John Paul II, quoted in "Pope John Paul II Taught Love for Animals," North American Liberation Press Office, http://www.animalliberationfront.com/Philosophy/Religion/PopeTaughtLoveAnimals.htm.

Transforming Oppressor and Oppressed

Like the Buddhists, we take a broad view of liberation. It is more than freedom from worldly oppressions, but also includes spiritual liberation from whatever karmic and blinded circumstances in which an individual, or community, or nation chooses to dwell. Yes, we must fight oppression, even as Moses, Jesus, and Muhammad did, on behalf of the *Minjung* or the *ochlos,* the poor, oppressed, and suffering. In fact, because many of our own church congregants came from abusive childhoods, there is a singular commitment to the liberation of children from suffering and abuse. At the same time, we recognize that the struggle is not just on the physical plane and not just with the oppressed.

We are hoping to change hearts and minds, and that must, of necessity, include the oppressor—also our brother and sister in bondage. Their enslavement is somewhat different, however, for it is a prison with thick bars of ignorance; long, darkened halls of blindness; and razor sharp barbed wire barriers of fear. And, in some lifetime, as our many years of past life regressions have repeatedly shown, we have been "them."[29] In 1971, the comic strip character, Pogo Possum, divined this when he said, "Yep, Son, we have met the enemy and he is us."[30] No one has been an innocent or a saint in every lifetime, yet, somehow, we eventually manage to escape our dank prison cells and, then, the liberating knowledge is ours to share. Of course, this viewpoint requires looking at the world radically differently and openly leaving judgment in abeyance.

On our crowded planet, oppression affects everyone, oppressor and oppressed. None escape unscathed. Not to diminish the suffering of the oppressed, but I have never met an oppressor who was truly happy or secure. On the contrary, their lives were generally depressing and caught up in vain, meaningless worldly attempts to stave off their loneliness, disaffection, lack of love, and unhappiness. From a shamanic perspective, we approach this duality another way. Like multi-dimensional shamans, we are simultaneously working in this material plane of existence and on the spiritual plane,[31] although they are one and the same in the end. So, even

29. *Other Lives, Other Selves* (New York: Bantam, Books, 1988). For more information on the darker side to our past lives, see Dr. Roger Woolger's work as a Jungian psychologist who brought a distinctive new perspective to the field.

30. From Walt Kelly, *Pogo: We Have Met the Enemy and He is Us* (New York: Simon and Schuster, 1987).

31. Mindell, 23, 39.

as we are activists for justice here, so are we activists in our prayers and meditations "up there" as well. Oppression is oppression, no matter the form it takes and no matter who it targets. Liberation is liberation if it transforms the divisiveness of oppression into the loving oneness of community, even a community of two. Such is our work, and such is our prayer.

In the end, how can one not be a liberationist if one is faithful to the teachings of his or her spiritual founders and great teachers? In Judaism, we have Moses liberating the enslaved Hebrews and the prophets repeating the message of caring for the poor, the widow, and the orphan. In Christianity, this message is echoed strongly through the teachings of Jesus and eminent role models such as St. Francis of Assisi and Mother Theresa. In Islam, Muhammad, an orphan himself, always extolled the virtues of caring for the poor and being generous. In Buddhism, the central theme is the liberation from suffering, and poverty absolutely continues to be one of the greatest areas of worldly suffering for so many.

Meeting the dilemma head on, Father Gustavo Gutierrez, the great Liberation Theologian, insists that if we accept poverty and oppression, we then live with the sin of the "premature and unjust death of many people" around the world.[32] Ada Maria Asasi Diaz is even more explicit. She notes that the poor and oppressed Latina *mulatez* (mulatto) and *mestizaje* (Amerindian) woman quickly educates herself about the five modes of oppression she faces on a daily basis: exploitation, marginalization, powerlessness, cultural imperialism (ethnocentrism), and systematic violence (police brutality, rape, and domestic violence).[33] This is the work of the poor and oppressed—to become so empowered that they are no longer just the problem, but an essential part of the solution. It is also the work of the Liberation Theologian and my challenge to all of us. It is the work of all peoples of faith regardless of their religion.

At the end of this chapter, we will read some of the words and quotes from the great spiritual teachers, which should suffice to make the message crystal clear. When studying the words and teachings of these teachers and so many more, it must be unmistakably apparent by now that Universalism embodies Liberation Theology at all levels. Within its principles, vision, and hoped-for practice, there can be no oppression, no injustice, no war, no division. Racism, sexism, classism, heterosexism,

32. Christopher Rowland, "Introduction: The Theology of Liberation," 3; and Gustavo Gutierrez, "The Task and Content of Liberation Theology," ed. Christopher Rowland (Cambridge: Cambridge University Press, 1999), 24.

33. Diaz, 38, 78.

handicappism, ageism, religiocentrism, and ethnocentrism cannot exist within the walls and halls of these principles, nor within a seeker of loving truth, a follower of universal ways, for this is not being true to the body, mind, heart, and soul of this faith or to the House of God.

Universalism and Personal Liberation

Certainly, there is no sociopolitical or socioeconomic comparison with the urban and rural poor of North America, Latin America, Europe, Asia, and Africa, and the "typical" individual involved in a postmodern spiritual quest. The world of the oppressed and suffering is inflamed by war, famine, disease, tyranny, violence, and poverty. It is generally not a world of choices. The world of the postmodern spiritualist, and certainly those in a typical American Universalist scenario, would appear to involve more social choices simply by virtue of his or her participation in an educated middle class. Nonetheless, in my experience as a minister and pastoral counselor, a significant number of Universalists have come from severely impoverished childhoods and/or have lived under either the tyranny of the home (child abuse and domestic violence) or the state. In essence, many of the Universalists or their families have at one time or another lived on the margin. However, most would now agree that they hold a free will choice to explore their spirituality, which often meant they had to rebel against or basically leave the center: the mainstream belief system. Needless to say, those prior life experiences likely had a strong hand in that choosing. Yet, is there another way in which some Universalists have been marginalized as well?

Since non-Christian Universalists are not completely accepted by mainstream Western society and religion, they represent a spiritual margin. Not so long ago, a number of Universalists could recount episodes in which they had been spiritually oppressed, ostracized, or rejected for their beliefs. They can cite examples of churches and/or family members turning their backs on them or accusing them of being Satanic, of turning away from God and Heaven, of choosing a path of sin and evil, of belonging to a cult, of being lost, and so on. As noted earlier, the perspectives of mainstream denominations about postmodern spiritual groups have ranged from feeling threatened to believing they are Satanically-inspired, to a bemused, patronizing attitude, to reaching out and networking. Except for this last interfaith approach, these are not acceptable stances.

Nevertheless, until Universalists develop and communicate a clearer message and theology, we will remain misinterpreted and misunderstood. Clarity may not bring acceptance or tolerance, but it may at least affirm the serious intent and profound spirituality of our church folk.

Another strong bridge in our Liberation Theology is a postmodern emphasis on liberation and freedom for the individual. Suffice it to say that many postmodern spiritualists express a strong empathy and compassion for the dispossessed, although, like so many others in our busy world, their words may not always be followed by action. Part of this empathy is their own compelling need for freedom, in this case, spiritual freedom. For many, as mentioned earlier, part of this compassion is based on their own real-life experiences of oppression. And lastly, part of it is their willingness to delve into and study the theologies of other peoples; to unearth a spiritual solidarity with Native American, Buddhist, Yogic, Shamanic, Hindu, and other traditions not within the North American and Eurocentric epicenter. In so doing, of course, there is a vast broadening of multicultural experience and understanding, not to mention a remembrance of past life experiences.

One of our church members has likened this to being a "Bridgewalker." We locate or create the bridges between people, peoples, cultures, and religions, and within our church's theology, even other dimensions and other times.[34] In line with these traditions, much of Universalist theology is focused upon spiritual transformation, often occurring within a period of suffering and crisis. Many people of faith have experienced a spiritual awakening, a call to enlightenment. This is what St. John of the Cross (1542–1591) called the "dark night of the soul." We are purged of our worldly and spiritual illusions in order to come closer to God and be in the spirit of God's love.[35] Spiritual transformation is not just for the individual, but also the whole world. The keystone of Universalism is the hope of a better, more tolerant, more transformed world for all, the gift of the "kin-dom" of God.

Finally, there are some similarities among Universalist groups with the aforementioned Ecclesial Base Communities in Latin America, another *koinonia* impetus. Generally, like those groups, there is much

34. Lorraine Sheldon, interview by Thomas Norris, *The Church of the Way of the Messiahs*, December 3, 2005.

35. St. John of the Cross, *Dark Night of the Soul* (Grand Rapids: Calvin College Christian Classics Ethereal Library, 1994), Book I: Chapter 14, http://www.ccel.org/ccel/john_cross/dark_night.html.

less preaching than teaching. Also, the communal atmosphere of a Universalist church mirrors these communities. There is much less of the older 19th and 20th century "follow the guru" ethos among postmodern groups today. Instead, there is a more egalitarian environment, and it is a watchword that we are all students and teachers. Like the Base Communities, Universalist groups, too, are small and many seem to function well in the mode of a spiritual study group. Similarly, the teachings in the Base Communities are often integrated with practical, day-to-day concerns, as well as some socio-political concerns. Thus, many of the teachings seem to be geared not just toward greater spiritual awareness but also social awareness. As Paolo Fernando Carneiro de Andrade notes,

> The community . . . provides not only the context of faith within which the text is read but also the interpretive framework for the concrete social conditions of life. Thus, community and social reality are related to one another, giving birth to the "location" from which the text is read.[36]

If we substitute "spiritual teachings" for biblical "text," then the interpretive location of our Universalist base community provides the context for our faith as well. As an aside, it is noteworthy that the Bible is not ignored in Universalism, for it is one among many sacred scriptures.

This section lists the many teachings of the great religions and great teachers relating to liberation and freedom. How any follower of these faiths could ignore these crucial scriptural passages is beyond me. There is nothing to debate; no gray areas here. The messages of compassion and liberation are emphatically clear.

The Words and Teachings of the Mahatmas (Great Ones)

Judaism and the Hebrew Bible (The Tanakh)

- *If any of your poor kin fall into difficulty and become dependent upon you, you shall support them . . .* Leviticus 25:35

36. Paolo Fernando Carneiro de Andrade, "Reading the Bible in the Ecclesial Base Communities of Latin America: The Meaning of Social Context," *Readings from This Place, Vol.* 2, ed. Fernando Segovia and Mary Ann Tolbert (Minneapolis: Fortress Press, 1995), 247–248.

- *Since there will never cease to be some in need on the earth, I therefore command you: "Open your hand to the poor and needy neighbor in your land."* (Moses to the Hebrew community) Deuteronomy 15:11
- *Justice, and only justice, you shall pursue.* Deuteronomy 16:20
- *He has told you, O mortal, what is good; and what does the Lord require of you but to do justice, and to love kindness, and to walk humbly with your God?* Micah 6:8
- *Remove the evil of your doings from before my eyes; cease to do evil; learn to do good; seek justice, rescue the oppressed, defend the orphan, plead for the widow.* Isaiah 1:16–17
- *Ah, you who make iniquitous decrees, who write oppressive statutes, to turn aside the needy from justice and to rob the poor of my people of their right, that widows may be your spoil, and that you may make the orphans your prey! What will you do on the day of punishment, in the calamity that will come from far away? To whom will you flee for help, and where will you leave your wealth, so as not to crouch among the prisoners or fall among the slain? For all this, his anger has not turned away; his hand is stretched out still.* Isaiah 10:1–3
- *And I will . . . lay low the insolence of tyrants.* Isaiah 13:11
- *How is the oppressor has cease! How his insolence has ceased! The Lord has broken the staff of the wicked, the scepter of rulers that struck down the peoples in wrath . . .* Isaiah 14:4–6
- *See, a king will reign in righteousness, and princes will rule with justice. Each will be like a hiding place from the wind, a covert from the tempest, like streams of water in a dry place, like the shade of a great rock in a weary land. Then the eyes of those who have sight will not be closed, and the ears of those who have hearing will listen. The minds of the rash will have good judgment, and the tongues of stammerers will speak readily and distinctly. A fool will no longer be called noble, nor a villain said to be honorable. For fools speak folly, and their minds plot iniquity: to practice ungodliness, to utter error concerning the Lord, to leave the craving of the hungry unsatisfied, and to deprive the thirsty of drink. The villainies of villains are evil; they devise wicked devices to ruin the poor with lying words, even when the plea of the needy is right. But those who are noble plan noble things, and by noble things they stand.* Isaiah 32:1–8

- *The effect of righteousness will be peace . . .* Isaiah 32:17
- *Why do we fast, but you do not see? Why humble ourselves, but you do not notice?" Look, you serve your own interest on your fast day, and oppress all your workers. Look, you fast only to quarrel and to fight and to strike with a wicked fist. Such fasting as you do today will not make your voice heard on high. Is such the fast that I choose, a day to humble oneself? Is it to bow down the head like a bulrush, and to lie in sackcloth and ashes? Will you call this a fast, a day acceptable to the Lord? Is not this the fast that I choose: to loose the bonds of injustice, to undo the thongs of the yoke, to let the oppressed go free, and to break every yoke? Is it not to share your bread with the hungry, and bring the homeless poor into your house; when you see the naked, to cover them, and not to hide ourself from your own kin?* Isaiah 58:3–7.
- *He [God] has sent me to bring good news to the oppressed, to bind up the broken-hearted, to proclaim liberty to the captives, and release to the prisoners . . .* Isaiah 61:1
- *Hate evil and love good, and establish justice in the gate . . .* Amos 5:15
- *But let justice roll down like waters, and righteousness like an ever-flowing stream.* Amos 5:24 (In his "I Have a Dream" speech, Martin Luther King, Jr. used a different translation and said, "No, no, we are not satisfied, and we will not be satisfied until justice rolls down like waters, and righteousness like a mighty stream.")
- *When the poor and needy seek water, and there is none, and their tongue is parched with thirst, I the LORD will answer them. I, the God of Israel, will not forsake them.* Isaiah 41:17
- *Thus said the Lord of hosts: Render true judgments; show kindness and mercy with one another; do not oppress the widow, the orphan, the alien [stranger], or the poor; and do not devise evil in your hearts against one another.* Zechariah 7:9–19
- *These are the things that you shall do: Speak the truth to one another, render in your gates judgments that are true and make for peace, do not devise evil in your hearts against one another, and love no false oath; for all these things I hate, says the Lord.* Zechariah 8:16–17
- *I will be swift to bear witness against . . . those who swear falsely; who oppress the hired workers in their wages, and the widow and the*

orphan, against those who thrust aside the alien, and do not fear me, says the Lord of hosts. Malachi 3:5

Christianity and the New Testament

- *The bulwark of the Christian commitment to social justice (diakonia) and especially of Liberation Theology is found within Jesus' famous message: "When the Son of Man comes in his glory, and all the angels with him, then he will sit on the throne of his glory. All the nations will be gathered before him, and he will separate people one from another as a shepherd separates the sheep from the goats, and he will put the sheep at his right hand and the goats at the left. Then the king will say to those at his right hand, 'Come, you that are blessed by my Father, inherit the kingdom prepared for you from the foundation of the world; for I was hungry and you gave me food, I was thirsty and you gave me something to drink, I was a stranger and you welcomed me, I was naked and you gave me clothing, I was sick and you took care of me, I was in prison and you visited me.' Then the righteous will answer him, 'Lord, when was it that we saw you hungry and gave you food, or thirsty and gave you something to drink? And when was it that we saw you a stranger and welcomed you, or naked and gave you clothing? And when was it that we saw you sick or in prison and visited you? And the king will answer them, 'Truly I tell you, just as you did it to one of the least of these who are members of my family, you did it to me.' Then he will say to those at his left hand, 'You that are accursed, depart from me into the eternal fire prepared for the devil and his angels; for I was hungry and you gave me no food, I was thirsty and you gave me nothing to drink, I was a stranger and you did not welcome me, naked and you did not give me clothing, sick and in prison and you did not visit me.' Then they also will answer, 'Lord, when was it that we saw you hungry or thirsty or a stranger or naked or sick or in prison, and did not take care of you?' Then he will answer them, 'Truly I tell you, just as you did not do it to one of the least of these, you did not do it to me.' And these will go away into eternal punishment, but the righteous into eternal life."* Matthew 25:31–46
- *Quoting Isaiah, Jesus said, "The Spirit of the Lord is upon me, because he has anointed me to bring good news to the poor. He has sent me*

to proclaim release to the captives and recovery of sight to the blind, to let the oppressed go free, to proclaim the year of the Lord's favor." Luke 4:18–19

- *In the Beatitudes, Jesus said:*

  "Blessed are you who are poor, for yours is the kingdom of God.

  Blessed are you who are hungry now, for you will be filled.

  Blessed are you who weep now, for you will laugh . . .

  But woe to you who are rich, for you have received your consolation.

  Woe to you who are full now, for you will be hungry.

  Woe to you who are laughing now, for you will mourn and weep.

  Woe to you when all speak well of you, for that is what their ancestors did to the false prophets." Luke 6:20–26

- *Jesus is seen throughout his ministry repeatedly reaching out to the ochlos, the common people and those with the least social status—the poor, women, Samaritans, lepers, children, prostitutes, and tax collectors. Jesus did not turn away those at the upper end of the social scale, but he made it clear that all, regardless of social position, needed to change in order to receive the Kingdom of God. For this reason, he invited the rich young man to sell all of his possessions and give the proceeds to the poor.* Matthew 19:16–30, Luke 18:18–30, Mark 10:17–31
- *Jesus' commandment to "Love your neighbor" did not just mean the people next door or the people down the street. His definition of "neighbor" was far more inclusive, defining our neighbor as anyone who is in need. "But when you give a banquet, invite the poor, the crippled, the lame, the blind, and you will be blessed . . ."* Luke 14:13–14. (His parable of the Good Samaritan also reminds us that our good neighbor can be anyone, even Samaritans, who were despised by the Jews of his day. Luke 10:25–37)
- Jesus practiced what he preached. Crowds of 4,000 (Mark 8:1–13) and 5,000 (Mark 6:30–44) had assembled to listen to Jesus. When they became hungry, his disciples suggested that Jesus send the people away to buy food. He answered, "I have compassion for the crowd . . ." and "you give them something to eat." We all know of the miracle of the five loaves of bread and two fish that fed thousands.

- *If a brother or a sister is naked and lacks daily food, and one of you says to them, "Go in peace, keep warm and eat your fill"—and yet you do not supply their bodily needs—what is the good of that?* James 2:15–16
- *"In the poor, we find Jesus in distressing disguise."* Mother Theresa

Islam and Muhammad[37]

- *Allah has revealed to me that you should adopt humility so that no one oppresses another.* Riyadh-us-Salaheen, *Hadith* 1589
- *Do not turn away a poor man . . . even if all you can give is half a date. If you love the poor and bring them near you . . . God will bring you near Him on the Day of Resurrection.* Al-Tirmidhi, *Hadith* 1376
- *He who has been a ruler over ten people will be brought shackled on the Day of Resurrection, until the justice (by which he ruled) loosens his chains or tyranny brings him to destruction.* Al-Tirmidhi, *Hadith* 1037
- *Kindness is the mark of faith; and whoever has not kindness has not faith.* (254:76)
- *Almsgiving is a duty unto you. Alms should be taken from the rich and returned to the poor.* (22:39)
- *The best of almsgiving is that which springeth from the heart, and is uttered by the lips to soften the wounds of the injured.* (21:39)
- *Muhammad said, "It is indispensable for every Muslim to give alms." The companions asked, "But if he hath not anything to give?" He said, "If he hath nothing, he must do a work with his hand, by which to obtain something, and benefit himself, and give alms with the remainder." They said, "But if he is not able to do that work, to benefit himself and give alms to others?" The Rasul (Muhammad) said, "Then he should assist the needy and oppressed." They asked, "What if he is not able to assist the oppressed?" Then he should exhort people to do good." They asked, "And if he cannot?" He said, "Then let him withhold*

37. When no source is given after the quote, Muhammad's quote comes from the work of Allama Sir Abdullah Al-Mamun Al Suhrawardy, *The Wisdom of Muhammad* (New York: Citadel Press, Copyright Philosophical Library, 2001). The number and page are given after each quote.

himself from doing harm to people; for verily that is alms and charity for him." (24:39)

- *Who so desireth that God should redeem him from the sorrows and travail of the day, must delay in calling on poor debtors, or forgive the debt in part or whole.* (113:55)
- *Feed the hungry and visit the sick, and free the captive, if he be unjustly confined. Assist any person oppressed, whether Muslim or non-Muslim.* (147:60)
- *That person is not of us who inviteth others to aid him in oppression; and he is not one of us who fighteth for his tribe in injustice; and he is not one of us who dieth in assisting his tribe in tyranny.* (174:63)
- *That person is not a perfect Muslim who eateth his fill, and leaveth his neighbors hungry.* (179:64)
- *God is not merciful to him who is not so to mankind.* (212:70)
- *To gladden the heart of the weary, to remove the suffering of the afflicted, hath its own reward.* (247:76)
- *He who helpeth his fellow creature in the hour of need, and he who helpeth the oppressed, him will God help in the Day of Travail.* (248:76)
- *Shall I not inform you of a better act than fasting, alms, and prayers? Making peace between one another: enmity and malice tear up heavenly rewards by the roots.* (340:90)
- *It is difficult for a man laden with riches to climb the steep path to bliss.* (384:97)
- *While a man was walking along a road, he became very thirsty and found a well. He lowered himself into the well, drank, and came out. Then [he saw] a dog protruding its tongue out with thirst. The man said, "This dog has become exhausted from thirst in the same way as I." He lowered himself into the well again and filled his shoe with water. He gave the dog some water to drink. He thanked God, and [his sins were] forgiven. The Prophet was then asked, "Is there a reward for us in our animals?" He said: "There is a reward in every living thing."* *Fiqh-us-Sunnah*, Volume 3, Number 104

Eastern Religions

In the Te Tao Ching, Lao Tzu wrote:

- *The Way of Heaven is to benefit and not cause any harm; the Way of Man is to act on behalf of others and not compete with them.*[38]
- *Those who assist their rulers with the Way (the Tao), don't use weapons to commit violence in the world. Such deeds easily rebound. In places where armies are stationed, thorns and brambles will grow.*[39]

Confucius said:

- *I have heard that a man in charge of a state or a family doesn't worry about there being too few people in it, but about the unequal distribution of wealth, nor does he worry about poverty, but about general dissatisfaction. For when wealth is equally distributed, there is no poverty; when the people are united, you cannot call it a small nation, and when there is no dissatisfaction (or when people have a sense of security), the country is secure.*[40]
- *When a country is in order, it is a shame to be a poor and common man. When a country is in chaos, it is a shame to be rich and an official.*[41]
- *The material prosperity of a nation does not consist in its material prosperity, but in righteousness.*[42]

The Dalai Lama said:

- *It is necessary to help others, not only in our prayers, but in our daily lives. If we find we cannot help others, the least we can do is to desist from harming them.*
- *Today, more than ever before, life must be characterized by a sense of Universal responsibility, not only nation to nation and human to human, but also human to other forms of life.*[43]

38. LaoTzu, *Te Tao Ching*, Trans. Robert G. Henricks (New York: Ballantine, 1989), Ch. 81, 37.

39. Ibid, Ch.30, 82.

40. *The Wisdom of Confucius*, 177.

41. Ibid, 181.

42. Ibid, 151.

43. "Dalai Lama Quotes," Thinkexist.com. 24 August 2007 http://thinkexist.com/quotes/dalai_lama.

Gandhi said:

- *Man becomes great exactly in the degree in which he works for the welfare of his fellow-men.*
- *An unjust law is itself a species of violence. Arrest for its breach is more so.*
- *Poverty is the worst form of violence.*[44]

Lord Mahavira and Jainism state:

- *Respect for all living beings is non-violence.*
- *Have compassion towards all living beings. Hatred leads to destruction.*
- *Where there is Love, there is Life. Violence is Suicide.*
- *All souls are alike. None is superior or inferior.*[45]

Vivekananda (1863–1902), a Hindu religious leader and follower of the great Hindu saint, Ramakrishna, asserted:

- *[A universal religion] will be a religion which will have no place in its polity for persecution or intolerance, which will recognize divinity in every man or woman, and whose whole scope, whose whole force, will be centered in aiding humanity to realize its own true divine nature.*[46]
- *So long as the millions live in hunger and ignorance, I hold every person a traitor who, having been educated at their expense, pays not the least heed to them.*[47]

Indigenous and Shamanic Religions

- As noted in the *Wiccan Rede* following Wiccan ("Wise Ones"), Druidic, and Celtic traditions, their fundamental tenet is: "An' it harm

44. "Mohandas Gandhi Quotes," Brainymedia.com, 24 August 2007 http://www.brainyquote.com/quotes/authors/m/mohandas_gandhi.html

45. "Jain Data Base: Quotes," July 1, 1997, http://www.ibiblio.org/jainism/database/index.html , (accessed 24 August 2007).

46. Vivekananda, quoted in "In Search of a Universal Religion," *Ahimsa Voices*, (Berkeley, CA), January 1997.

47. "Vivrekananda's Quotes," Vivekananda Vedanta Network (Boston: Ramakrisna Vedanta Society), 24 August 2007, http://www.vivekananda.org/quotes.aspx.

none, do what thou wilt." In other words, do good for all and harm to none.[48]

- In tribal groups, there were no poor, unless all were poor. There were no poor classes until urbanization. In Arabic tribes, it was the chieftain's duty to make sure all was given out equally.[49] In Native American tribes, the Giveaway or Potlatch is a bedrock part of their spiritual beliefs as a community.[50]

48. Raymond Buckland, *Buckland's Complete Book of Witchcraft* (St. Paul: Llewellyn Publications, 1993), 9.

49. Armstrong, *A History of God*, 133–134.

50. "Giveaway: North American Indian Custom," Britannica Online, http://www.britannica.com/EBchecked/topic/1080979/giveaway#tab=active~checked%2Citems~checked&title=giveaway%20—%20Britannica%20Online%20Encyclopedia (accessed July 15, 2008); and lectures by Barrett Eaglebear, Lakota Sundancer, as told by the Lakota Elders, 1994.

CHAPTER 13

All the World's a Stage

(On the Nature of Divine Purpose)

All the world's a stage, And all the men and women merely players; They have their exits and their entrances, And one man in his time plays many parts . . .

WILLIAM SHAKESPEARE, *AS YOU LIKE IT*

In the end, it's not the years in your life that count. It's the life in your years.

ABRAHAM LINCOLN

What we do for ourselves dies with us. What we do for others and the world remains and is immortal.

ALBERT PINE

Were there no weeds, what would gardeners do?

CHUANG TZU

We can easily forgive a child who is afraid of the dark; the real tragedy of life is when men are afraid of the light.

PLATO

Awaken

As proponents of the evolution of the soul, Universalists envision a day when each and every soul will awaken to a higher purpose. When enough soul lessons have been learned, when enough of creation and its mysteries have been explored through many lives and innumerable experiences, then the soul cannot help but aspire to a plane of higher meaning and fulfillment. This is the moment when humans reach a level of oneness with Creator and Creation. This is the moment when we are "touched to the soul" and incorporate the elements of godliness into our being that up, until this point, we have been merely emulating. In Buddhism, this "awakened thought" is called *bodhicitta*, the moment when one seeks enlightenment to benefit others.[1] In yoga (meaning "to join" or "union") and in all mysticism, this is the mystical union and reunion with God.[2] The old realms of materialism and singular service to self quickly lose their luster. This new realm of higher awareness bestows a compelling vision of possibility and hope into the person's consciousness. Whether we call it Buddhist liberation from suffering (*nirvana*), Christian salvation, or Hindu enlightenment (*moksha*), from a Universalist's perspective, it is not just the path to God. It is the path of God. This vision is incorporated in Principles 9 and 11 below:

> 9. We will come to an understanding and a life whereby we recognize our Oneness with the Divine Creation Spirit and dedicate our lives to the Divine Love, Will, Purpose, and Creation Work of Great Spirit, according to our unique talents, skills, and gifts. This is our Awakening, our Enlightenment, and begins the Conscious Path of Love and Service.
>
> 11. We are here to co-create Light, Harmony, and Balance in all things of creation by example, teaching, charity, compassion, prayer and meditation, and the guiding principle of unconditional love.[3]

As can be seen, this is not an otherworldly exercise. Like the Sikh ideal, we concur that "the purpose of life is to realize God within the world, through the everyday practices of work, worship, and charity,

1. Nystrom, et al," Buddhism" in *Exploring World Religions* (Oxford: Oxford Press, 2008 unpublished manuscript), 36.

2. Hopfe and Woodward, 96–97; and Singh, 3–4.

3. *A Universalist Spiritual Manifesto*, 6–7.

of sacrificing love."[4] Moreover, each of us will contribute according to our gifts and skills, so all will have their place in the sun. And the time to do this is now, not in some amazing future place called "heaven." In Universalist theology, heaven is not a place "up there," nor is hell a place "down there." As multidimensional expressions of creation, heaven and hell gather around, within, and through us. They are everywhere, and as co-creators, it is up to us how much or little of each we wish to bring into our lives and the world at any given moment. Heaven is co-creating and manifesting "Light, Harmony and Balance" in our lives and our neighbor's lives through our behavior, example, and love. Hell is co-creating Darkness, Disharmony, and Imbalance in our lives and our neighbor's lives through our behavior, example, and anger-fear. Jesus gave us a clue about our work in bringing heaven and earth together when he said in the Lord's Prayer, "Thy will be done on earth as it is in heaven" (Matthew 6:10). This is when the higher and lower dimensions of heaven and earth come together and become one. This is what he called The Kingdom of Heaven, where love and justice reign. We would add that we hardly need to wait for a Second Coming. Jesus noted that his currently robust God work indicated that "The Kingdom of God has come to you" (Luke: 11:20). It is already here and even more significantly, "the Kingdom of God is among you" (Luke 17:21). Again, similar to the shamans, who balance their work in the shamanic spirit world (Shamanic State of Consciousness) and the mundane, material world (Ordinary State of Consciousness),[5] our spiritual daily work is to balance the hand of heaven and the hand of earth and bring them together. It is our witnessing, our *martyria*, through our living praxis of the Kingdom or Kin-dom of God. Now, the question is, why do we do this?

Just Because

Throughout history, humans have been motivated through many religions to look forward to a better place—the afterlife—as Christian Heaven, Islamic Paradise, Buddhist Nirvana, Buddhist Pure Land, and so on. This promise of a heavenly reward is often given as a reason to "do good" and live a moral life, to be righteous so you can receive your heavenly treasures. In the end, is this still not a bribe, like promising a

4. Fisher, 160.

5. Michael Harner, *The Way of the Shaman* (San Francisco: Harper, 1990), 21.

child an ice cream cone if they clean up their room or help set the dinner table? Why isn't a rational, logical reason to do good and be good without bribes enough? There are rewards indeed. It feels good. It brings harmony to one's life and the world. It opens the heart through love. Yet, blessed is the person who is upright and moral and does not cause harm to others, simply because that is who they are. It is what they have learned in their lifetimes of growing wisdom and accepted as their purposeful way of living—without the inducement of rewards for good behavior. It is their "I AM," their highest God Self.

Perhaps, it is time to let go of the little child perspective that we be good little "do bees" because we are supposed to, just because our mommies and daddies say this is what good little boys and girls do. Rather, as we are now the grown children of the Creatress-Creator or even new partners in co-creation, isn't it time to accept full responsibility for our choices and our values? Values are not rules, and as the old adage says, "Rules are made to be broken." When I break a rule, it seems easier to rationalize it and shrug it off (unless I am caught with my hand in the cookie jar). However, when I go against my own values, this is a profound violation of myself, my wholeness, and my integrity. Not so easy to shrug that off. So, I don't need to be told "Thou Shalt Not Kill." It is no longer just a rule for me, and I no longer need it as a commandment either. No one needs to command me not to kill, simply because it is part and parcel of who I Am now. It took a lot of lifetimes to learn that, among other hard-earned lessons—to move beyond the "Thou Shalt Nots." So now we need to strive for goodness and loving kindness "just because." It is no longer tied to cause and effect—hellish punishment for bad behavior and heavenly reward for good behavior. It is "just because" it's the right thing to do.

No Coincidences

Carl Jung's principle of synchronicity is especially relevant to this section. Not all coincidences are coincidences. He asserted that there are acausal events that are complementary and compensatory to cause and effect but are outside of causal phenomena. He understood that this was a difficult concept for many to accept, as we are so wedded in our Modernism to cause and effect interactions.[6]

6. Victor Mansfield, "The Rhine-Jung Letters: Distinguishing Parapsychological from Synchronistic Events—J.B. Rhine; Carl Jung," *Journal of Parapsychology* (March

As Universalists, we have seen synchronicity at work in a number of ways. For example, we have observed time and time again that people begin a spiritual awakening precisely at the time in their lives when the need becomes evident. As many look back, they are surprised at the seemingly random, serendipitous route they took to reach that day, and, yet, in retrospect, it did not appear coincidental. Since we acknowledge the idea that we are co-creators in our lives, then we are obviously co-manifestors of what we need as well. Consciously or unconsciously, when the request is made, we feel Spirit respond.

For weeks, even months, a friend kept hearing about a certain spiritual book but didn't get around to purchasing it. One day, at Barnes and Noble, she was drawn to a book that had fallen on the floor. It was the same book. The next day, a co-worker placed a copy of the book in her office mailbox. Those were more than enough signs for her and she immediately read the book that night, unable to put it down. Reading the book was a spiritually transformative moment for her, and she felt she had been unmistakably guided to it.

Another time, a man was waiting for his order in the grocery deli, and for some reason, Cate and I were drawn to speak with him. As we casually talked, he asked what we did, and we mentioned that we were ministers. He inquired further as to the type of church and then, with great passion, exclaimed that is exactly what he had been looking for. He was thrilled such a place existed and wanted to attend our services. We don't usually speak to strangers in the deli, so we can only assume that we were guided to this man as well. We can multiply these stories by the hundreds. In the end, we believe it is simply what Rabbi Jesus knew to be a universal truth. "Ask and it will be given you; search and you will find; knock and the door will be opened for you" (Luke 11:9). No coincidences.

Let There Be Light

As Principle 11 also denotes, part of our work is to co-create light. Here we begin to see direct links with Judeo-Christian symbol and metaphor, although, in our church, many so-called symbols are taken literally. Our church generally conceives of these symbols as the essence of what is

1998), FindArticle, http://www.findarticles.com/p/articles/mi_m2320/is_n1_v62/ai_21227885#continue.

being described and that they exist etherically or multi-dimensionally alongside our earthly dimension.

"Light" is a perfect example. "The Light" is more than a symbol for God and goodness and Spirit but is perceived to be the evanescent nature of the Creator and Spirit. Light (God energy) not only makes up our very life force (*prana* in Sanskrit), it is also used literally for healing and transformation. Julian of Norwich discerned the three qualities of God are "life, love, and light." For her, God is Light, "our endless day."[7] There is even evidence from modern quantum physics that there are higher and higher levels of light energy and that light is the central force of creation.[8] So it is not surprising that we often refer to ourselves and all who are committed to the Light as Lightworkers. We are doing God's work, using God energy and God force, whether it is through prayer and meditation, healing the sick, revelation, social activism, or spiritual growth and transformation.

Yet, it would scarcely be fair for Judaism, Christianity, or our Universalist Church to claim light as their original divine metaphor. It is a primeval symbol that goes far back in human memory. It visibly cannot be missed each day and every day—in the sun. Its distinct nature is life-giving, warming, revealing, and illuminating. C.K. Barrett confirms that the concept that "God is light" comes out of the Gnostic traditions and their earlier oriental forebears. Madanjeet Singh reports these originated from ancient oriental religions of the sun, which frequently depicted divinized men with rays emanating from their heads.[9] Thus evolved the symbol of the sun as cosmic light or truth, and possibly sparked the artistic tradition of painting halos around Jesus and the saints in the Middle Ages.[10] These sun theologies later had a significant impact on Greco-Roman thought, particularly in the form of *Mithraism* and through the Hermetic presentation of a revealer-god.[11] Other influences on the Greco-Roman and Middle Eastern world (eventually the Christian world) must also

7. Julian of Norwich, 206–207.

8. Fritjof Capra, *The Tao of Physics* (New York: Bantam Books, 1984), 67.

9. Madanjeet Singh, *The Sun: Symbol of Power and Life* (New York: Harry Abrams and UNESCO, 1993), 13.

10. Singh, 277, and throughout his book, we see depictions of prophets, saints and Jesus with sun halos, sun chariots (Elijah) and other sun-related themes, but, of course, this is seen in many other ancient and modern religions around the world.

11. C.K. Barrett*The Gospel According to St. John* (London: SPCK, 1967), 277.

include Manichaeism, centered in North Africa, and Zoroastrianism, emerging from the Persians.

> With the development of metaphysical thought, the sun's spiritual responsibilities also multiplied. The sun god Mithra (Vedic Mitra) became the charioteer of Ahuru Mazda, the Zoroastrian Creator God of Light who is opposed by the evil darkness of Angra Mainyu or Ahriman . . . Zoroastrianism [Zoroaster c. 628–551 BCE] and Manichaeism were among the great dualistic world religions which the sun inspired and, even though Manichaeism has since all but disappeared, the religion was once professed by many peoples, from Spain in the west to the eastern coast of China . . . It was truly an "ecumenical" faith, embracing all people, as Mani tried to integrate diverse religions such as Gnostic Christianity, Zoroastrianism, and Buddhism, in a strongly dualistic philosophy based on the eternal struggle between good and evil, light and darkness. The Manichaean sun god, also known as the Third Messenger (*Neryosang*), resides in the sun along with the Mother of Life and the Living Spirit ("Holy Trinity").[12]

Manichaeism later adapted to Christianity.[13] Interestingly, although he later renounced it, St. Augustine was at one time a Manichaean before his conversion to Christianity.[14] As we will see below, it is not hard to speculate that these theologies of light and dark would have influenced the early Jews, including the Essene writers of the *Dead Sea Scrolls*. The Zoroastrian and Manichaean Persians under Cyrus the Great inherited the Israelite territories from the vanquished Babylonians in 539 BCE. They held them until Alexander the Great overthrew the vast Persian Empire in 331 BCE. Later, this sun theology directly impacted Christian church architecture, whereby Christian churches adopted the pagan tradition of orienting their shrines towards the sunrise.[15] They also had a bearing on the early theology of the Christian church, particularly in the Gospel of John.

There is no other gospel writer that presses the theme of light and dark more than John, as we see in the following passages.

12. Singh, 49, 51.

13. Ibid, 276.

14. R. S. Pine-Coffin, "Introduction" in *Confessions* by Saint (New York: Penguin, 1961), 12–13.

15. Singh, 81.

- Speaking of the Creator, the gospel affirms: "In him was life; and the life was the light of all people. The light shines in the darkness; and the darkness did not overcome it" (John 1:4–5).
- Speaking of John the Baptist and Jesus, the gospel writer professes: "He came as a witness to testify to the light, so that all might believe through him. He himself was not the light, but he came to testify to the light. The true light, which enlightens everyone, was coming into the world" (John 1:7–9).
- In speaking with Nicodemus, Jesus says: "And this is the judgment, that the light has come into the world, and people loved darkness rather than the light because their deeds were evil. For all who do evil hate the light and do not come to the light, so that their deeds may not be exposed. But those who do what is true come to the light, so that it may be clearly seen that their deeds have been done in God" (John 3: 19–21).
- Speaking of John the Baptist, Jesus asserts: "He was a burning and shining lamp, and you were willing to rejoice for a while in his light. But I have a testimony greater than John's" (John 5:35–36).
- Again, Jesus spoke to them, saying: "I am the light of the world. Whoever follows me will never walk in darkness but will have the light of life" (John 8:12).
- In healing the blind man, Jesus notes: "We must work the works of him who sent me while it is day; night is coming when no one can work. As long as I am in the world, I am the light of the world" (John 9:4–5).
- Later, Jesus said: "Are there not twelve hours of daylight? Those who walk during the day do not stumble, because they see the light of this world. But those who walk at night stumble, because the light is not in them" (John 11:9).
- And finally, Jesus stated: "I have come as light into the world, so that everyone who believes in me should not remain in the darkness" (John 12:46).

Interestingly, we hear very similar light terminology and themes in the Nag Hammadi Gnostic Gospel of Thomas: "There is a light within a person of light, and it shines on the whole world. If it does not shine, it is dark" (Thomas: 24).[16] This point is especially relevant because the Gospel of John was also a key Gnostic Christian text and was only reluctantly accepted into the Christian canon.[17] So, although we may have some Universalist disagreements with the God-Jesus that John created, going somewhat beyond the three Synoptic Gospels of Matthew, Mark, and Luke, we love the mystical, Gnostic John who parallels Jesus as an earthly version of the Holy Spirit. We might also interpret this as Jesus being a human empowered by Holy Spirit.

The Qumran documents known as the Dead Sea Scrolls were apparently written by the Essene community in Qumran[18] between the 4th century BCE and the 1st century CE.[19] They may be one ancient source for this "qualified dualism" in the Gospel of John using a light versus dark motif.[20] From *The Rule of the Community* and *The War Rule* scrolls emerges a theology of dualism between two warring angelic spirits. These are the Spirit of Truth or Prince of Light, which inhabits the light and has dominion over the "sons of righteousness" or the "sons of light"; and the Spirit of Perversity or Angel of Darkness, which originates in a "spring of darkness" and has dominion over the "sons of perversity."[21] This is not a dualism paralleled in Greek, Roman, or Egyptian philosophy.[22] John adopted much of this Essene dualism, but modified it as a dualism within the world between those who see (in the light) and those who are blind (in the darkness), rather than a war of angelic forces at a cosmic level.[23]

16. Stephen Patterson and Marvin Meyer, "Gospel of Thomas", *The Complete Gospels*, ed. Robert J. Miller (San Francisco: Harper, 1994), 310.

17. Pagels, 119.

18. James Vanderkam and Peter Flint, *The Meaning of the Dead Sea Scrolls* (San Francisco: Harper Collins, 2002), 240, 254; and Michael Wise, Martin Abegg, and Edward Cook, *The Dead Sea Scrolls* (San Francisco: Harper, 1996), 16.

19. Vanderkam and Flint, 32.

20. James L. Price, "Light from Qumran upon Some Aspects of Johannine Theology," *John and the Dead Sea Scrolls*, ed. James H. Charlesworth (New York: Crossroad, 1991), 18.

21. James H. Charlesworth, "A Critical comparison of the Dualism in IQS 3:13—4:26 and the 'Dualism' Contained in the Gospel of John," *John and the Dead Sea Scrolls*, ed. James H. Charlesworth (New York: Crossroad, 1991), 18; and Vanderkam and Flint, 261–264.

22. James Charlesworth, "The Dead Sea Scrolls and the Gospel According to John," *Exploring the Gospel of John*, ed. Alan Culpepper and C. Clifton Black, Black (Louisville: Westminster John Knox Press, 1996), 70.

23. Price, 18–19.

Although there is no proof that John actually copied from the Essene *Rule of the Community*, there are a number of literary expressions John shares with the *Rule*. And, we have already seen the similarities in the light-dark motifs of both texts.[24] Obviously, it carried some weight in the formulation of Johannine theology and terminology.

A few more comments are in order here regarding the parallel metaphors John uses in conjunction with the light. For example, in John 1:4–5, light is undeniably equated with "life."[25] In John 8:12, Jesus masterfully utilizes the Feast of the Tabernacles to proclaim he is the light of the world. The backdrop for this proclamation was the ritual lighting of the great golden lamps in the temple court.[26] The people could hardly miss the symbolism, and Crossan adds,

> The symbol of light had become associated with the great future moment of eschatological or messianic salvation since it recalled the pillar of fire which had led the Israelites through the desert toward the promised land.[27]

We know that light has already been equated with "truth" and "life" from the Essene influences and gospel references. This makes Jesus' second significant proclamation even more meaningful, as he continues the theme of light in John 14:6. Jesus said, "I am the way, and the truth, and the life." Finally, we see that Jesus, through John, neatly brings the light motif full circle with the story of the blind man. He said that "those who do not see may see, and those who do not see may become blind" (John 9:39).[28]

These light-dark motifs are not far removed from much of Universalist thought. We especially discover it in the modified light-dark dualism of our theology and the equating of light with goodness, enlightenment (not being blind), life, truth, and the way (the path of light). Universalism carries forward a rich tradition with some aspects of Gnosticism and Essene theology, as well as Jewish and Christian beliefs. Of course, it has also purposely and pluralistically included other traditions as well,

24. Charlesworth, 103.

25. F. Davidson, ed., *The New Bible Commentary* (Grand Rapids: Wm. B. Eerdmans Publishing,
1965), 867.

26. Dominic Crossan, *The Gospel of Eternal Life* (Milwaukee: Bruce Publishing, 1967), 90–91.

27. Ibid.

28. Raymond Brown, *An Introduction to the New Testament* (New York: Doubleday, 1997), 348.

including Buddhism, Hinduism, Yin-Yang, Sufism, Sikhism, and so on. What is fascinating is that many of these other religions also carry light-dark motifs that absolutely parallel some of the work discussed above.

Even in our everyday life, we perceive light in energy terms. High energy equates with brightness and low energy equates with dimness (even to darkness), whether it is a 100-watt light bulb versus a 40-watt light bulb lighting our desk, or the sun at midday versus the sun at sunset. In physics, light is a form of electromagnetic wave energy, along with magnetism, electricity, radio waves, microwaves, X-rays, ultraviolet rays, and so on. Different colors of the visible light spectrum represent lower frequency vibrations (reds and yellows) versus higher frequency vibrations (blues and violets).[29] This sense of high vibrational energy versus low energy is even translated into our good and bad emotional states. When we are happy, we are "up" and feel "light"—high frequency. When we are depressed, we are "down" and feel "heavy"—low frequency. Several studies on color have even noted that blue (high frequency) has a calming effect and that red (low frequency) is agitating (danger and alarm). Unfortunately, the psychological field has yet to accept the psychology of color as an entirely legitimate area of inquiry.[30] In any event, light is all around us every day. Perhaps this is why Jesus and so many faiths were so successfully able to use light as a metaphor for our spiritual growth and moods. We might add that, in the end, physicists and scientists do not think of vibrational energy in "good" or "bad" terms. Energy is energy, whether high or low, and all energy is good energy. It is the stuff of the universe. That is not a bad paradigm metaphysically, as well; all energy is good energy. All energy is god energy.

As can be seen throughout this theology of light, it is a theology of expansion, recognizing the limitless, energy-filled nature of God. Hence, it is our God-modeled purpose as humans and as souls to continue expanding as well, to peek through the crack in the universe and contemplate the infinite. Another word for this might be ascension, and as Principle 28 acknowledges, it is the grand adventure of all time.

> 28. The whole point is the Gestalt, the Uniqueness, Partness, Wholeness, and Oneness of all things, whether viewed from a

29. Fritjof Capra, *The Tao of Physics* (New York: Bantam, 1983), 48–49; and Brian Greene, *The Fabric of the Cosmos* (New York: Alfred A. Knopf, 2004), 40–43.

30. Saberi Roy, "The Psychology of Color: On studying the psychology of color as effects on human emotions and human cognition," *E-Zine Articles*, http://ezinearticles.com/?The-Psychology-of-Color&id=1488976.

> scientific, moral, artistic, legal, economic, spiritual, or philosophical perspective. The parts and the whole are equally necessary for the definition, effectiveness, and integrated beingness of anything, whether human body, national constitution, power saw, government, Theory of Relativity, sculpture, star, molecule, law, universe, Divine Creatress-Creator. The Universe is not lonely. Rather, it is filled with the parts and the sum of all things infinitely expanding beyond infinite time and space. It is Divine Creation Spirit growing, and we are adventurously part of the continual rebirth and renewal of Creation.[31]

In this moment of God reunion, of God-realization, then, such a person is blessed and helps bring the world one step closer to its ascension, to a higher world consciousness, to a true worldly and spiritual liberation. When there are enough people "working the light program"—that is, growing in and sharing their Light while actively practicing the ways of God (life, love, and light) as the very essence of light service—it will not be such a high step.

31. *A Universalist Spiritual Manifesto*, 13.

PART III

The Praxis—Light Living

So many books would end after engaging in a dialog about their subject and then presenting the author's point of view with a nice summary and conclusion. We could have done that here, but, in fact, the subject would be incomplete if we had only offered *The Dialog* (Part I) and *The Theology* (Part II) sections. Universalism is not just about a congenial philosophy of life or theology of belief. It is a living, growing, changing dynamic and will not be imprisoned within words (scriptures), beliefs (doctrine), or practices (rituals). As a result, this section on *The Praxis: Light Living* (Part III) is essential to rounding out the book and the living theology of Universalism. Praxis means our *living practice*—the ways we live and practice Universalism every day, as individuals and communities. In Part IV, we will broaden the view to include living within and developing spiritual organizations, our "Lightwork." Hence, we provide a practical, down-to-earth discussion of this living practice, as well as principles for putting it into action—from sacred texts to societal reflections and, later, to organizational realities. This is a significant break from academic and theological tradition. These tend to reside in the ivory towers of pure thought and lofty reason while neglecting the real world of humans, politics, workplaces, home life, finances, and the marketplace. This is where we move beyond academic references and logic and get opinionated. This is where we get up close and personal. We get our hands dirty and break new ground in practical theology.

CHAPTER 14

Lost in Translation

(Universalism and Sacred Texts)

Those who read many scriptures, but who fail to practice what they contain, are like counting someone else's cows. They gain nothing for themselves.

BUDDHA

A belief is not merely an idea the mind possesses; it is an idea that possesses the mind.

ROBERT OXTON BOLT

Is Scripture Everything?

IN BRINGING A UNIVERSALIST way of life into being, it is essential to discuss the role of oral and written narrative in Universalist thinking. As Universalists, it would be oxymoronic to be Absolutists or Literalists and insist on the inerrancy of scripture,[1] or, for that matter, to insist upon any

1. Apparently, within every religion at the conservative end of the spectrum, there are orthodox, fundamentalist, absolutist adherents who believe that their holy scriptures (the Bible, the *Torah*, the *Qu'ran*, the *Vedas*, and so on) and literally every word in those scriptures, are infallible, come directly from God, and contain no errors. William H. Barnes, "Fundamentalism," *The Oxford Companion to the Bible* (New York: Oxford University Press, 1993), 236–237; and Fisher, 18–19.

particular set of sacred texts and doctrine. We must politely disagree with some of our Absolutist, Literalist Christian Fundamentalist, Orthodox Jewish, and Islamic Fundamentalist friends. They believe not only that their religion's scriptures (the Holy Bible, *Tanakh*, and *Qu'ran*, respectively) are the only authentic scriptures, but that they were dictated directly by God. They believe these texts represent God's words without human input and contain no errors or contradictions. This chapter will attempt to place into perspective this potential "catch-22" of honoring the wisdom of scripture without situating them on a rigid and dogmatic pedestal.

In Christianity, in Judaism, in Islam, the text is everything. Their foundation stones are based upon the Old and New Testaments, the *Torah* and *Tanakh*,[2] and the *Qu'ran*. This is not as true of Hinduism, which encompasses a broad range of belief systems and has many sacred texts, such as the *Vedas*, the *Upanishads*, the *Law of Manu*, and the *Bhagavad Gita*, to name but a few. Likewise, in Buddhism, there is the *Dharma*—the teachings and words of the Buddha—but these are not organized as a formal scriptural canon. For so many Western mainstream religions, however, scripture is an indispensable base for their faiths. It would be hard to imagine Christianity without the Holy Bible, or Judaism without the *Torah*, or Islam without the *Qu'ran*. It is questionable if they could even carry on without their guiding words. There is nothing wrong with this, as these scriptures are filled with marvelous God-inspired wisdom, ideas, stories, ethics, and rules for living. Even societies built upon oral tradition use their stories and teachings to fulfill the same role. From a Universalist perspective, however, being tied to scripture eventually leads to being bound to doctrine, which can lead to being slaved to rigid dogma.

Interestingly, the word religion derives from the Latin *religio*, meaning "to tie back" or "to tie down,"[3] or alternatively, "the fear or awe one feels in the presence of a spirit or god."[4] This is one reason why postmodernists and Universalists will frequently say, "I'm not very religious, but I am very spiritual." We don't like being tied down, and we don't believe we need to be afraid of the Creator-Creatress. In many ways, this phrase represents the tension in the shift from religion to spirituality.

2. The Tanakh is the Hebrew Bible, which consists of the Torah, the *Neviim* (the prophets), and the *Kethubim* (*The Writings*, such as Psalms, Proverbs, Ruth, Wisdom of Sirach, and so on). Henry Jackson Flanders, Jr., Robert Wilson Crapps, and David Anthony Smith, *People of the Covenant* (New York: Oxford University Press, 1996), 3.

3. Fisher, 12.

4. Hopfe and Woodward, 5.

Being spiritual is somewhat mystical and implies a personal, individual relationship with the Creator-Creatress (although it may be shared in community), as opposed to a personal, individual relationship with a particular religion. Our spiritual identity is not tied to a specific sect or denomination, but exists in relation solely to the divine—which includes just about everything.[5] This has been quite threatening to many of the established, mainstream religions because the spiritual person is self-directed to Great Spirit and the divine through their own efforts and beliefs. It is a highly independent venture that does not require a restrictive doctrine, dogma, ritual system, or priesthood and clergy.

How sacred is a sacred text? We know that agreement on the Christian canon (official scriptures) was a political drama as much as anything else. When the church was deciding upon the canon, they threw out many books, gospels, and letters, which many Christians considered sacred and included some that others felt were not as sacred or authentic. Although it took centuries for the final Christian canon to be accepted, the impulse began in the second half of the 2nd century as a reaction to Gnosticism, Marcionism, and other so-called heresies. It was the Roman Church's attempt to define itself and its followers, and it was definitely not just a religious exercise but a political undertaking as well.[6] Many books were excluded from the "official" canon of twenty-seven works, finally established at the end of the 4th century CE in the Councils of Hippo (393 CE) and Carthage (397 CE).[7] Many Christians were alarmed because these other books had been accepted by various Gnostic and Christian sects for some time. Needless to say, these "other" scriptures did not often agree with the institutionalized Roman church and its doctrines.[8] It did not hurt that the Christian Roman Emperor appointed most of the delegates to the Councils, and he had very definite Roman ideas about absolute obedience to the party line. Consequently, the acceptance of a text as sacred appeared to involve more of a political compromise and consensus by the

5. From conversations with Rev. Cathleen Norris on defining religion, The Church of the Way of the Messiahs, January 5, 2009.

6. Justo L. Gonzalez, *A History of Christian Thought*, vol.2 (Nashville: Abingdon Press, 1970), 148–150; and Pagels, 104.

7. Michael Baigent, *The Jesus Papers* (San Francisco: Harper, 2006), 85; and Brown, 15.

8. Andrie B. Du Toit, "Canon," *The Oxford Companion to the Bible* (New York: Oxford University Press, 1993), 102–103; Raymond Brown, *An Introduction to the New Testament* (New York: Doubleday, 1997), 11–15; and Pagels, 102.

institutional group in power than an inclusive process neutrally evaluating all potentially sacred texts. In no way does this denigrate the sincere and devout efforts of many of the decision-makers. It merely points out that the process of selection was based on an intrafaith and interfaith struggle, inevitably bringing it within the realm of church politics.

The Theology of Story

So, how do many Universalists view sacred texts? Our church is not very text-oriented and has more of an oral tradition, but as Universalists, we are so fortunate. We get to pick and choose from the best of the best, from all the divinely inspired words and spiritual teachers from thousands of cultures over many thousands of years. There are so many beautiful teachings spoken and written already. It's easy to adopt them, especially since so many track the same trails of love, service, devotion, spirit, peace, and light. As one of our members said, "We pick the best and leave the rest." We borrow the existing texts and stories from many religions—review, argue over, interpret, and intuit them—then we make them our own, just as people have been doing since time immemorial. No matter where we start, by virtue of everyone's input and experience, the text or story soon becomes our co-creation with Great Spirit. We bring it to life. We bring it into the now and into our daily lives. It comes alive because we are co-creating a new, positive canon inclusive of all the great teachings and great teachers—bringing the best of the Old Age into the best of the New Age. It is our way of breaking through the density of the old, outmoded paradigm of negativity and fear, where God was to be feared and religion became a straitjacket. Somehow, humanity lost its way and lost the teachings of love and light that these Great Ones brought to us time and time again, and in so many ways. We are rediscovering the spiritual truths of these many messengers of light and returning their message to the planet.

In this way, we are constantly co-creating our own sacred texts and stories. Sometimes, as we speak and share among ourselves, we even become the sacred text, the sacred story. This sharing of our inner truths and visions is absolutely central to our spiritual practice. At these moments of inspiration, it becomes apparent to us that Holy Spirit is speaking to and through us—and we become the living text. We call it the Theology of Story. Thus, from our church's Sacred Circle Buddha Nights, our Muhammad Nights, our White Buffalo Calf Woman Nights, our Jesus Nights, our Goddess Nights, and so many more,[9] we discern and tease out the universal themes and truths revealed in the teachings.

Since we follow more of an oral tradition, we don't generally like to write down our own sacred texts. We do not want to freeze the thoughts into dogma, forever carved in stone. For example, although written, our *Manifesto* is purposely not called a *Statement of Beliefs*. They are guiding principles, freely accepted or rejected, not rigid rules and doctrine. In this way, we hope, instead, to catch the pure spirit of the teachings and the truths, letting the essence and not the text be our guide. In this respect, theologically, we might be called Essentialists, in which, "The important thing is the inner faith, the inner 'essence' of religion."[10] In Buddhism, the *Dharma*, the universal truths and teachings, is enough all by itself to instruct, guide, and enlighten all who wish to listen. Likewise, the Native American Rainbow Nation prophecy contends that the teachings of Great Spirit are for all people—red, black, yellow, and white (the Rainbow Nation)—not just Native Americans. The teachings and truths of Great Spirit are universal; they are for everyone, and they have a place in every life.[11] They have a place in our life. We attempt to bring these teachings to life in our prayers, meditations, services, liturgy, classes, and daily life. It is a pathway, perhaps trail-blazed by great teachers and prophets long ago but now broadened and straightened by our determined footsteps. And the teachings are a continuing revelation through each of us.

As we have intimated, we are storytellers, not text-reciters. This is when we are at our best. We share our personal revelations from Self and Sprit. We narrate our own unique, sacred stories—the paths we have followed, the visions that have been revealed, and the lessons we have learned. We also embrace the many teaching stories from other traditions, such as Jesus' parables, Native American lore, Hindu and Buddhist tales, Wiccan traditions, and so on. The Native cultures learned long ago that storytelling is an extremely helpful teaching tool, one I use in my college courses to great effect. Storytelling animates and lends color to

9. The church's Sacred Circles are held in the evenings on various days of the week at several locations throughout South Florida, and the topics cover all aspects of Universalist teachings and spirituality.

10. Russell T. McCutcheopn, "What is Religion," *Introduction to World Religions*, ed. Christopher Partridge (Minneapolis: Fortress Press, 2005), 12.

11. Hyemeyohsts Storm, "To All of Earth's People," an internet response to "Declaration of War Against Exploiters of Lakota Spirituality," 1993; and Barrett Eaglebear, Lakota Sundancer, as told by the Lakota Elders, 1994.

the teaching, and good stories are rich with mystery, suspense, spiritual symbolism, and deeper levels of meaning.

We find that a good story can be told many times. The Native American Story of Jumping Mouse is beloved by five year-olds and fifty-five year-olds alike, for each telling leads them down a slightly different path. Storytelling allows us to taste, touch, see, hear, and smell the lesson from the outside in and the inside out. This is Lyotard's postmodern "narrative knowledge." In addition, in our Universalist Church, we incorporate the great universal symbols of life in our teachings and stories. One example is the Native American Medicine Wheel, a complex and overarching symbol for life, growth, soul evolution, mission, service, meditation, and so on. Oh yes, Universalism is rich with the wisdom wealth of all humanity and Great Spirit for tens of thousands of generations. These are the treasures and inheritance of the House of Humanity and the House of God. As we wend our way through the scriptures, stories, legends, metaphors, poems, and verses of the ages, it is our spiritual "Walkabout" through the lands of revelation.

CHAPTER 15

Reflections on a Societal Theme

The Times, They are a' Changin'

In 1963, Bob Dylan wrote a song that became one of several anthems for the questing, defiant generation of the Sixties "The Times They are 'a Changin'."[1] He wasn't kidding. In the 1980s, Marilyn Ferguson dubbed this revolution the "Aquarian Conspiracy," yet another moniker for postmodernism.

> It is a conspiracy without a political doctrine. Without a manifesto. With conspirators who seek power only to disperse it, and whose strategies are pragmatic, even scientific, but whose perspective sounds so mystical that they hesitate to discuss it. Activists asking different kinds of questions, challenging the establishment from within.
>
> Broader than reform, deeper than revolution, this benign conspiracy for a new human agenda has triggered the most rapid cultural realignment in history. The great shuddering, irrevocable shift overtaking us is not a new political, religious, or philosophical system. It is a new mind—the ascendance of a startling worldview that gathers into its framework breakthrough science and insight from earliest recorded thought.[2]

The past fifty-some years have brought about a sea change in technology, spirituality, and behavior. When my daughter was in college a few years ago, she innocently asked me if my professors had allowed us to take

1. Dylan, Bob, "The Times They are A-Changin'," (Sony Music Corporation: 1963).
2. Marilyn Ferguson, *The Aquarian Conspiracy* (New York: Putnam,1980), 23.

a calculator into math and science exams. She looked in utter disbelief when I told her that in 1968 handheld calculators had yet to be invented. I was only permitted to take into the exam an ungainly little manual instrument called a slide rule. It was supposed to help make complicated calculations easier, but I think there are many generations of non-math majors who have routinely cursed that little "helper." I think, at that moment, she must have felt I was born in the Age of Dinosaurs. It made me reflect on the tremendous changes we have witnessed in such a very short time. I love reminding my students that there was a time, not so long ago, when there were no answering machines or cell phones. If someone called and they did not reach you, it was no big deal. They would just try again later. No one minded, and no one panicked if they weren't home. No one was upset if their boyfriend or girlfriend did not text them back within a few minutes. Now we are followed in the car, in the bathroom, in the bedroom, in the closet, and on vacation by little rectangles of electronic communication ring toning incessantly for our attention.

To further push the point, I also remind my students that, when I was a child in the 1950s, my family would go on vacation for a few weeks and leave the house unlocked. No one could reach us by phone, except by leaving a message at the General Store in the Upper Minnesota lake area, where we stayed. We knew the house was safe and our neighbors would keep an eye on things. We knew there were few emergencies worthy of interrupting our annual lake pilgrimage. Today, with higher crime rates and a Brinks Alarm System required by our insurance company, people would think we were crazy to leave the house unlocked, even if we left for just an hour. A sad corollary to this is that few of us know our urban neighbors well anymore, if at all, so they don't keep much of an eye out for us or we for them.

If you reflect upon it, how did people like my grandparents, who were born into a relatively quiet, stable farming community in Minnesota at the very beginning of the 20th century, adjust to this new, fast-paced world? In one lifetime, they witnessed the advent of automobiles and airplanes, the Great Depression, two World Wars, jets, the atom bomb, the Civil Rights Movement, computers, cell phones, and Neil Armstrong landing on the moon. From the Wright Brothers at Kitty Hawk to the Apollo Program on the moon, all in less than 100 years. It must have been mind-boggling at best and disorienting at worst. This is an aspect of postmodernity we only briefly addressed in the introduction.

As we discussed earlier, until recent times, philosophers, social scientists, and others assumed that the world could be nicely and neatly ordered, something called "structuralism." Worldview, social structures (e.g., government, religion, marketplace), language, and social mythology were somewhat fixed, stable, unchanging constants in the world. One can see why. Until the past few hundred years, people's lives and societies seemed relatively steady and unvarying within one lifetime. There may have been wars and natural disasters, but even those were so ubiquitous throughout so much of human history that they were often accepted as the "normal" landscape in many societies. Then, along comes the 20th century. My grandparents experienced more social change, technological innovation, and scientific advances in their one lifetime than had been observed in all five million years of human history up to that point. And it is accelerating. How will this new world of ours look as we progress through the New Millennium? What will you see in just your lifetime that our grandparents and parents could not have even imagined? What will stick and what will be left behind? What will be the "old school" and "new school" ways of thinking, perceiving, behaving, and being? Can you, and can we, make the necessary adjustments? Hence we see the emergence of post-structural theory as an aspect of postmodernity. There are no unchanging social structures or language constants, or unyielding world views. As the old saw goes, "There is only one constant in the universe and that is change."

Some examples? I live in South Florida. Sometimes, when I go out to a restaurant with my family, I wonder what the average white person of fifty years ago would think if they walked into *Bahama Breeze* or *Red Lobster* or *Hooters* today. They would be overwhelmed by the number of Hispanics and people of color casually integrated into the social scene. They would be astonished to see white servers serving a family of color. A few years ago, an African American student told me a story about a birthday party for her eighty-four year-old great grandmother. They took her to *Bahama Breeze* for dinner. They had to leave early because she had panic attacks throughout dinner. She apologized and said she just couldn't get used to eating at a restaurant with all these "white people." When she was a woman well into her forties, she participated in the Civil Rights Movement. Attempting to eat at "white" restaurants as a protest led to her getting thrown out, beaten, and jailed in Miami. There were still lynchings in the Deep South. She was never able to let go of the trauma, and it is certainly understandable within her generation.

As a young girl in the 1960s, Cate remembers there were still "Colored Only" bathrooms and drinking fountains in Miami. Schools were segregated, and until 1968, African Americans could not visit Miami Beach without a work permit. They had to swim and picnic at the "Colored Beach" on Virginia Key. In a related vein, as a sign of immense linguistic change, the word "nigger" has been one of the harshest of racial slurs for over 300 years. When uttered by a white person toward a person of color, it evoked a strong fear response, even into the 1960s. More recently, it had been used as an affectionate, joking term between African American youth and in the hip hop genre. But, after the deaths of George Floyd, Breonna Taylor, and Ahmed Arbery in 2020, it has returned as a deadly reminder of the continuing systemic racism permeating our country and our history.

Another language example is the word "bitch," originally a term for a female dog. It has also been a sexist term of male domination for centuries, particularly frightening for battered women when uttered by their abuser. They know what is coming next. Today, women use the term with each other teasingly, and it has even morphed into a relatively harmless hip hop term, "biatch." We should remember, nevertheless, that these words are not totally free of their domination origins. It is still utterly inappropriate for a white person to use a racial slur or a man to call his wife or girlfriend a bitch, even in jest. There has been too much suffering shed through those words to ignore the history. In postmodernity, then, the intent seems to be the key, and the intent has changed considerably.

Some other examples must include that a Black man has been elected the president of the United States, and the nomination almost went to his female rival. One hundred years ago, when women were just receiving the right to vote (19th Amendment) and most African Americans were deprived of their right to vote, this was unimaginable. Finally, just thirty years ago, most astronomers might have frowned at the unproven idea that there were other planets around other stars. Today, an astronomer who opposed the idea would be laughed out of the profession. Since 1995, thousands of extrasolar planets have been discovered orbiting other stars, some with enticing qualities that might presage life.[3] I think the post-structural point is made. In any event, Dylan's song could probably be the theme song not just for the 1960s but for the poststructural and postmodern period as well.

3. Nasa and Jet Propulsion Laboratory, Planet Quest, accessed September 2014, http://planetquest.jpl.nasa.gov/page/whatsTheDifference.

Following this train of thought, let's look at some of the paradigm shifts and postmodern issues we must tackle:

- The human connection and technology
- The human connection and population density
- The new function of religion and the postmodern transition, away from the rigidity of the old, mainstream orthodoxies and faiths
- The ongoing struggle between science and religion
- The place for spirituality in the corporate place and in a global economy
- The ongoing struggle pitting conservative fundamentalism against pluralism and universalism

Although we have looked at pieces of this jigsaw puzzle in preceding chapters, we will return now for a closer look. As we discover more pieces over the next few pages and see how they fit, I suspect, in the end, it will raise far more questions than provide answers. Such is the nature of the beast and I make no apologies for not being able to comprehend and solve the complex puzzle we call humanity and human behavior. It is a never-ending quest that began with the first human who asked, "Why?" Niels Bohr, the great Nobel Physicist, once summarized it well as, "Understanding nuclear quantum mechanics is child's play compared to understanding child's play." What I will do is attempt to outline some of the challenges we face as humanity passes into its postmodern adolescence. I will also suggest some possibilities and landmarks for realizing a vision of a kinder, more peaceful, more respectful, and more connected world. Envisioned is a world evolving to a higher light and love consciousness.

The Human Connection: Living in the Xbox

Coping with human connectedness in the face of a technological onslaught is a key survival challenge for humanity. It is alternatively breathtaking and terrifying to contemplate that what was once wild science fiction has turned into a scientific reality. We have the potential to forestall and reverse global warming, end major diseases in our time, increase food production so none will starve, travel to the stars, educate everyone, and create new energies free of pollution. Or we can use these very same technologies to create the most terrible weapons ever known to humanity and continue to enrich the few at the expense of the many. We can invest our technology in our future, our children's future, and our grandchildren's future as a whole people. Or we can continue down the same old rat hole of war, power, and greed. I am not saying anything new here and what has not been said far better by others, but the point for a spiritual person is clear and direct. The postmodern challenge is to enhance our emotional, cognitive, and spiritual evolution, not to allow the continued devolution of all we are and can be.

As Universalists, we contest the musty notion of original sin from classical Christianity or the many other doctrines from all manner of religions that view human nature as essentially (or only) corrupt and flawed—like the belief that only through some form of divine intervention or rigorous, ascetic discipline is humanity capable of salvation and enlightenment. I don't disagree with the Hindu sages or Jesus that the path to a spiritual life or enlightenment is difficult and narrow. "Sharp like a razor's edge, the sages say, is the path, difficult to traverse."[4] Or, "For the gate is narrow and the road is hard that leads to life, and there are few who find it" (Matthew 7:14). But it is not beyond human capability. So, now I have thrown down the gauntlet and, like Confucius and his disciple, Mencius, I propose that human nature is inherently good.[5] Let us see how we might bear witness to this humanistic stand.

This is not a time for only individuals to step up to the plate and begin making the necessary changes in their lives. Equally importantly, our world must develop a leadership base that is finally and genuinely interested in and passionate about public service. Politicians have some of the lowest ratings among professions in terms of people's respect,[6] probably right up there with hitmen, grifters, and con artists. It is no wonder, considering the dearth of great leaders in the world today. At the same time, as individuals, as neighbors, as bosses, as employees, as parents, as grandparents, as aunts and uncles and brothers and sisters and sons and daughters and nephews and nieces, we have not demanded that our leaders improve. We have not taken care of our precious human selves because we tolerate leadership that frequently cares little for each of us.

4 Katha Upanishad 3:14, "Death as Teacher," *The Upanishads*, trans. Eknath Easwaran (Tomales, California: Nilgiri Press, 1987), 89.

5. Yutang, 18–20, 280–281.

6. Associated Press, "Bush, Congress: Low Approval," *Miami Herald* (July 16, 2008), 6A. For example, in July 2008, President George Bush received a record low 28% approval rating among Americans, and Congress fared even worse at 18%.

And we have not taken care of our precious human family by tolerating leadership that often cares little for all of us.

I am not of the school that all politicians and public officials are corrupt and self-serving, for I have known and worked with many dedicated, unselfish, caring public servants. I was once one of them. But they and I often worked in bureaucratic systems that discouraged teamwork, dissent, creativity, and individuality. It seemed no better with my experiences in the corporate arena and it is a complaint echoed by many in both bureaucratic systems today. A century ago, Max Weber (1864–1920) predicted that these governmental and corporate systems would turn into an "iron cage."[7] Its mechanistic culture and structure would absolutely work against the healthy organizational attributes of teamwork, dissent, creativity, and individuality. We will return to Weber later as we discuss the challenge of the hoped for non-bureaucratic church.

For individuals and leaders to step up to this challenge of social transformation, they must be actively engaged in the world. In Modernity, we believed that we needed to interact face to face to create bonds and build relationships with real people (not virtual people). We could hold accountable, argue with, discuss with, negotiate with, shake hands with, make love with, and hug tangible, actual human beings. Now we may attend a net conferencing Zoom meeting with people halfway across the country or halfway around the world. Can we still create those bonds and build those relationships even if we cannot touch or embrace our virtual meeting partner? I imagine the jury is still out, but it is inevitable that we must make the attempt. In the not too distant future, the net conferencing meeting or phone call will truly be out of this world, as is already the case for the astronauts on the International Space Station. What if we never come face to face with the people we work with on a regular basis? How many of us already will never come face to face with our community, corporate, and world leaders? How do we, and how will we, relate to each other?

Already, we walk around more and more with our little headphones or earbuds on or surfing our computer or playing fantasy games with unseen allies and opponents or sifting through hundreds of e-mails and texts, and replying with short bursts of half sentences and phrases that would drive our English teachers to apoplexy. More and more, we do not come face to face with real people to take care of business, to take care of

7. Randall Collins, *Four Sociological Traditions* (New York: Oxford University Press, 1994), 91.

friendship, to take care of love, to take care of work, even to take care of ourselves. This can potentially become a disconnect, and it can actually disconnect us from reality.

Virtual reality. What an oxymoron! I have never given change to a virtual homeless person. I have never kissed a virtual soul mate. I have never hugged a virtual friend. I have never helped a virtual daughter or son with their homework. I have never thrown a ball to a virtual pet. I have never attended a virtual baptism or funeral. I have never been harmed by a virtual enemy. I have never visited a virtual concentration camp memorial. I have never debated a virtual politician or leader. When they are virtual, they are not real and generally do not engender genuine emotion. When they are real, I feel real compassion, real caring, real loving, real friendship, real anger, real fear, real disagreement, real sharing, real excitement, real sorrow, real pain, real pride, real joy. These are all the things that make me human and challenge me, that impel me to grow.

Yet, for some, they have confused this virtual world with reality, and they believe they are experiencing authentic moments and genuine emotions rather than playing out some unresolved drama from their past or in their psyche. Perhaps it began with the first prehistoric play, but in modern times we can certainly concur that it crescendoed with radio and television, and now the Internet. Soap opera stars are frequently accosted by people who approach them on the street or in the supermarket. They demand to know why they are cheating on their television spouse or abandoning their television son or running away from their television problems. We might think this is a bit far-fetched and that these sad folks sorely need to get a life. However, I know some young people who measure their popularity by the number of "friends" on their Facebook or Instagram pages, even if they have never met many of these "friends." I know gamers whose whole life is spent in front of an Xbox or Nintendo. I know families who spend more time in front of the television or computer or smartphone in a month than they participate together, for family activities, in a year. I frequently hear spouses complain that their partner is always on the computer (it used to be sports or the television) or phone and that they don't talk anymore. I have counseled people whose only sex life is in front of the computer. These are clearly disconnects.

Leonard Pitts, a consistently insightful *Miami Herald* commentator on the human condition, recently decried the decision at Fossil Hill Middle School in Fort Worth, Texas (and others around the country) to ban all hugging and hand-holding by students. As he noted:

> Now we have hugging bans. As if there was not already enough in life to make you feel disconnected, disaffected, alienated, isolated . . . Sometimes—times of pain, times of commiseration, times of affection, and times of joy—you just need to be held . . . I guess kids who need consolation, kids primed for celebration, kids who just want to know that they are not alone will henceforth have to write text messages instead. And progress marches on.[8]

I'm also remembering that one of the greatest joys of my high school years was holding hands with my girlfriend as we walked to class. Not all the best education about life occurred in the classroom. As Pitts notes, we are not talking about sexual groping or sexual harassment, which the rules already cover.[9] Instead, we are talking about encouraging appropriate expressions of warmth, caring, and emotional bonds in young people who are just beginning the journey into adulthood. Do we want them to make this arduous journey connected or disconnected?

I understand the reasoning behind these policies, especially with my years working with sex offenders and child molesters as a psychotherapist. Nevertheless, I'm still unsure what it says about our society when a kindergarten teacher is prohibited from giving a hug to a crying five year-old. Likewise, in my seminary, we held a number of ethical debates about the propriety of ministers giving hugs to parishioners. Many denominations now ban it because of the potential for abuse and the fear of lawsuits. Sadly, we have some of our wayward brothers in the clergy to thank for that. However, our Universalist Church stubbornly resists this trend simply because, if we have any meaningful ritual at all in our church, it is hugs. It is part of the connection between the members of our spiritual family. So, at the risk of over-reliance on Leonard Pitts:

> Am I the only one who feels this is just the latest step in a troubling trend? Am I the only one who sees businesses, schools, and public institutions moving inexorably as a Terminator, toward the standardization and regulation of even the most mundane of human interaction? In so doing, they seek to remove the defining element of human interaction: humanity . . . I understand the thinking. If you can standardize all interactions, you ensure

8. Leonard Pitts, Jr., "What Robots We've Become," *Miami Herald*, October 3, 2007, 23A.

9. Ibid.

> a consistent level of quality. I'm just not convinced what we gain is worth all that we lose.[10]

Amen!

So, how long before we are not merely wired in, but become the wire in? As technology and behavior become more interconnected, will we actually become more interconnected ourselves, or will we become the insulated, isolated, headphones-on, wired-in virtual selves stuck in our little electronic worlds? There is a satirical moment between Sylvester Stallone and Sandra Bullock in *The Running Man*, an eminently forgettable science fiction movie. Still, the point is well made in this particular scene. He is an aggressive, even violent, police officer from the past who is taken out of a cryogenic, frozen state and revived to help the people of the future fight crime. They don't know how to handle violent criminals anymore. One of his police guides is an attractive young woman (Bullock) who casually suggests they have sex. He is somewhat taken aback but is even more appalled that she means something quite different from anything in his experience. He learns there is no more physical contact in the future, and the lovemaking transpires through virtual reality helmets. What a metaphor!

Some Sociological Musings

This thirst for spiritual meaning, this quest for the Divine, this search for connection raises some fascinating and foundational sociological and theological questions. Why do humans need religion? What functions do God and religion serve in society and for the individual? How are our religious needs changing in this postmodern world? There have been some sociological schools over the past two centuries that have commented upon or theorized about the role of religion in society. These include Utilitarian, Marxian, Durkheimian, Weberian, and Microtinteractionist sociological theories, to name a few. If we move through each of these and also look into the heart of Liberation Theology, we can secure a better picture of the historical role of religion, as well as its postmodern role today. Sometimes, we will use the Universalist experiment to measure one aspect of the modern to postmodern paradigm shift.

10. Pitts, 23A

Utilitarian Consequences and Durkheim's Glue

It is not difficult for a Universalist to find the Utilitarian Theory of Jeremy Bentham (1748–1832) and John Stuart Mill (1806–1873) lacking. It was a brilliant step forward in looking at the social advantages and disadvantages (consequences) for any action. They developed a morality based upon social and individual benefit, a modernist philosophy based primarily on scientific objectivity and reason.[11] Emile Durkheim (1858–1917), one of the fathers of sociology, was to comment later that people did not make thoughtful, rational choices for rewards and punishments, investments, and payoffs. Rather, he demonstrated that the surface level of rationality is not what holds a society together but the non-rational foundation from which it emerges.[12] As he so cogently noted about rational theory, ". . . individual choice could not possibly hold society together. A combination of rational individuals only leads to a war of all against all."[13] As we have observed, Universalist theology has its logical, rational side but is not solely aligned with theories of reason and rationality. It is even more attuned to the non-rational and mystical.

Durkheim's sociological theories, although highly scientific in approach, are not neat and rational by the very nature of the messy, complicated subject to be studied—humans and human society. On the surface of this new 19th century social science were objective social groupings, symbols, and rituals. However, according to Durkheim, concealed underneath lurked the vast, subjective, real structure of society; the non-rational and the subconscious.[14] Sigmund Freud brought this home a few years later with his theories about the unconscious mind. This non-rationality is especially appreciated through the study of religion. As Randall Collins noted about Durkheim's exposure of the underbelly of society, "This intellectual tradition focuses on themes of emotional forces, morality, the sacred, and religious—and declares that these are the essence of everything social."[15] Emotions are non-rational forces within the human psyche and are frequently driven by the unconscious mind. Thus, the

11. Anthony Falikowski, *Moral Philosophy for Modern Life* (Scarborough, Canada: Prentice Hall Allyn and Bacon, 1998), 64–65.

12. Randall Collins, *Four Sociological Traditions* (New York: Oxford University Press, 1994), 193.

13. Ibid, 197.

14. Ibid, 181.

15. Ibid.

theory implies that society, social groups, families, communities, religions, and religious groups are primarily guided by unseen non-rational and unconscious motives. Once that was set out, Durkheim's lasting value was his ability to cut to the heart of the question, in this case: What is the glue that holds society together?[16] He asserted that religion was the glue, especially since it was built on a non-rational base of faith, not reason. It would naturally speak to the emotional, subjective, and unconscious mind reaching the deepest roots of human longing for feeling valued and relevant and for belongingness.

Durkheim postulated a formula for this glue, his "Law of Social Gravity." Put simply, the actual physical distance between people and groups of people has a profound impact on their thinking, their customs, their rituals, and their group patterns. There is a lot of physical distance in tribal and rural communities. There is less density in their communities and their social groups are smaller. As society becomes denser (urbanization), the physical and emotional space between people is lessened, and there are far more interactions between individuals and groups. Durkheim hypothesized that the greater the social density, the more interdependent the society, while simultaneously, individuals become more specialized—a complex division of labor develops.[17] For a while, this works in favor of forming groups with durable social and belief bonds (such as religion). Or so it seemed in the 19th century.

One of the social phenomena he studied to make his case was suicide, especially as it represented a foil for the "normal" social structure. Something broke down. He discerned that groups, such as religious groups with a high social density, created a "moral cocoon" around individuals within their physical and social arena. The binding for the cocoon is ritual, "a moment of intense social density." Group bonding rituals usually work best when there are greater numbers of people. For example, many Christians speak of a sense of deep reverence during their Communion ceremony. Jews have a similar reaction when the Torah is carried through the congregation. Participating in the *hajj* (the once-in-a-lifetime pilgrimage to *Mecca*) has been a life-transforming experience for many Muslims.

Rituals craft a common, esteemed focus for the group, transcending the ordinary and mundane. Eventually, individuals begin to identify with

16. Collins, 186.

17. Ibid, 186–187.

the group's symbols and rituals as they concentrate more on the group than themselves. This is the cocoon of "moral density." It is when these social bonds weaken that suicide can become a real possibility. Durkheim suggested that there was less suicide among the highly ritualized and interdependent Jewish and Catholic communities than the more individualistic and minimalist ritual Protestants.[18]

Over 100 years later, as we move out of modernity, one cannot help but ask: Why is the social glue, particularly religion, no longer holding? The societal threads are unraveling. The aging, threadbare fabric of social ties is tearing. Have we lost the essence of community, of *koinonia*? In our very crowded world, is there too much social density and specialization, resulting in an opposite, self-protective reaction of emotional distance? This may very well be preventing the rigid cocoons of outdated, worn-out rituals and uninspired group consciousness from protecting or welcoming or enfolding the individual as they once did in a society affording more social cohesion.

Within the postmodern impulse, there seems to be a deep longing to return to less emotional distance between individuals while still retaining one's individuality and socially sophisticated ideas that were the advantage of the denser civilization. We want the benefits and emotional closeness of the tribe combined with the satisfactions of the higher world awareness of the urban milieu. This countervailing tendency is the new glue—tribal warmth and urbane sophistication, what we call Metrotribalism.[19] Along these lines, in his treatise on postmodern theology, Anselm Min calls for a further shift in the postmodern individualistic, deconstructionist paradigm:

> . . . not for a theology of difference but for a theology of solidarity; not the solidarity of the same but precisely the solidarity of the different, the solidarity of strangers, the solidarity of those who are other to one another.[20]

This last might well describe the motivation of many postmodern people seeking spirituality. They come from all walks of life, and they are coming together as a spiritual family with a minimum of ritual and symbol. Far more than ritual or symbol, emotional closeness seems to be

18. Collins, 184, 190.

19. From discussions with Rev. Cathleen Norris, who coined the term "Metrotribalism," The Church of the Way of the Messiahs, October 2008.

20. Min, 82.

the moral cocoon for our church and many other postmodern groups. Still, some are still drawn to the emotional comfort of ancient or newly-fashioned ritual and ceremony.

Marx's Opium

Emile Durkheim, the scientist, was the thinker in observing the human social condition. Karl Marx (1818–1883), the reformer, was the mover-thinker in changing the human social condition. His theory provides one of the foundation pillars for Liberation Theology and emphasizes a profound concern for the oppressed.[21] The plight of the European worker deeply moved Marx. Everywhere he looked, he observed adults and children working under appalling conditions in mills, mines, fields, and factories. There was no regard for the worker who actually produced the products that allowed society to survive and thrive. There was no concern for safety, sanitation, health, or rights. Wages were uniformly minimal; there was no sick leave or vacation leave, and there were no laws to protect workers from abusive employers. He saw the "haves"—the owners, executives, and royalty of Europe, who produced nothing themselves—living off the backs of the "have-nots." Even religion was brought in to support the social norm. Workers would hear from their priests and preachers that it was a sin and against God's law to disobey their boss, much less protest or strike. Thus, we are reminded of Marx's famous quote: "Religion is the sigh of the oppressed creature, the heart of a heartless world, and the soul of soulless conditions. It is the opium of the people."[22]

Cate and I came across a perfect example of worker exploitation a few years ago while on vacation in Colorado. We were visiting one of the old silver mines from the 1800s. In the crew shed was a large drill with a sign hanging from it, "The Widowmaker." When we asked the tour guide what this meant, he related that whoever was assigned to the drill usually died within the year from the inhalation of the dust created by the drilling. Sadly, there was a simple, relatively inexpensive fix. If the owners pumped water through a hose into the mine and attached it to the drill,

21. Juan Luis Segundo, *Liberation of Theology*, trans. John Drury (Eugene, Oregon: Wipf and Stock Publishers, 1999), 16.

22. Karl Marx, *Contribution to the Critique of Hegel's Philosophy of Law* (Moscow: Progress, 1957), 38–39.

the water spray captured the dust and washed it away harmlessly to the tunnel floor. The owners resisted this inexpensive change for a long time.

If only this were ancient history. However, we have had several serious mining disasters in the Americas over the past few years—West Virginia's Sago Mines explosion in 2006 (twelve deaths) and Utah's Crandall Canyon cave in 2007 (nine deaths). Many believe some workers could have been saved if they had been issued a relatively inexpensive PED (Personal Emergency Device). This would allow them to contact the surface in an emergency and pinpoint their location to any rescuers. Several American mines and most Australian mines have had them, some as early as 1990. Sadly, for budgetary reasons, many American mine corporations have resisted this and related safety measures, such as breathing units that last more than an hour.[23] In the 2010 Chilean San Jose mine disaster, thirty-three miners were imprisoned half a mile underground for sixty-nine days. Legislators discovered that the men could have been rescued much sooner. The mine might not even have collapsed if the mine operators had simply installed the contractually required safety equipment.[24]

Nevertheless, beyond the aspect of social conscience, Marxism generally holds little appeal to postmodern thinkers. This is largely because it is a modernist socioeconomic theory and, of course, associated with the failed Communist experiment. It is my guess that Marx would not have endorsed the manner in which his utopian ideas were implemented by the Soviet Union or China, but that is an academic matter of endless dispute. In any event, in tune with their individualistic bent, postmoderns tend not to think in these particular global or Newtonian scientific terms, which are too materialistic[25] and outdated for their tastes. Father Gustavo Gutierrez, the great Liberation theologian, was highly critical of this, as he noted:

23. Senator Robert Byrd, "No More Excuses, Make the Mines Safer" (U.S. Senate), February 1, 2006, http://byrd.senate.gov/speeches/2006_february/mine_safety_bill.html; U.S. Mine Safety and Health Administration (MSHA), "Description of MSHA-Approved Technologies," 4; and "An Unnatural Disaster," *The Mountain Eagle*, http://www.themountaineagle.com/news/2007/0829/Opinion/017.html.

24. Bonnefoy, Pascale, "Inquiry on Mine Collapse in Chile Ends With No Charges," *New York Times*, August 1, 2013, http://www.nytimes.com/2013/08/02/world/americas/inquiry-on-mine-collapse-in-chile-ends-with-no-charges.html?_r=0.

25. Fisher, 13. According to Mary Pat Fisher, over the past two centuries, scientific materialism has gained prominence, which suggests that "the supernatural is imaginary; only the material world exists." This is clearly the outcome of Modernity, but is less of a postmodern trait.

> Individualism and spiritualism . . . combine to impoverish and even distort the following of Jesus. An individualist spirituality is incapable of offering guidance . . . to those who have embarked upon a collective enterprise of liberation.[26]

This is accentuated because there is some truth to the criticism, although many like Father Gutierrez miss the point that many spiritual people are acutely concerned about the human condition and experience. However, their global and scientific view is more metaphysical, post-Newtonian,[27] and mystical, so their solutions to the sufferings of the world will definitely differ from those of Marx and other earlier social reformers. Still, the thought that postmodern spiritual solutions may be a little too otherworldly, mystical, and unrealistic is worth consideration. This is why a considerable portion of this book addresses the issues of the poor and oppressed with an eye toward supporting more social awareness and social action. To truly be Universalist, one must be inclusive of all people, including the poor and oppressed, who represent the majority of the population in the world. The theological basis of Universalism cannot neglect the underlying truths of a Liberation Theology.

Despite these differences, postmodern thinkers tend to resonate with Marx's rejection of organized religion. In Marxian terms, religion is an error,[28] just another ideology or intellectual construction.[29] Universalists, too, are generally impatient with inflexible orthodoxies or traditional religious institutions, which have so often supported or devolved into the very bureaucracies that devalue the individual. Thus, at the heart of their spirituality, postmoderns are not just seekers but also reformers and rebels. One might say that the mid-20th century move away from the Modern Era was a quiet revolution born of postmodern misgivings. Becker expands upon this trend through the work of Jurgen Habermas, who tracked the demise of classical religious consciousness. As she notes:

26. Gustavo Gutierrez, from *We Drink from Our Own Wells: the Spiritual Journey of a People*, trans. Matthew J. O'Connell (Maryknoll, NY: Orbis Books, 1984), reprinted in *Invitation to Christian Spirituality*, ed. John R. Tyson (New York: Oxford Press, 1999), 451.

27. Holland, "An Excerpt from . . . Pax Romana in Postmodern Planetary Civilizations," *28th Plenary Assembly, Pax Romana*, September 21, 2000, International Catholic Movement for Intellectual and Cultural Affairs, 1–3.

28. Segundo, 59.

29. Jose Miguez Bonino, "Marxist Critical Tools," *The Bible and Liberation*, ed. Norman K. Gottwald and Richard A. Horsley (Maryknoll: Orbis, 1993), 108.

> In a secularized world, it is no longer necessary or even desirable to be religious. Philosophers and sociologists since Karl Marx have predicted that secular philosophical systems would fill the void in meaning that religion had previously given people's lives. But secular philosophy has also failed. Why? Secular thinking faced not only the fixations of a technocratic consciousness but also, at the same time, the collapse of religious consciousness. Since the secular interpretation of the world depends precisely on coexistence with a widely influential religion of the masses, its ability to provide "substitute meaning" is an illusion. Only religion can speak to people en masse of hope, because it alone speaks in symbols, signs, images, rhythms, and icons to which people can relate emotionally as well as intellectually.[30]

Durkheim could not have said it better himself.

The postmodern spiritual movement, then, is a socio-religio reaction to the increasing displacement of the human individual in a capitalist, bureaucratic society. Postmodern and New Age spiritual adherents abound in the former Communist countries as well,[31] where a ruinous devaluing of the individual most certainly occurred over the past century. As Joseph Holland points out, in the deepening stages of industrial mechanization, there was a social impact in the breakup of craft guilds soon to be replaced by factories; a physical impact as human muscle was replaced by machine; and a cybernetic impact with the replacement of workers by computers. There has been an ongoing movement of alienation and anomie of the individual from their work, from each other, and from their society.[32] This stage of late capitalism represents a profound global, cultural transformation moving us out of and beyond the past 500 years of Modernity[33] into an era of hopefully "regenerative" Postmodernity.[34]

Weber's Iron Cage

Approaching religion from a very different angle, we come to Max Weber (1864–1920), noted for his preeminent theory of bureaucracy. He

30. Becker, 24–25.

31. Ibid, 254–257.

32. Holland, "The Evolution of Modern Industrial-Capitalist Society and the Birth of the Postmodern Electronic-Ecological Era," 9.

33. Ibid., 10.

34. Ibid., 17.

postulated that the state and all social institutions unfailingly evolve toward bureaucracy. His is a mechanistic, rationalistic sociological analysis. There certainly seem to be some deep-seated truths to the theory as our current mechanistic, corporate, bureaucratic society and state are ample proof. He called it the "iron cage."[35] In religion, he saw this occurring when the original, charismatic leadership passes on. Then, "the center of the movement may shift to people with managerial prowess and those who turn the original inspirations into routine rituals and dogma." He called it the "routinization of charisma."[36]

This Weberian bureaucratic death sentence is anathema to postmodern spiritual people. It is the very thing they are attempting to escape. It counteracts any attempts to create and maintain a spiritual family (*koinonia*), the moral cocoon of emotional closeness. It is perhaps the greatest challenge of any reform or revolution—to avoid becoming that which they have just overthrown. We recognize the necessity of having an organizational structure with its attendant leadership, outreach, networking, fundraising, and administrative functions. So, how does an organization prevent the organization's managerial needs and internal politics from crushing the life out of its initial spiritual goals and emotional bonding processes? It certainly is the greatest challenge for a Universalist Church, which attempts to balance spiritual and emotional intimacy among its members with an organizational structure that can grow and succeed.

In what ways can a Universalist Church or postmodern spiritual group wrestle against this hypothesized inevitable institutionalization? We can begin by noting such an organization works very hard to prevent bureaucratization and institutionalization. It utilizes a more lay-centered, democratic, and less priestly approach through a congregational (committee of the whole) style, which is less leadership-centered. Also, it incorporates a limited number of rituals, generally created and/or adopted by the congregants themselves. The emphasis is on the emotional bonds between members and a non-hierarchical decision-making and facilitator leadership style.

In the attempt to create a new spirituality, Universalists also try to create a new spiritual pathway for organizations to evolve. Thus, in the face of the practicality of organizational life, we cannot minimize the role of our central faith (the non-rational, subjective force). We do not believe

35. Collins, 91; and Holland, "The Evolution of Modern-Industrial-Capitalist Society . . . ," 19.

36. Fisher, 38.

we are entirely alone in this venture of new creation. We have a partner in spirit. Utilizing a spiritual approach with the renewed guidance of Great Spirit may help prevent the very thing that previously seems to have undermined religious ventures throughout history, becoming ordinary, mundane, and bureaucratic over time. Once, these religions, early in their saga, were also greatly spirit-inspired and then something "happened" along the long corridors of history. It is almost as if success plants the seeds for eventual "iron" bureaucracy. Success seems to drain the original life force energy of passionate faith in Spirit and faith in each other. Instead, it is replaced with procedures, administrative rituals, policy manuals, and hierarchies of organization. In the new paradigm, we hope to avoid this by taking the best of the Old Age and bring it, refreshed, into the new creation of the New Age.

I am reminded of the scene in the movie *Joshua* where Joshua (played by Tony Goldwyn) returned a beautiful crystal Christmas tree to a friend. She had thrown it angrily to the ground in a moment of lost faith and despair. It broke into dozens of shattered fragments, just like the woman's life. When he returned it to her, he had miraculously refashioned it anew as a beautiful crystalline angel, and she held and looked at it in wonder that such a shattered thing could become so beautiful. Such is what we are hoping for in this renewal of the postmodern spirit. The postmodern church models we are suggesting in later chapters will hopefully break free of Weber's "iron cage" and refashion the shattered Christmas tree into the delightful angel of hope and promise. Only time will tell if this is a futile or fruitful course of action.

Micro Stories

As Universalists, we also use some sociological tools, such as ethnomethodology, which comes out of sociologist Harold Garfinkel's Micro-interactionist work. Part of this is simply listening to people's stories to discover their underlying meanings.[37] Sadly demonstrating the truth of Weber's thesis, one element that seems to have been lost in many mainline churches is the ability to provide a genuine focus on the individual. What is particularly lost are the individual stories of personal and spiritual growth, of the person's sufferings and triumphs. The number of church services, congregants, and bureaucratic responsibilities combined with a

37. Collins, 276–277.

lack of staffing frequently undermines the determined *koinonia* resolve of many churches, mosques, and temples and their priests, ministers, imams, and rabbis. Consequently, the individual focus is often relegated to the pastoral counseling arena, and the larger group then loses the history, struggles, life meaning, and wisdom of its individual members. For many postmodern groups, the focus is not only upon the group but the individuals within it, so there is, hopefully, balance and cooperative interplay between the group and individual consciousness. Again, the emphasis is on *koinonia*, but as a collection of individuals who have come together for the common purpose of spiritual questing, growing, and acting.

Reflections on a Sociological Theme

While Utilitarian and Weberian theories are generally discarded by the Postmodern movement, their models prove useful as a counterpoint for what Universalists desire to avoid. We wish to sidestep basing our spiritual work on a solely material rewards and benefits model or becoming a bureaucratic nightmare. Durkheimian and Marxian ventures prove far more helpful in describing some of the social structural and socioeconomic developments of the Modern Era and their influence transitioning into postmodernity. Durkheim's emphasis on investigating the "glue" that holds society together provides crucial clues to comprehending the Postmodern Era, since the old social cohesion bonds no longer seem to be holding. The collapse of Modernity, and with it, the decline of long-established religious institutions,[38] has provided fallow ground for the emergence of insurgent cultural, artistic, philosophical, and spiritual movements in the Postmodern Era. One of these is Universalism.

Our brief sociological overview offers some valuable insights into modern and postmodern thinking, most notably regarding the overriding postmodern theme of individualism-within-community. Moreover, even though the Universalist movement can be seen as a radical break from tradition, it and the rest of postmodernity is not entirely new. The

38. The Pew Forum on Religion and Public Life, "U.S Public Becoming Less Religious" (Pew Research Center, 2015), https://www.pewforum.org/2015/11/03/u-s-public-becoming-less-religious; *Transitioning* (Grand Rapids: Zondervan, 1999), 13–14. Dan Southerland reports that recent studies have shown that 80% of North American churches are plateaued or in decline. Recent Pew Center research has found that 23 percent of Americans now say they are unaffiliated with any religion, a significant increase from years past (16.1 percent in 2007), and they are youthful.

flowering of the tree is recent, but the seeds were planted long before. In hindsight, one can see the seeds of postmodernity germinating and sprouting centuries ago, so it is less of a revolutionary process than an evolutionary progress. From this perspective, a Universalist Church of interfaith tolerance is just another natural, logical evolutionary step. It opens a new age as society struggles in an increasingly complex, global world to find the balance between tribal family unity and postmodern individualism, the new Metrotribe.

CHAPTER 16

The New Paradigm

The Age of Aquarius

More than one metaphysical author has pointed out that there has been a quantum shift in the nature of leadership as we are moving out of the Age of Pisces and into the Age of Aquarius. The 2,160-year cycles measure the precession of the equinoxes. Somewhere around 2060 CE, the constellation Aquarius will rise in the east each morning for another 2,160 years and usher in the Age of Aquarius.

Whether one believes in astrology or not, let us at least look at it symbolically, especially with an eye toward the goal of human spiritual evolution. What is the next step for humanity? What is the new paradigm? Are we always to remain in the role of obedient children, forever under the all-seeing eye of a loving but strict father, or are we finally supposed to grow up? It has been noted that the time just before the Age of Pisces and throughout the Age of Pisces was the time of the great spiritual leaders. What a time it was in the 5th and 6th BCE. Luminaries such as Lao Tzu (Taoism) and Confucius in China, Mahavir (Jainism) and Gautama Buddha in India, Socrates in Greece, Zarathustra (Zoroastrianism) in Persia (now Iran), Viracocha (pre-Incan and Incan Creator god),[1] and the Hindu sages who wrote the *Upanishads* all appeared on the world scene.[2] Their work changed the face of much of South America, the Far East, and The Middle East for the next 2,500 years and even had strong

1. Adam Zeidan, "Viracocha: Inca deity," *Encyclopedia Britannica*, https://www.britannica.com/topic/Viracocha.

2. Fisher, 120, 135, 184, 231.

influences on the Judeo-Christian world. In approximately 6–4 BCE, Jesus of Nazareth entered the stage.[3] Not so much later, some 1600 years ago, White Buffalo Calf Woman appeared to her people among the Plains Indians,[4] and Quetzalcoatl emerged in the Mayan and Aztec civilizations of Central America.[5] In 610 CE, Muhammad received his first revelations from Angel Gabriel, which eventually developed into the *Qu'ran* (*The Recitations*) and the religion of Islam.[6] This was followed by Hasan al-Basri and Jalal ad-Din Rumi from the 8th-13th centuries, advancing the mystical side of Islam, *Sufism*.[7] In the 15th century, Guru Nanak, in Northern India, arrived to redeem the people from "the dark ages," and *Sikhism* was born.[8] We can think of so many more: The Ari (Isaac Luria, 1534–1572), pre-eminent in the *Kaballah* traditions; St. Francis of Assisi (1181–1226); Martin Luther (1483–1546), the founder of Protestantism; Bahá'u'lláh (1817–1892), the prophet of the Bahai faith; Mahatma Gandhi (1869–1948); Martin Luther King, Jr. (1929–1968); Mother Theresa (1910–997); and Tenzin Gyatso, the 14th Dalai Lama (1935-present), to name a few. All of these luminaries impacted religion and spirituality in ways that can be seen to this day. Perhaps the Age of Pisces was the old paradigm of the Age of the Gurus, the Great Masters who led humanity to a higher awareness for those who dared to listen. It was the Age of the Great Teachers, certainly not the only time of great teachers, but most certainly a prominent age. How is the Age of Aquarius or our next evolutionary step going to be different?

Consider the purpose and hope of all the great spiritual teachers who have come to planet Earth. They are a humble group. None wanted to be kings or political leaders. None wanted worldly riches or worldly fame. Instead, they hoped that the teachings and the revelations they had received and shared would help enlighten everyone who followed the path laid out by God, Goddess, or *Dharma* (Absolute Truth). Once this goal of enlightenment was achieved, then what? Do we need a Guru or a Master Teacher anymore? Our premise is that the next human step,

3. Hopfe and Woodward, 273.

4. As told by Dakota storyteller and spiritual leader, Woableza of the Cheyenne River Reservation, in a Miami Sacred Circle at our church (October, 1999).

5. Adam Augustyn, "Quetzalcoatl: Mesoamerican god," *Encyclopedia Britannica*, https://www.britannica.com/topic/Quetzalcoatl.

6. Armstrong, *Muhammad*, 82–83.

7. Armstrong, *A History of God*, 225, 240–241.

8. Fisher, 435–436.

perhaps symbolized by the Age of Aquarius, also ends the Age of the Guru (Age of Pisces). Humanity has a grand opportunity. We no longer need to look outside ourselves for a savior, but finally to look within. Will we take advantage of this "new" age?

Daddy-King God

First, we must overcome an annoying and persistent human trait. Invariably, we must make gods out of our heroes. I call it the "We Need a Mommy-Daddy God Syndrome" or, alternatively, the "Daddy-King Syndrome." Perhaps Sigmund Freud wasn't so far off the mark when he postulated that most people's concepts of God and religion are based upon a deep, unresolved, even infantile neurosis. This neurosis revolved around the young child's view of parents as handing out rewards when he or she is a "good" little boy or girl or meting out punishment when he or she is a "bad" little boy or girl. In the face of an uncertain and frequently unforgiving universe, God is created to make some sense of it all—to protect, reward, and punish just like a parent, like a strict father.[9] One friend cannot even hear the term "God the Father" without becoming enraged. As a little girl in Nazi-occupied France, her mother told her that God was angry with her whenever it thundered. Between the stormy weather and the thundering German artillery, she was a very shamed and frightened child. To this day, she is still angry at this punitive father figure (and with an angry, abusive mother for creating the image).

This idealization of God and our spiritual heroes is akin to the new "pseudo religion" of the West, Romantic Love. Buddhist professor Judith Brown proposes that our Western obsession with finding our soulmate—the one person in the universe, our split-apart, who will complete us—keeps us relentlessly falling in love with a fantasy. We cling to an idealized version of our partner who does not and cannot exist. Naturally, this leads to constant disappointment when our idealized partners (as well as our idealized selves) fail to live up to our heightened expectations, but worse, it implies we cannot love real people. We will reject real people for a fantasy.[10] Similarly, have we not done this to Jesus and other great spiritual teachers?

9. Sigmund Freud, *The Future of An Illusion*, trans. W.D. Robson-Scott (Garden City: Anchor Books, 1964), 24, 27, 32–35, and 47.

10. Judith Brown, of Naropa University, in a lecture at Florida International

What I love about Jesus is his humanness. I can relate to him because I know he knows what a bill is and sometimes how hard it was to pay it on time. He knew how painful splinters were. He was a carpenter's son and a carpenter himself who used to help his dad with jobs in the community. He knew what hard work was. He understood sorrow when his father died and left his mom a single parent in a peasant community. He understood what it was like to be the oldest child in the family, helping to raise younger brothers and sisters. He knew what it was like to be a teenager throbbing with hormones and having a crush on a girl down the lane who didn't even know he existed. He knew what it was like to have the flu or diarrhea. He knew what it was like to be you and me.

Then, there is the idealized church version of Jesus with light skin and light hair like he is from Sweden or Denmark. He often appears so frail that it looks like he could hardly lift a hammer, and of course, he never had a bad or erotic thought in his life. That Jesus I cannot relate to. That Jesus leaves me cold, and I don't believe that "church Jesus" has a clue about our lives, our issues, our problems—about you and me. I don't believe the "church Jesus" ever existed. Have we often not done the same to Muhammad or Gautama Buddha and the rest? By robbing them of their humanity, by removing them from the earthly plane of real life, we remove them from us. We make them so different from us by idealizing them and consequently devaluing ourselves that it destroys all hope that we might have that we could be like them. They cannot be immanent, down-to-earth role models and teachers, but must be transcendent, distant, unobtainable gods. We have set the bar to perfection and concluded that, as humans, we are never able to be perfect. To be like them, we will have to attain some mythical, fantasy level of perfection with never a sinful thought or moment of human weakness. We set ourselves up for constant disappointment. We are forever in love with a fantasy and reject our wonderfully fallible human selves with all of our strengths, courage, hopes, determination, good works, good intents, and imperfections. Perhaps we finally reject our gods and goddesses and their messengers as well, never accepting their role within humanity. As a pantheist and believing that God is part of everything, must I not only honor God's magnificent, immanent life within humanity, but God's transcendent magnificence within greater creation too?

University, "The Pseudo Religion of Western Romantic Love," February 14, 2007; North Miami, Florida.

In religious and spiritual circles, we see this idealization occur all the time, and not just with the Pope, but also with cult figures like Rev. Moon of the Reunification Church and L. Ron Hubbard of Scientology—or at the extreme—Jim Jones of Jonestown, with his "drink the Koolaid" answer, or David Koresh of Waco, Texas with his narcissistic, self-destruction answer. In the New Age, the tendency continues to elevate leaders to sainthood or Godhood, whether it is J.J. Hurtak of the *Keys of Enoch*, Drunvalo Melchizedek of the Flower of Life Teachings, or even the channeled beings of Seth (via Jane Roberts) or Abraham (via Esher Hicks), to name a few. I personally have great respect for much of their enlightened work and teachings, and it is ironic that they remain, as a whole, relatively humble individuals. This does not seem to deter some of their followers any more than it did the followers of Buddha, Jesus, and Muhammad. Near death, Buddha exhorted his followers to resist appointing leaders of the *Sangha* (Buddhist community) after his death, as the *Dharma* (The Teachings) should be enough. They did not listen for long.[11] Jesus was a reform Jew and would probably not have known what to make of the new Christianity of St. Paul that began emerging several decades after his death. It wildly diverged from his beloved rural, pastoral, Galilean reform Judaism.[12] After his death, Muhammad's friend, Abu Bakr, addressed Muhammad's followers. He asked why they were crying, for only a man has died.[13] Nevertheless, the later Sunni-Shia schism was centered around the very issue of elevating leaders to near-prophet status, a point still debatable as to the Prophet's real intent.[14]

Part of this idealization may have formed in our earliest years. If we are honest in the Western world, many of our Judeo-Christian views of God were molded when we very young children attending Sunday school, Bible school, or Hebrew school. We listened to adults explain God to us through pictures and stories. Strip away our more sophisticated adult images of God, reach only a little way down into our subconscious, and the first thing that pops into our mind is a stern, but kind, stately, grandfatherly man with long white hair, a long white beard, and white robes who

11. H.W. Schumann, *The Historical Buddha*, trans. M.O'C. Walshe (London: Penguin Books, 1989), 246; and Robert Allen Mitchell, *The Buddha: His Life Retold* (New York: Paragon House, 1991), 266.

12. For example, David Wenham, *Follower of Jesus or Founder of Christianity?* (Grand Rapids: William B. Eerdmans Publishing, 1995), 3–4; and Baigent, 77–78.

13. Armstrong, *Muhammad*, 257.

14. Hopfe and Woodward, 339–340.

is sitting on a throne "up there." The archetypal image is a larger-than-life Albus Dumbledore from Harry Potter or Gandalf the White from *The Lord of the Rings*. It certainly does not represent our adult consciousness of the Creator-Creatress, but this childlike imagery and symbolism still shapes much of our thought about the divine. These would reflect Stage I (Intuitive-Projective Faith) and Stage II (Mythic–Literal Faith) that James Fowler describes for preschool and school-age children in his "Stages of Faith Theory." Some adults do not progress much beyond these stages, and, according to Fowler, very few people ever reach Stage VI (Universalizers). I believe that is beginning to change. We will see more and more people embracing a Universalist vision and moving into its attendant loving "Lifeway." As Fowler describes it:

> Stage VI is exceedingly rare. The persons best described by it have generated faith compositions in which their felt sense of an ultimate environment is inclusive of all beings. They have become incarnators and actualizers of the spirit of an inclusive and fulfilled human community. They are "contagious" in the sense that they create zones of liberation from the social, political, economic, and ideological shackles we place and endure on human futurity.[15]

Fowler notes that Universalizers are frequently considered a threat to the established religious structures, oftentimes killed by the authorities. They became martyrs posthumously honored and recognized for their "special grace." For these people, he notes, "Life is both loved and held too loosely. Such persons are ready for fellowship with persons at any of the other stages and from any other faith tradition."[16]

In the more traditional and childlike images of the Creator noted above, there is also an outdated aspect of kingliness, and we are "his" subjects. There is a sense of distance. God is a king on a distant throne high above us, overlooking His vast kingdom. Moreover, we cannot ignore the inherent sexism as God must be a "He." Finally, of course, as subjects of our Sovereign Lord, we must obey his orders—always. We are not in control of our own lives as vassal subjects of his kingdom, and he is in charge of us. It is his job to protect, guide, punish, and reward us. He determines if we are going "up there" or "down there" as a stern judge of

15. Fowler, "Stages of Faith," *Women's Spirituality: Resources for Christian Development*, 348.

16. Ibid.

our earthly sojourn. Looked at this way, it seems rather childish and as if it is determined by the historical model of Oriental potentates, medieval kings, and strict parents from millennia past. Anthropologists have long observed that earlier, urban, hierarchical societies tended to see God "as a monarch to whom tribute is due, with attendant imagery of servants and subjects honoring a supreme ruler."[17] It certainly is not modern, much less postmodern.

If we are to outgrow these infantile Daddy-King images, if we are to grow into loving and mature partnership and friendship with our Creator-Creatress, it requires a rejection of this "old school" perspective and the embrace of a new, postmodern relationship with the Divine. Like all children, we must eventually grow up and leave the comfort of our home. If we don't, we have failed in the most fundamental task of adulthood: independence. Certainly, a loving parent Creator-Creatress would want her or his children to grow and become competent adults. Is this any less true spiritually? So, it is at this independence crossroads where we can begin to discover the Guru Within, the God Within, the Goddess Within, the Christ Within, the Messiah Within, the Buddha Within, the Prophet Within, the Yogi Within, and the Shaman Within.

As part of our healthy Declaration of Independence, each individual begins to take responsibility for his or her own sins, actions, thoughts, feelings, and karma without looking to Satan, dysfunctional families, or uncaring societies to blame for their situation—or to a Savior Daddy-King God to save them from themselves. Maybe, at last, with the aid of spiritual teachers and guides, we are here to enlighten and save ourselves. We have come to work together as a Team of Gurus, Gods, Goddesses, Christs, Messiahs, Buddhas, Prophets, Yogis, and Shamans; as a Family of Creation; as a Family of the Creator-Creatress acting for once like a healthy, functional family. Maybe, after nearly 10,000 years of the old patriarchy paradigm, we can also bring in a new paradigm of the Yin-Yang balance of feminine energy (*Shakti* and Holy *Shekinah* Spirit). In this way, we can learn authentic partnership with each other and our Mother-Father-Partner-Friend Creatress-Creator. Maybe, at last, we can accept and acknowledge the humanity of our great spiritual teachers and enter into genuine friendship and partnership with them and their message.

In this mandate for change, we don't want to eliminate tribal, clan, or community groupings. They provide legitimate comfort, support, and

17. Fiona Bowie, "The Anthropology of Religion," *Introduction to World Religions*, 19.

social identity pieces that enhance our uniqueness as individuals and cultures. Vive le' difference. However, it is time to evolve to a place where they are no longer competitors or enemies, but partners in Civilization Earth. Hearkening back to the point made earlier by Christian theologian Yung Young Lee, it is time to leave the Western "conflicting dualism" of Aristotelian "either/or" thinking. It is time to embrace the "complementary dualism" of the Yin-Yang "both/and" way.[18] This new paradigm requires a new type of language. The old language of polarity must be replaced by a renewed language of unity. Dietrich Bonhoeffer saw this as the fatal flaw in Nazi and White Supremacist ideology. It was the disintegration of true community since "True community is not constituted by like-minded people associating, but by participating in mutual ethical relationships."[19] Instead of just the idea of the law of the jungle or survival of the fittest, perhaps it is time to honor the concept of the Human Cooperation Gene as an essential element for survival.[20]

This new paradigm also requires a new type of organization, a new kind of leadership, and a new style of leader. A contemporary term for this is "Lightwork," so we call them Lightwork organizations and the people who work within them Lightworkers. A Lightworker is simply someone who is dedicated to making this world a better place. They bring light to darkness, and it is clear this does not need to be tied to religion or even spirituality. A parent raising her or his child in a nurturing, loving environment is a Lightworker. An activist on a Greenpeace ship trying to save the whales is a Lightworker. A bank executive fighting to end discriminatory lending practices is a Lightworker. A third-grade teacher who uses her own money to make enough study sheets for her children and to create a nurturing, loving learning environment in her classroom

18. Yung Young Lee, *The Trinity in Asian Perspective* (Nashville: Abingdon Press, 1996), 31–33.

19 401 John de Gruchy, 'Introduction: Christology and Reality,' *Dietrich Bonhoeffer: Witness to Jesus Christ*, ed. John de Gruchy (Minneapolis: Fortress Press, 1986), 5; and Thomas Norris, "Six Decades Later: A Liberation Retrospective of Dietrich Bonhoeffer from the 21st Century," unpublished paper, Florida Center for Theological Studies, July 30, 2006.

20. A number of recent researchers have explored and advanced this theory including: Ernest Fehr, Urs Fischbacher, Samuel Bowles, Herbert Gintis, and Simon Gachter, et al. Bowles and Gintis are involved in an international effort to meld economics and biology in researching this theory: "International Effort Explores Evolution of Human Cooperation," *Santa Fe Institute Update*, December 2007, 1, 3, http://www.santafe.edu/events/update/files/12_07newsltr.pdf.

is a Lightworker. An atheist fighting for human rights is a Lightworker. The coworker, whether white collar executive or blue collar construction worker, who greets people with a smile and treats her or his brother and sister workers with equal respect is a Lightworker. The dedicated social worker trying to alleviate the suffering of the poor and oppressed in the community where he or she works is a Lightworker. The physician who donates his or her time to treat disadvantaged children for free on the weekends is a Lightworker. Not all Lightworkers will fulfill visible, traditional leadership roles, but all in some way will take the initiative to work on behalf of a growing, evolving, enlightening, and transforming world.

All We Need is Love

John Lennon and Paul McCartney had it right in their 1967 song "All You Need is Love." Postmodernity is the New Age of Love rediscovering the Old Age of ancient understanding that "love is all you need." I love you with all my heart, body, mind, and soul is the path and the being of the peaceful warrior, the Universalist. I love all creation with all my heart, body, mind, and soul is the path and the being of the peaceful warrior, the Universalist. Each moment, each person, each experience, each creature, each creation, each life, each existence is embraced fully and warmly as the lesson, the blessing, the awareness, the gift, the presence of life itself, the soul of the universe. There are no halfway measures in love. You don't "sort of" love someone or something. The essence of love is its fullness of heart and expansiveness of soul. Mind and body step out of the way for the moment as love is experienced until they are brought in to revel in and savor the moment in time. You don't think about love. It just is. It just happens—in a spontaneous burst of emotion and heart-opening. You don't love solely for physical, body reasons. Even if physical and body reasons are an element of initial attraction when love enters the picture, everything about the person is enhanced. So love is an expanding, enhancing, filling, bursting, lightening, accelerating, nurturing, augmenting, and uplifting encounter with the divine within (Self) and the divine without (Other).

Now it is easy to love our child. It is easy to love our sister or brother. It is easy to love a kitten or puppy. But this love we are talking about is not exclusive. It is inclusive. So, we need to add the not-so-easy: our abusive parent; our drunk Uncle Al; our neighborhood bully Johnny, who terrorized us in middle school; our meddling Aunt Tilly; our nosy, gossiping neighbor; our dictatorial boss; our backstabbing coworker; our jealous stepsister; our unfaithful spouse; our cheating golf legend; our corrupt senator, our "Big Lie" former president. Not so easy, this list, is it? But we are not done. How about Adolf Hitler, Ted Bundy, Timothy McVeigh (Oklahoma City Bombing), Osama bin Laden, the Columbine Kids, Fidel Castro, Saddam Hussein, and Derek Chauvin (convicted of murdering George Floyd)? Now we are really pushing it. This last group has caused so much pain for so many people. How can they be loved?

They, too, are part of creation. They, too, are brothers and sisters. And in some lifetime, we have been them.[21] And in each case, we had a hand, as a society, in co-creating them; whether we ignored how they grew up to be such sad, angry, hateful, and blind people or whether we ignored the signs of who they really were and what they were about. Hitler was voted in by a despairing, hungry, depressed, resentful, predominantly Christian population hoping for a way out of their desperation and looking for scapegoats.[22] Timothy McVeigh was an enraged army vet taught in the military to think in terms of "collateral damage" rather than human beings. Osama bin Laden was our ally at one time, and we ignored the signs of his people's growing distrust of the West.

So, if we have been "them" and "they" have been us, what right do we have to judge any other human being? Our movers stole a camera that Cate had given to me as a birthday present. We didn't have a lot of money, and it meant a lot to me. A member of our church was astounded when, in our Sacred Circle service, Cate prayed for the robbers. She answered that they really needed the prayers far more than we did. In what lifetime was I a thief? How many of us have never taken one thing that did not belong to us at least once in this lifetime? As Jesus so cogently noted, "Why do you see the speck in your neighbor's eye, but do not notice the log in your own eye?" (Luke 6:41) An old Oriental proverb adds, "Take

21. Woolger, 219.

22. Although historically this is an accurate statement accounting for many of the reasons for Hitler's initial rise to power in the face of the weak, failing democratic Weimar Republic, and a devastated economy, it in no way excuses Hitler, his government or the people of Germany for the unconscionable, horrific anti-Semitic policies that later led to genocide against the Jews of Europe (six million killed in the Holocaust); seven million more Russians, Poles, gypsies, intellectuals, gays, and handicapped killed in the extermination camps; and a war that not only devastated Germany, but all of Europe. Throughout history, other nations have faced terrible economic circumstances, and only a few have resorted to genocide.

revenge and feel good for a day, forgive and feel good for a lifetime." Now we are moving onto the steep, rocky path of unconditional love (back to Principles 16 and 23). Perhaps this is truly what it means to be a Universalist. We are one with all things and beings. In the end, in the unity of light, there is no "us" and "them." Welcome to the New World.

New Models for a New Way

As a constructionist postmodern Universalist movement, we are not here to destroy or take away from what has come before. We are more than happy to build upon the wisdom of our forebears, but we also hope to avoid the religious and organizational pitfalls they encountered. We are here to help construct a new vision and a new way of expressing spirituality in the world—and the watchword for this new vision is "tolerance." Our central theme is that we are all Messiahs/Buddhas/Christs/Yogis/Shamans, and as such, we hold the potential to not only change ourselves but to change a world. If that change unfolds one person at a time, we are patient enough to accept that. After all, what are a few dozen more lifetimes or a few more centuries when we have lived so many before? Yet, our Liberation Theology side will not let us meekly lie down and accept that premise without a fight. We trust that love, education, compassion, prayer, and direct action can accelerate the process of spiritual freedom and liberation from oppression. Enough people with vision and enough people in action can make the difference. That is our mission as Messiahs, Christs, Buddhas, Yogis, and Shamans—to help save a world.

All of that is very nice, of course, but the reality is far different. It is much easier said than done. Based on a Universalist theology, our experience with other religious institutions, and our personal commitment to change, we are developing a model for postmodern people in postmodern organizations in a postmodern world. It is broken down into three major areas: organizational structure, organizational leadership, and organizational mission. All are hopefully supporting the three pillars of *koinonia* (spiritual community), *martyria* (witness to a new way), and *diakonia* (service and justice) we have discussed before. We remind you that this is a work in progress, an early blueprint at best.

CHAPTER 17

Structure or Prison?

(On the Nature of Organizational Structure)

Breakout from the Iron Cage

IN OUR UNIVERSALIST CHURCH, we tease that we are the "No Rules Church." This does not mean that we can be the "No Structure Church." Here is the paradox in a nutshell. We highly individualistic postmoderns immensely dislike the prison of structure, yet to function, every organization needs some structure. To survive, every organization must attend to certain managerial and real world practicalities. The question is the balance: too little (chaos) versus too much (rigidity). This is a touchy issue for many newer postmodern spiritual groups. They have appropriately reacted to the stifling bureaucracy and rigid dogmatism of many mainstream religious, corporate, and governmental institutions. Through trial and error and harsh lessons, we have all learned from the unwritten intuitive manual on *Spiritual Organizations: What Not To Do*. Unfortunately, that does not mean we have grasped the manual on *Spiritual Organizations: What To Do*. Has it even been written yet? Nevertheless, in this third-dimensional, down-to-earth world (in the process of moving into higher fourth and fifth-dimensional energies), it appears that no organization can survive without some structure. The key lies within the type of structure and how it is implemented. Every successful organization—whether it is the neighborhood "Boys Only Treehouse Club," Microsoft Corporation, the White House, or the Dalai Lama's Government of Tibet in Exile—must address matters of organizational structure, leadership, outreach and networking, marketing, administration, size, human and financial resources, and communication.

Wheel, Spokes, and Hub

Universalist and Lightwork organizations,[1] philosophically and theologically, will not work effectively within the old hierarchical structures and leadership. We just are not built that way. If we are all equally valued, unconditionally loved sons and daughters of God, the old top-down pyramid table of organization undermines that egalitarian vision of humanity. A Universalist model is intentionally the opposite of the traditional pyramid hierarchy with a "boss" CEO, authoritarian leader type at the top and everyone else fitting somewhere in the organization underneath. (See Figure 2 below.)

1. As a reminder, a Lightwork organization is any organization committed to giving back more than it takes. It wishes to be in a good give-and-take balance with the community and clients it serves. This can be a corporation, a governmental organization, an entrepreneurial venture, or a nonprofit agency. For example, Peaks Potential, the multinational company that trains and sponsors many of the top trainers and public speakers in the world has a company mission committed to global peace. It is a very successful, for-profit company, but sees its training and teaching work as transforming lives.

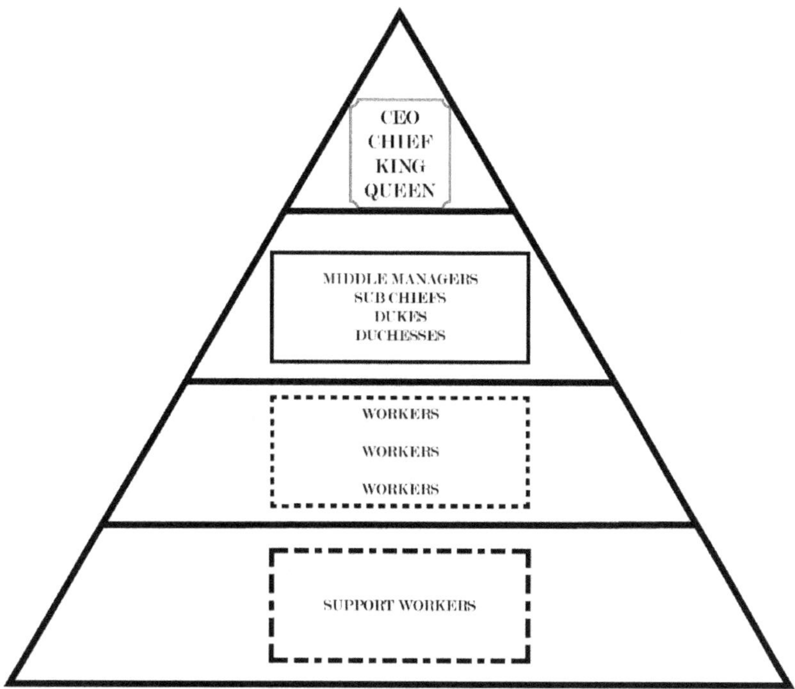

Figure 2: Traditional Hierarchy Model of Organization

In discussing methodologies within feminist theologies, Letty Russell reports,

". . . these methods have to take into account the struggle to move beyond the competitive and hierarchical forms of patriarchal methods, which seek a truth that is made secure through the vanquishing of all other truths."[2] Lightworkers and Universalists are not interested in vanquishing all other truths. In fact, we wish to revel in the shared glory of millions of years of hard-won human wisdom, adding our little piece as we go along and working to bring it all together in our lifetime. We are bridging the best of the Old Age and carrying it into the best of the New Age.

We are also intrigued with Russell's continuing metaphors of the church in the round. Sitting together at the kitchen round table for table talk, with its town hall atmosphere, creates a spiral of interaction (action and reflection) at the table rather than a static, closed circle.[3] It is

2. Letty M. Russell, *Church in the Round* (Louisville: Westminster/John Knox Press, 1993), 30.

3. Ibid, 34.

a dynamic metaphor and reflects one that our church embraces as well. Russell also notes that non-hierarchical, non-linear, non-vertical, non-patriarchal, more horizontal, circular organizational setups facilitate better communication and keep people from being marginalized.[4] Nor do we just take these principles only from modern feminism, but from much older sources.

The indigenous peoples of the world revered the circle as they witnessed the neverending, marvelous, multitudinous cycles of life all around them, all of the time. This reverence was not based on an intellectual or aesthetic appreciation only but was a clear survival issue for people who lived off the land and remained intimately in contact with Mother Earth at all moments. Their understanding of these many life cycles allowed them to live in harmony with the natural order. Being "in the flow" of life meant survival and being ignorant of or resisting the flow of life, often invited death and disaster. I can think of few movies beyond *Avatar* and *Dances with Wolves* that have so movingly captured the essence of the interrelationship, harmony, and flow of life between the people of the land and their planetary Mother.

For Native Americans, it was their symbol of the Medicine Wheel, the sacred hoop of life (and the logo chosen for our church). Some native peoples have wondered if the move away from circular architecture, circular council meetings, and other honorings of the wheel of life has not undermined their sacred energies and power. The Circle has been replaced by a European square and rectangular architecture. If you think this is trivial, remember how this can affect even peace negotiations. In 1972, during the Vietnam War, the United States and North Vietnam finally began peace negotiations. The very first thing they had to agree upon was the shape of the conference table. As Edwin Moise relates,

> A compromise was finally reached involving one large circular table and two smaller rectangular ones, arranged in a way that the United States could interpret as representing a two-sided negotiation, and the Communists could interpret as representing a four-sided negotiation.[5]

This took months, but the circle won. No one can dominate by position in a circle. Native Americans certainly had a core understanding

4. Russell, 25, 35, 46.

5. Edwin M. Moise, *The Vietnam Wars* (Electronic Publication: Clemson University, 1998), Section 9.

of this principle. Balance and harmony dictated the structure, format, and procedures of their meeting councils where, for example, the people of the Zero Chiefs (Pueblo Nations) met in the Circle of Law. This was an actual circular meeting lodge oriented to the Four Directions. Eight female and eight male chiefs were equally paired according to their tribal function (law chiefs, peace chiefs, hunters and workers chiefs, medicine/spiritual chiefs, war chiefs, and so on) and sat around the circle following the four directions of the Medicine Wheel. None was more important than the other. This facilitated their governance by consensus rather than simple majority rule.[6]

Honoring our circular logic and the lessons from our indigenous and feminist friends, an updated postmodern organizational model might likewise utilize the circle. In this instance, elements of the previously discussed Yin-Yang circle emphasized balance and the harmony of the whole lying within its boundaries. There is no center, and there is no margin. One cannot be marginalized within this model. It is meant to demonstrate equilibrium between male and female, young and old, mind and heart, action and non-action, minister and congregant, and so on. It is the very essence of the Yin-Yang both/and balance.

One way to achieve success is to create an organizational structure that supports organizational needs for effective, efficient administration and communication. At the same time, it must buoy up a Facilitator Model of Leadership (see chapter 18). We have already introduced the idea of a circle as our model within the Yin Yang and Native American Medicine Wheel symbology. Thus, a workable model for a Universalist organization is the wheel and the hub. Based on our earlier discussions, there is no coincidence in choosing this structure. We agree with our indigenous friends that the circle is not just an important spiritual symbol but also an excellent organizational tool. This has been partially recognized in modern business theory as well, where the Matrix Model, while not exactly a circle, is a much more integrated model for project-oriented organizations—in our sample, it's a cube. (See Figure 3 below.) As Stephen Fitzgerald reports, the matrix is a mixed bag of pros and cons.

6. Hyemeyohsts Storm, *Lightningbolt* (New York: Ballantine, 1994), 411–415.

Spiritual Center Administration	Marketing Manager	Events Manager	Technical/Design Manager
2015 National Conference Manager	Marketing Team Member	Events Team Member	Technical/Design Manager
Light University Curriculum Updating Manager	Marketing Team Member	Events Team Member	Technical/Design Manager
2015 Fall Kickoff Marketing Team Manager	Marketing Team Member	Events Team Member	Technical/Design Manager

Figure 3: Sample Matrix Model of Organization

Theoretically, for large organizations, it was a legitimate attempt to handle their complexity: "However, in reality, power cannot be evenly balanced, and conflicts inevitably arise."[7] We are not absolutely sure we agree with his conclusion, but the warning is so noted. On the other hand, I have a friend who is a senior executive at a large, global corporation. She just laughs when I ask her how anyone manages to get any work done in their Matrix Model organization. Between team meetings, the personal coaching meetings about how she handles her teams, the coaching meetings with her teams, and her meetings with her boss' management team, it almost seems they have daily meetings about meetings. She admits it's hard to get her work done with the high number of meetings, which is one of the criticisms of the Matrix Model—too many meetings

7. Stephen Fitzgerald, *Organizational Models* (Oxford: Capstone, 2002), 24.

can exhaust staff. At the same time, there are many good communication channels, and teamwork is definitely enhanced.

Along these lines, Adam Kleinbaum, Toby Stuart, and Michael Tushman report that modern business theorists find "that in contemporary organizations, leadership is disassociating from formal hierarchies and is migrating to lower levels of the organization."[8] Many companies veer away from traditional organizational theories that emphasize the dominance of formal organizational structures. We find most useful those findings that indicate contemporary organizations are characterized by "free-flowing, lateral, and collaborative interaction patterns," and they are defined as "boundary-less" or "networked" organizations.[9] They are not rigid, mechanistic models but are organic in nature.[10]

In Universalist organizations, the organizational structure must support an Open System versus a Closed System. Open Systems allow for receptive interaction with the community and within the organization. There is a good give and take (with feedback loops) in internal and external communication; cooperation and partnership with other groups and organizations with similar missions; and an openness to evolution and change within the organization. This keeps it relevant, up-to-date, and vibrant. Organizations that foster a relaxed, team-oriented organizational culture are set up to be more informal. They are more organic, horizontal, inter-related, and circular in their communication modes; and tend to be more "open" in their internal and external relations. It reminds us of the descriptions of the early Apple Corporation, when everyone worked together in the garage as a team and created innovative new products in the infant computer industry.

In the Wheel and Hub Model, the outer wheel rim is the actual work and executed mission of our church but can apply to any Lightwork organization. It is where the rubber meets the pavement, and the vehicle of action travels along the various avenues of its work. The spokes are the members and workers who provide the strength, backbone, and structure of the wheel. The hub is the organizing center of the wheel. The Facilitator Leaders are the central administrators, area managers, project managers, trainers, and teachers within the hub. The communication from the center

8. Adam Kleinbaum, Toby Stuart, and Michael Tushman, "Communication (and Coordination?) in a Modern, Complex Organization," *Working Knowledge* (Harvard Business School, July 31, 2008), 9.

9. Ibid, 8.

10. Ibid.

radiates out through all the members/workers (the spokes) to the outer wheel rim, where it is translated into action. Likewise, communication and feedback from those affected by the church's actions (community members, service recipients, other organizations) and from the church members radiate back into the center. All are connected to the central hub and the outer wheel rim, so the flow of ideas, development of goals, and good communication involves everyone and assigns the wheel its direction. The wheel collapses if it is missing any of its three major components. When all the pieces are in place, it is in harmonious balance.

Lastly, a wheel moves. As it moves through time and space, it creates a spiral of evolving movement and direction from the past, through the present, to the future. It also passes through earthly and higher realms of consciousness and through the spiritual energies of teaching, guidance, healing, leading, connection, and emergence. Thus, this is not a circle that just goes round and round, stuck in one place. It progresses down a road of purpose and realization. (See Figure 4 below.) It echoes Russell's evolving spiral of ongoing action and reflection. In this case, reflection is a form of organizational self-evaluation and feedback. As a dominant metaphor, it also facilitates the relaxed, informal, team-oriented corporate culture we highlighted earlier. It is no longer based upon fear of the "Daddy Boss" (not unlike the "Daddy God" highlighted earlier). Replacing Fear Consciousness with Mission Consciousness is always an underlying principle in a Lightwork organization.

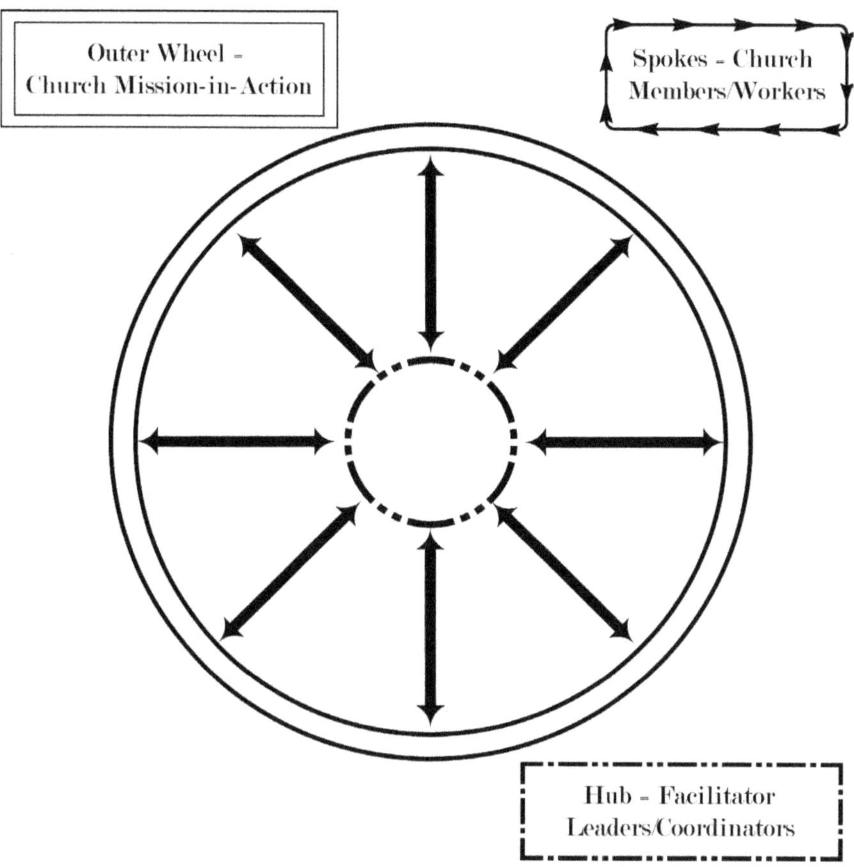

Figure 4: The Wheel, Spokes, and Hub Organizational Model

In the Wheel and Hub Model, the secretary is as important as the minister. The Sacred Circle participant is as important as the committee member. A member of the community is as important as a member of the church. An oppressed person is as important as any other person on the planet. Circles demonstrate equality. Tolerance demands equality! We are all in the same leaky boat, and everyone needs to bail, for if we all bail together, we may successfully sail to our spiritual and organizational destinations.

It is About the Size (and the Message)

To use as one example, in our Universalist Church, perhaps the most crucial element to its success as a spiritual community is its size. The church purposely keeps its individual Sacred Circle[11] groups small (at this time, primarily based on location). Consequently, one Sacred Circle is about the same size as any other Sacred Circle. If one becomes too large, it splits into two groups. This enhances the *koinonia*, spiritual family feeling within the church as much as the members' love and sincerity. Many have come from churches and temples which lost touch with their mission and their members simply because of size. Their churches and temples became bureaucracies and institutions. The members became tithing budget numbers, distant faces in the back pews, and social acquaintances. We cannot emphasize enough the transformative impact of the social, emotional, and spiritual intimacy the church members experience every week by sharing and knowing each other's "stories." This is a variation of the Metrotribalism mentioned earlier—creating our loving tribe within the larger, highly complicated postmodern world—and was also clearly illustrated in the previous section on "Sacred Texts."

There is a caveat here. This church and any new postmodern spiritual group face the catch-22 dilemma that the more successful it becomes, the larger it becomes. The larger it becomes, the greater the chance that its core spiritual identity and purpose will be unintentionally tossed to the wayside. It may become a "power" and, as such, become more of a political and institutional animal. If that were to happen, it would become imprisoned in Weber's "iron cage." It would no longer be a Universalist Church known as *The Church of the Way of the Messiahs*, holding true to its original principles. Nor would any other group retain the fresh, innovative, and inspired organization of its first creation. At the same time, like any organization, our Universalist spiritual organization wishes to be successful. *The Church of the Way of the Messiahs* emphatically believes in its compelling and needed message of unity, tolerance, love, joy, and peace. It is a world message that can reunite us as neighbors once again.

One method to prevent the size from becoming an issue involves developing a growth model that establishes size guidelines. There is nothing

11. Reflecting our appreciation of the sacred circle symbol, the term "Sacred Circle" was adopted for the church's weekly worship services. It is a weekly group meeting run rather informally, involving prayers and blessings, discussion and study, and meditation.

to prevent this church or any competent spiritual organization from taking off and eventually involving many thousands or even millions of people in its work. However, to do so with integrity, it cannot become consumed with size, budgets, numbers, and power. The message will become lost among the numbers. The members will be lost in the numbers. Therefore, something akin to a home church model might prevail. It certainly worked for the early Jews in their home synagogues and for early Christians in their home churches. It is a flexible model in that services and meetings can also occur in spiritual bookstores, storefronts, and spiritual centers. There is definitely room at the inn for online communities as well. The model intends to purposely limit the size of any one congregation.

Based on the church's experience, an ideal size for each Sacred Circle group would be around forty active members, with a mailing list in the hundreds. Usually, that means the average Sacred Circle service attendance is twenty or thirty members. This allows them to retain their spiritual closeness, but the group is not so large that they have to do away with the individual prayers or limit the discussion and meditation. The large mailing list allows for a decent pool of interested persons for classes and workshops.

Going back to our Wheel and Hub Model, it will work as the organization grows nationally and internationally as well. The hub will now correspond to the central facilitation leadership for all the Sacred Circle groups. The spokes will represent the individual branch groups. The wheel will still be the mission in action, where the rubber meets the road.

One might immediately notice that this is in danger of becoming an economically distressed organizational structure. At this point within *The Church of the Way of the Messiahs*, we just don't know if it is viable. Nonetheless, we envision that a Facilitator Leader[12] might facilitate several homestyle congregations in her or his local area or online. Since many Universalist organizations do not seem to be wedded to Sundays, any day of the week will work. Many of the Facilitator Leaders will probably choose to be bi-vocational, just as today the economy of many smaller churches dictates that necessity for their ministers.[13] Current Circle

12. Depending upon a particular organization's needs, these leaders may go by various titles. In our church, they are ministers. Although they are trained in leadership skills and in a diversity of spiritual traditions, they are not meant to institute a formalized clergy. Rather, the name just designates their particular role with a specialized ministry or mission as Facilitator Leaders.

13. In what used to be a high status/low stress profession, the clergy has become

Facilitators are teachers, healers, artists, and counselors. Until proven otherwise, this is a model worth exploring. In the future, we note that we plan to write a book about Light companies and organizations. This book will encompass some of these principles, whether they are a large corporation, small business, government agency, nonprofit organization, or a church. The old organizational models just do not work well with postmoderns—their need for individuality, positive engagement, and innovation within any organization cannot be denied. I see it every day with my college students.

Obviously, this is a model that will valiantly attempt to stave off institutionalization and bureaucratization. A lot of kinks need to be worked out, and our operational model is a work in progress, just beyond the blueprint stage. However, hopefully, we will leave Max Weber and his "iron cage" of bureaucracy behind in the far off mists of old modernity as we co-create a new, uncaged, poststructural Postmodernity. Likewise, we hope not to fall into the trap that eventually it becomes all about the institution and not the message. Many Christians and non-Christians have commented that the Christian Church moved away from its founding principles when it made the message all about Jesus and not the message of Jesus. From all we can discern, Yeshua ben Joseph (Jesus) was a highly humble being. One can only wonder if he really wanted it to be all about him and a huge church, and not his beautiful message about the coming Kingdom of God, where love and justice will prevail. Similarly, when did the Roman Church cross the line, and it became all about the survival of Mother Church (the institution) and not the message? This seems to happen to every institution, whether Protestant, Roman Catholic, Greek Orthodox, Christian, and non-Christian. We will have succeeded as Universalists if we can stay on message and not remain stuck within the prison walls of vast buildings, complicated budgets, aging, bloated scriptures, and profit barometers of success. The memorandum from Spirit and its many teachers is this simple. As Jesus said, "Split a piece of wood; I am there. Lift up the stone, and you will find me there" (Gospel of Thomas: 77).

---

a low status/high stress profession. Many smaller congregations can no longer afford to pay their ministers a living wage, scarcely above the minimum wage. David Gasperson, "The Polarization of Ministry," lectures in the *Integrational Seminar*, Florida Center for Theological Studies, Miami, Florida, April 3, 2003.

Virtual Circles

In this age of computers and social networking, any spiritual and Lightwork organization that ignores its online connections does so at its own peril. It is long past time to recognize that face-to-face interactions in an ever-growing and ever-crowded world are frequently a luxury more than a necessity. Many people are or will be working at home (or eventually off-planet), and the computer is the link to their office and the world. We envision connecting people online when it is too difficult for reasons of geography or culture to attend Sacred Circles. For example, why should someone be deprived of the opportunity to participate in a Sacred Circle if they are a homebound senior citizen in Los Angeles, or a rancher in Montana sixty miles from the nearest large town, or a homemaker in a small town where there is not enough interest or public support for a Universalist Sacred Circle? This is where the internet and social networking sites come in handy. Some of these online Sacred Circles may have formats in line with the weekly circles conducted in person. However, others may be specialized circles, reaching out to single parents, the disabled, college students, people addressing addictions, LGBTQ communities, and so on.

Networking and Marketing

There is an old joke in which God is talking to Abraham and reminding Abraham, "Without me, you would be nothing!" Abraham replied, "Yeah, and without me, nobody would know about you!" Apparently, God did not strike Abraham down with a lightning bolt, so the Creator must have recognized the fundamental truth in Abraham's response-with-attitude. No organization can survive unless people know about it, wish to learn more about it, and most importantly, support it in some way. This is the bailiwick of networking and marketing—getting the message out and developing relationships with potentially interested persons.

Although a non-profit organization is not motivated by profit, it still has customers to satisfy and must provide the necessary services to provide such satisfaction. Like all organizations, it will succeed or fail based on the demand for services and the quality of the services. An important point to make in this new age is that spiritual organizations must reject fear-based marketing: "If you don't believe, you are going to hell." Or, "If you don't go to church, you are going to hell." Then there is the, "If you are not saved, you will be 'left behind'" and the, "If you don't stay with the 'true' church, you are condemned."

Even the New Age blame game and pointing fingers are counterproductive: "If you stay with your old traditional church, you will never be enlightened." These old messages just do not work for many postmoderns, and certainly not for Universalist groups. Nobody is left behind, and we honor all faiths. By the very nature of the organization, a Universalist message wishes to create an inclusive (as opposed to exclusive) ambiance. We want to develop positive reasons for someone to join, open up to our mission, and stick around. This is an open system at its best.

All Our Resources

Earlier, I suggested that non-profit organizations, such as churches, are not founded upon the notion of a profit motive. They are not an IBM or a "Mom and Pop" grocery store on the corner, both of which live or die by the profit margin. However, this does not mean that non-profit organizations do not need to garner financial resources or establish sound budgets. On the contrary, this seems to be a weakness in many non-profit groups, often ruled by an abundance of idealism and good intent, but not necessarily by good fundraising, marketing, and accounting practices. I understand this. My ministry and mission as a Universalist are about making this a better world. I love to perform this mission through teaching, counseling, ministering, networking, and writing. I didn't go into this work to become a reliable manager, to develop administrative skills, or to learn fiscal procedures (like budgeting, accounting, or tax code). Nonetheless, I needed to develop those capabilities if I wished for our spiritual organization to succeed. And I certainly did not get into the field for "pressing flesh" or focusing on that dreaded word, fundraising, which means asking people for money. It is the most challenging thing for me to do, even though I so firmly believe in the beautiful message of Universalism and know that it cannot be shared without resources.

My reluctance is not unfounded. It is a stew mixed with a drop of bitters from Buddhism (letting go of possessions and attachments), a dash of resolve from Jesus (easier for a camel to go through the eye of a needle than for a rich man to enter the kingdom of God), and a sprinkling of personal experience with unwise choices. Money does not have the best spiritual reputation. All of us are a bit leery of the neverending requests for money from legitimate groups, scam artists, and even the high school football players standing on the street corner with outstretched hands holding helmets as donation baskets to buy team uniforms. The "give me" messages are everywhere, and we have all been brought up on the old biblical adage that "Money is the root of all evil." Actually, this is a misquotation. The actual passage reads, "For the love of money is the root of all evil . . ." (Timothy 6:10) Now, mind you, it does not say that money itself is evil, just how it is utilized.

We can all lament the power of materialism and greed in our world (and on Wall Street), especially relevant at this point a decade after the Great Recession and the Occupy Wall Street Movement. However, railing about the stranglehold of materialism really doesn't address the equally relevant issue that we need money to accomplish things in this postmodern world. A more enlightened view of money visualizes it as simply energy—an energy resource at that.

I used to take a dollar bill and rip it up in front of my Liberation Theology class to make a point. They were even more horrified when I took out a ten dollar bill. I would look at them innocently and say, "What? I am just tearing up a piece of paper. Why does it matter if I tear up this piece of paper?" They answered anxiously, "Because it is worth something!" And I replied, "Why?"

Clearly, the actual, physical paper or metals in our money do not create an energy of exchange. It is the societal contract that we have all agreed upon which determines specific values for these papers and metals. These accepted values give them their energy as a medium of exchange. As energy, then, they are a means and not an end. Money energy is simply the means to accomplish something. Money itself is morally and ethically neutral, so it is up to the user how any ethics or morals are applied in its usage. That frees us to view money simply as a resource, and resources allow us to share a message, maintain an organization, and carry out our work. Instead of bartering a chicken, we now use a piece of paper. Moreover, financial resources are not the only resources an organization must consider. People are resources, too, and definitely the most essential. Now all of this is the most elementary management and organizational theory, but it is something that some idealists working within nonprofits do not address adequately. Consequently, part of being a successful organization is awareness of and sound utilization of resources. This requires good management and fiscal knowledge, as well as an organizational structure that effectively utilizes all its resources.

We cannot leave this subject without noting that postmodern spiritual groups also need to be educated about their own role as a resource. Resource seems like such an impersonal word, but if you add the notions of rich resources, treasures, and valued members, people are beginning to sound pretty good. If the New Testament commandment is truly to love your neighbor just as you love yourself, then you must start with valuing yourself. We have enough "wounded messiahs" among Lightworkers to last a lifetime. You are a co-equal, co-creative resource within the Universalist Church or your Lightwork organization and can be nothing less without short-changing yourself and those around you. I have never met a worthless person. I have met people who devalued themselves horribly and acted worthless in their actions; however, whether they are a criminal or they live without goals and effort or they have simply lost hope and become lost souls in the process, it always comes back to insecurity, low self-esteem, and devaluing messages somewhere in their past. Many look down on these people condescendingly and call them weak, or deviant, or beyond hope. It is here that I bring up Howard Gardner's Multiple Intelligences Theory.

Gardner was correctly reacting to a psychological and educational system that measured intelligence along only two parameters: linguistic (language) and mathematical-logical. Instead, Gardner asserted that his theory presents:

> . . . a pluralistic view of mind, recognizing many different and discrete views of cognition, acknowledging that people have many different cognitive strengths and contrasting cognitive styles.[14]

Essentially, he says that the traditional Binet IQ intelligence test (developed in Paris in 1900) overlooked the native intelligence of many children and adults. They are very bright, or even geniuses in their own intelligence arena, but may score poorly on traditional IQ tests.[15] For example, we might not be surprised that Danny Marino (Hall of Fame Miami Dolphins quarterback) or Michael Jordan (Hall of Fame Chicago Bulls shooting guard) were not interested in getting their doctorates in theoretical physics (Logical-Mathematical Intelligence) or writing the Great American Novel (Linguistic Intelligence), any more than ballet

14. Howard Gardner, *The Development and Education of the Mind, The Selected Works of Howard Gardner* (New York: Routledge, 2006), 47–48, http://www.netlibrary.com/Reader.

15. Ibid.

giant Mikhail Baryshnikov was. What all three have in common, however, is their genius in the Bodily-Kinesthetic Intelligence arena. Likewise, Madonna, Drake, John Lennon, Stevie Wonder, Lady Gaga, and Mozart would be similarly disinterested in sports or accounting careers, areas outside their genius in Musical Intelligence. We can go on. Socrates, Immanuel Kant, and John Rawls probably would not score very high on Interpersonal Intelligence (diplomats, counselors, teachers, politicians, union negotiators) or Spatial Intelligence (artists, architects, movie directors, quarterbacks), but as philosophers, they are geniuses in Intrapersonal Intelligence.[16] Recently, an eighth area was added: Naturalist Intelligence (farmers, environmentalists, botanists, biologists, hunters).[17] I might have added Mechanical Intelligence (mechanics, inventors, engineers) out of great admiration for how my auto mechanic comprehends the inner mysteries of my car.

Additionally, there is Spiritual Intelligence, as some people seem to have special psychic, metaphysical, healing, and spiritual gifts. To my surprise, Gardner has explored the possibility of a Spiritual Intelligence but is still uncommitted to the concept. He prefers to call it Existential Intelligence, "the human capacity to raise and ponder large questions."[18] Over the years, as I polled my college students about their interests and talents, it soon became apparent that most people are very smart or even brilliant in at least one of Gardner's areas of intelligence, and often more than one. In other words, there are no stupid kids. Everyone has something to offer as a human resource. The challenge is finding it in them or helping them discover it in themselves.

16. Gardner, 49–50. Although the examples are mine, this material comes from Gardner's original discussion about the seven areas of multiple intelligences.

17. Ibid, 58.

18. Ibid, 59, 90.

CHAPTER 18

Who's in Command?

(On the Nature of Organizational Leadership)

UNIVERSALISTS ARE NOT SO naïve and idealistic as to believe an organization can flourish without leadership and guidance. However, it is the type of leadership that is at issue here. Just as we see God as partner, friend, and companion, we see our spiritual teachers in a similar manner. To put it plainly, we believe our spiritual leaders are at their best when they reflect Source with all the humility, kindness, love, and generosity that implies.

In a research survey investigating ministerial and teacher leadership styles conducted by our church, leadership roles and styles that were overwhelmingly rejected included: authority figure, parent, director, and lecturer. These would be the traditional roles of Modernity. The more postmodern roles and styles that were supported included: facilitator, guide, and, to a lesser extent, team leader.[1] Consequently, the successful model of Universalist and Lightwork leadership that is emerging is a Facilitator Model of Leadership, not so unlike Russell's Partnership Model of Leadership. As she denotes:

> In feminist styles of leadership, authority is exercised by standing with others by seeking to share power and authority. Power is seen as something to be multiplied and shared rather than accumulated at the top.[2]

1. Norris, *Universalism: The New Religion of Tolerance*, 169 and 181.
2. Russell, 57.

We might add that, as facilitators, it is our job to assist the members of the church or committee or team to share and multiply their own power as individuals and as a group. Hyemeyohsts Storm details how Pueblo leadership-community relations can even be represented by the circle.

> The Circle of Law of the community was seen as The Being of the Wheel, an individual. Also, the separate individuals within the Tribe saw themselves as individual Circles of Law.[3]

This certainly signifies reciprocity in the relationship between the leader and the individuals in a community. Taking it a step further, we are reminded that Universalists bear witness to the priesthood of all believers; that all are ministers in some way. We have also mentioned that Universalists tend toward a lay-centered community rather than a clergy-centered organization. Put another way, sometimes we are the teacher and sometimes we are the student; sometimes we are the minister[4] and sometimes we are the congregant; sometimes we are the leader and sometimes we are the follower; but everyone in a Universalist organization is a bit of each. Still, there is no way to get around the fact that there is something additional within the leadership role that requires insights and skills beyond the ordinary.

The Responsibilities of Command

In the movie *U-571*, starring Matthew McConaughey, the actor plays a young executive officer (XO) on an American submarine during WWII. The film portrays the actual Secret Ops conducted by the United States and its allies to obtain the *Enigma* code machine of the German submarine service. Nazi U-boats were decimating Allied shipping across the Atlantic. They were sending so many ships to the bottom with desperately needed supplies for the European battlefront; it truly was a matter of winning or losing the war to Hitler that made the missions so critical. Obtaining the secret code machine without the Germans discovering the theft required extraordinary measures, secrecy, and heroism. The story revolves around this young XO's baptism under fire and his belated understanding of the terrible burdens of command. Before that, his captain would not promote him to his own captaincy because he noted that he

3. Hyemeyohsts Storm, *Lightningbolt* (New York: Ballantine, 1994), 425.

4. Here we can easily insert rabbi, priest, priestess, lama, pastor, imam, shaman, guru, or any other name for the clergy leadership in a religion.

tried to be everyone's friend on the crew. The captain knew this to be a problem. How would the XO handle a situation where he might have to order a friend to his death to save the rest of the crew?

This seemed to be such a faraway leadership struggle until Cate and I sat next to a destroyer captain and his young XO at a Miami Marlins baseball game. This was just a few months after the movie came out in 2000. When the young XO left to get food, out of curiosity, I asked the captain how his XO was doing. He said he had a lot of potential but wasn't sure he was good officer material because he tried to be everyone's friend on the crew. When the XO returned and his captain left for a few minutes, I attempted to give the young man a heads up and possibly help his career. I mentioned the captain's remarks. The XO shrugged it off lightly, stating the captain was just old school and a "hard ass." He didn't seem very concerned, but it did point out an old theme in military commands. Over the years, I had seen the same thing among my police officer friends after they were promoted. The officer could no longer be just "one of the guys," because now he or she evaluated and gave orders to those same coworkers and friends. The officer could even fire them if necessary. It was always quite an adjustment.

Why am I giving examples from a hierarchical command structure dictated by war measures and law enforcement standards? Isn't that relatively removed from the day-to-day operations of the average governmental, corporate, or nonprofit organization? Well, of course the answer is yes. Outside of military, fire, police, and health agencies, rarely, if ever, are we engaged in true life and death situations. Or are we? When you think about it, the list of organizations affecting life, health, and death can get pretty long.

- What are the consequences of incompetent engineers and architects, shoddy construction, corrupt building inspectors, and politicians awarding building contracts based on expensive lobbying and campaign contributions? It is not such a distant example if it is your child's school, your office building, your mom's senior center, or the bridge you cross every day for work that collapses.
- How can peanut butter kill people? Just ask the victims of an unsanitary peanut plant in Georgia, which sold peanut butter recently that sickened hundreds with Salmonella and led to the deaths of eight people across the country.[5] Where were their quality control officers?

5. Gardner Harris, "Peanut Product Recall Grows in Salmonella Scare," *New York*

- In a macho, violent sport where one expects injuries, what do you say to the football coaches, team doctors, athletic directors, and general managers? How do you tell them it is not safe to send a high school, college, or NFL player back into the game after they have had their "bell rung." Until recently, no one knew how seriously concussions affected football players, often many years later. Symptoms have included depression, memory loss, disorientation, blackouts, brain hemorrhages, and dementia among relatively young retired players.[6] Now, what do we say to the players and their parents, spouses, and children?

So, maybe there is something to be said for the metaphor that the leader is still the captain of the ship, whether that ship is a naval vessel, a waste management company, a government budget office, a classroom, a basketball team, or a courtroom. All require reliable, strong leadership if they are to thrive and survive, coupled with a great respect for those they serve (clients and customers) and those crewing the ship (employees).

I have worked for several organizations where the leadership was utterly disastrous. Riven by politics and gossip, spineless decision-making, a dearth of management skills, and even embezzlement, these "captains" nearly took their ships down with them. At the least, they had no sense of their leadership responsibilities. I'm not sure if it ever occurred to them that real people relied upon them. That employees relied upon them for the paychecks that paid mortgages, fed children, assisted elderly parents, and hopefully stretched to nice vacations and a retirement fund. That clients relied upon them for crucial social services—food, shelter, abuse prevention, mental health counseling, addictions rehab, and so on. That students relied upon them to provide competent faculty, good books and resources, and a solid education essential to their futures in a difficult economy. That taxpayers relied upon them to spend their tax dollars wisely and ensure trash is collected, streets are paved, public hospitals are safe, water is uncontaminated, crime is prevented, mosquitoes are sprayed, fires are quenched, and so on.

Again, in even some of the more innocuous organizations, it seemed that some leadership actions had nearly life and death consequences

---

Times, January 29, 2009, A15.

6. Alan Schwartz, "Concussion Trauma Risk Seen in Amateur Athlete," *New York Times*, October 22, 2009, B14; and "N.F.L. Data Reinforces Dementia Links," October 24, 2009, D1.

because they so directly and painfully impacted people's lives. Tell the pregnant employee it was an inconsequential matter when she was laid off due to her boss's incompetence in meeting a grant deadline. Tell the student that it was a small thing when she could not afford to eat on a regular basis and had to drop out of school because she could no longer afford to attend. Meanwhile, unknown to her, the school administrators embezzled from her tuition money and did not exercise good fiscal control in the student loan office. Tell the hardworking employee that it means nothing after she suffered great mental stress and many sleepless nights because her bosses allowed malicious gossip[7] to run rampant in the agency. Tell the employee who was fired for reasons that turned out to be false that it was trivial that the human resources investigation was bungled. Tell the public housing tenant and her children that it was just an "oversight" when the contractors installed new toilets that leaked into her kitchen below and eventually fell through the ceiling. In fact, the shoddy work was duplicated throughout the entire housing project. Since 2008, tell the millions of Americans who lost their retirement savings, their jobs, their health insurance, and their homes that the American Dream is still alive and well in the face of the Great Recession. This is in the face of the unfettered excesses and greed of the captains of industry on Wall Street and the banking sector, as well as the lax oversight of our government. All of the captains of these various organizations ran their ships aground and sometimes sank them.

Of course, there are some really great leaders—people who transform the situation and often the lives of the people they lead. Temple Doors, Joan of Arc, Queen Elizabeth I, Abraham Lincoln, Franklin Delano Roosevelt, Mohandas Gandhi, Martin Luther King, Jr., Mikhail Gorbachev, and Nelson Mandela come to mind. Yet, not all great leaders need to stand out in the world arena. This real-life example highlights one of the critical qualities of effective leadership in any organization.

In August 1992, a few days after Hurricane Andrew hit, I worked with a VA mental health assistance team in the heart of the devastation near Homestead, Florida. A Vietnam vet and pediatrician at the University of Miami Miller School of Medicine was my colleague on the mental health team. He looked completely shaken as he recalled that it reminded him of the aftermath of a B-52 bombing raid. In many neighborhoods, nothing was standing higher than three feet and houses looked like piles

7. Is there such a thing as gossip that is not hurtful?

of matchsticks. The sense of grief and loss was leaden and palpable in the air. The Army's 82nd Airborne, fresh from Desert Storm in Iraq, was called in to bring order out of complete chaos. They miraculously managed this within twenty-four hours.

One of the company leaders was Sgt. Rodriguez, a genuinely remarkable non-commissioned officer (NCO). The people under his command said they would jump off a cliff for him if they had to, and the colonel and major first consulted with him before carrying out any operations. He commanded that type of respect. Quiet and unassuming, he was strict and fair—no favorites in his command. At the same time, he had an easy way about him and a good sense of humor. Being in the army and in significant combat, he must have ably proven himself to the men and women under his command. But there was more to it than that. There was just some quality about him that you could not quite pin down, but you listened to him. This is a quality that cannot be learned, only earned. No matter how many diplomas there are on your wall, insignia on your uniform, or signed documents touting your authority, the essence of leadership, what really makes it legitimate, is that quality of respect. It cannot be based upon fear of your power, as that will only breed contempt, lies, and spurious responses to your so-called "authority." Without genuine respect from superiors, colleagues, and subordinates, you cannot be an effective leader.

One last little story in this section underlining the responsibilities of a leader. It is called "Lincoln Democracy." The story goes that President Abraham Lincoln had a difficult wartime decision to make. As he polled his cabinet sitting around the table, each said "Nay" to the question. It was unanimous. Lincoln replied, "The Ayes have it." Sometimes he had to override his advisors and take the heat for the outcome of his decisions. His team would never have stood for that if he did not frequently follow their advice, but as President Harry Truman reminded people with the plaque on his desk, "The buck stops here." Leadership is not a wishy-washy affair, and it is not for the faint-hearted. Moreover, the old authoritarian ways will just not work anymore—at least not for long and not effectively.

Gurus Need Not Apply or God-King-Boss

Some organizations still look for the Daddy-God-Boss in their leaders. Some managers still need to be Daddy-God-Boss or Mommy-Queen Bee-Goddess. Every once in a while, I still run across a church member who looks up to me as some sort of Daddy-God-Savior-Guru. They really think I have all the answers. I remind them that an alternative name for *The Church of the Way of the Messiahs* could just have easily been *The Church of the Way of the Gurus*, but then that would not have been our Universalist way. There is no Neo from the *Matrix* or one Savior Guru. Going back to what we discussed earlier, the emerging Age of Aquarius is the aeon when we are supposed to search for the Guru Within, the Christ Within, the Buddha Within, the God Within, the Goddess Within, the Yogi Within, the Shaman Within, the Avatar Within, and the Wisdom Teacher Within. I remind them that our New Age challenge is no longer to search for the answers outside ourselves, but to seek the answers within. We all have the capability for that intuitive, spiritual connection which opens to better judgment and wiser decisions. Jesus reminded his followers in the Gospel of Thomas,

> If those who lead you say to you, "See, the Kingdom is in the sky," then the birds of the sky will precede you. If they say to you, "It is in the sea," then the fish will precede you. Rather, the Kingdom is inside of you, and it is outside of you. When you come to know yourselves, then you will become known, and you will realize that it is you who are the sons of the living Father. But if you will not know yourselves, you dwell in poverty and it is you who are that poverty.[8]

Perhaps, we are challenging them to find the Leader Within and stop being a "sheeple."

This is difficult for many people. In our collective insecurity, many are still looking for someone to guide them through the "valley of the shadow of death." They yearn for someone to show them the way, to tell them what to do, to save them. To do the work for them? How many times have I heard someone say that their life is completely in God's hands? I prefer Euripides response, "The gods help those who help themselves." Others will insist that there is no free will or that God knows all. They miss the point that, if true, what is the purpose of living if everything

8. *The Gospel of Thomas*: 3, *The Other Bible*, ed. Willis Barnstone (San Francisco: Harper, 1984), 300.

is pre-determined and pre-arranged by Daddy Sky God? Why go on if some of us are predestined to being the Elect, and some are predestined to be the Sons and Daughters of Perdition—and literally God only knows who is who? It is precisely this type of belief system that has stalked us for the past 8,000 patriarchal years. And it has created a male role model for authority with Daddy-King-God-in-the-Sky, while we play the role of his loyal, obedient, humble child subjects without any individual rights. The King must be unconditionally loved and obeyed. Long live the King!

I don't need a king (or a queen) anymore. Do you? Along these lines, I was very frustrated with the adulation and awe that accompanied Mel Gibson's 2004 movie, *The Passion of the Christ*. It elevated this idea of dependency upon an Almighty-God-in-the-Sky through the life of his innocent son, Jesus of Nazareth. When Cate and I saw it, we felt we had just wasted $18.00 and three hours to watch a horrifically brutal film in which the incredible life, ministry, and message of Jesus was wholly ignored while glorifying the agony of his death. People viewed it as such a realistic portrayal. So, even ignoring the anti-Semitic tone and the Hollywood script additions found nowhere in the New Testament, realistically, one has to ask if any human being could have stayed conscious or survived the first fifteen minutes of such a brutal beating.

I always sensed that Jesus would have been really angered by that film. I can imagine him saying, "Why would you focus on the last twelve hours of my life, and not my years of ministry toiling through countless wildernesses, country roads, villages, and cities throughout Palestine, preaching about love, forgiveness, and the Kingdom of God? Why would you call my death my passion, when my real passion was these teachings? Why would you focus on me and not my message, which I considered far more important than the messenger? Why is my death by crucifixion any more brutal than the tens of thousands who died in this horrific manner at the hands of Assyrians, fellow Jews, Greeks, and Romans over several centuries?"

Moreover, I have to add that I am just independent enough that I would never ask Jesus to die for my sins. Through my mistakes, failures, and sins have come some of my greatest lessons and accomplishments. They are my hard-earned lessons and issues to resolve. They challenge me to stay stuck and remain miserable or to change and grow and find a measure of peace. Why would I want someone else to do that meaningful work for me, much less die for me when I am quite capable of mastering my own sins or "energetic mistakes?"[9] What kind of Creator would give me the gift of creation and then remove free will from me so I cannot explore and learn and grow without the direst of consequences—eternal damnation? What kind of loving Creator would punish his creations forever with no opportunity to grow, evolve, or change beyond one lifetime? What kind of Creator would have so little trust in me—a me who he blessed with a brain, with the ability to make choices, and the ability to learn and change—that he had to send someone down to do my work for me? What parent does not encourage their child to grow and learn, even with the skinned knees, tears, adolescent heartbreaks, and growing pains of life? What kind of parent robs their child of any sense of competence and confidence in their own abilities by saying you can never do this by yourself, even with the help of your brothers and sisters on the planet? I will have to step in and do all your homework for you, and in return, you must give up all of your freedom of thought and will to me? That is just terrible parenting and psychology.

What kind of creator would want his subjects to love him because they have to—or else! If God is a being, then we might assume he or she or it is the most intelligent being in the universe. Why would the most intelligent being in the universe and the unimaginable creator of all universes and all things want humans to bow down, to kiss his toes, to adore and worship him? Why would the brightest and wisest being in the universe need such adulation? I don't know about you, but that has always sounded a tad egotistical and insecure to me. Moreover, the enormous contradiction in this is that God sent messenger after messenger, all of whom were supremely humble and uninterested in worldly gain or power. They did not wish to rule or be worshiped. One would surmise they were a reflection of their boss. Added to that, it has always sounded the slightest bit authoritarian to me for God to be a vengeful God, a wrathful God, a jealous God, and so on. What a view of God and what a view of the supreme leadership in the universe.

Of course, I am well aware that these notions contradict the teachings of a significant portion of Christianity. To illustrate the breadth of the divide, in 1999, I was working on my Master's Degree of Divinity at the Florida Center for Theological Studies, a Christian seminary. As I attended a lecture on Christian Evangelical Theology presented by a

9. Mistakes can be corrected. They do not imply eternal damnation for failing some of the tough lessons of life—but only imply that we need to take "the test" over until we get it right.

famous theologian from one of the Ivy League schools, I was still fairly unschooled in the subtleties of fundamentalist theology. I became more and more appalled as I listened to him berate our society from nearly every angle. He was particularly scathing about self-help groups, Twelve Step Programs (e.g., Alcoholics Anonymous), and modern psychology. I raised my hand during the question and answer portion of his talk and asked, "I am curious why you are criticizing Twelve Step Programs. As a psychotherapist, I have found that these groups help many people and have even led many people back to God through their emphasis on a Higher Power." He looked at me condescendingly and said, "Ah, and therein lies the gulf between us. You believe we can do something to help ourselves, and I do not." He was right. There was nothing more for us to discuss. I do think we can do something to help ourselves, and he does not. Such an abyss shocked and saddened me. As a social worker, psychotherapist, teacher, and minister, I have always advocated for the power of loving communication. I believe there are few differences that cannot be resolved or are irreconcilable. That day I was not so sure.

Now that we have finished our little theological foray into concepts of God, what does this have to do with leadership? It is simple; we are still stuck with a Classical Age and medieval paradigm on God and leadership. Monarch, head honcho, authoritarian ruler, Emperor, warlord, Czar, El Jefe, Oz, or Supreme Being on a golden throne, in a palatial office, visited only by a select few in a penthouse suite, at the top of the office tower (heaven). Monarchical religions and governments so dominated human society for the past several millennia, it is no wonder it is taking centuries for us to recover from the hangover. There seems to be a part of us that still longs for someone to tell us what to do or who to be. We see how society today is torn between the traditionalists, who wish to cling to the past with its so-called tried-and-true security blankets, and the progressives, who adventurously look forward to new ways of sharing and equality. As we have postulated throughout, the authoritarian, top-down models are just not an effective leadership model for maturing, postmodern, evolving humanity. You can cling to the past all you want, but time and change will march right past you without a backwards glance. It is the Tao, the Way, and nothing in all of human history can halt the forces of time and change.

Before leveling the playing field with the Facilitator Model of Leadership, let us explore some of the dos and don'ts of postmodern leadership style and performance.

Dealbreakers in Leadership and Organizational Success

It is an axiom in organizational theory that leadership sets the tone and culture of an organization in both the formal and informal organizational structure. Put simply, lousy leadership generates lousy results; effective leadership more likely leads to effective results. Again, these are not groundbreaking, earthshaking new revelations, but over the past fifty-some years, I have observed and studied what I call dealbreakers in organizational success, and it almost always stems back to leadership.

Love that Gossip and Those Cliques

As mentioned earlier, one agency I worked in was torn apart by gossip. It started at the top. The senior managers were inveterate gossips. During staff meetings, they would openly gossip about people in the agency, including a friend of mine in another unit. This hurt her deeply. When I summoned the courage to speak up one day and suggest that we not discuss the personal and professional problems of staff, especially when they were not present, it was the start of a long downhill slide in the relationship with my boss. The feedback was not only unappreciated but met with outright hostility. It was a very sick agency, and accordingly, there was a lot of tension in coworker relationships, including feelings of distrust and betrayal. Morale was low throughout, and this clearly affected our productivity and mission to help prevent crime.

I want to be clear I am not just picking on this agency, which also did a lot of good, but it does give us some clear-cut examples of poor leadership. I have observed some of these same problems in other organizations as well—government, corporate, private enterprise, and nonprofit. Sadly, it seems endemic to human groups of all kinds. It causes all manner of disruption on the planet, whether within a couple, a family, a neighborhood, a workplace, a community, a country, and even between nations. How many wars have been launched or almost launched because of erroneous suspicions, unhealthy alliances, and faulty communication, which are the international equivalent of gossip and cliques? For example, the 1962 Cuban Missile Crisis has been particularly well-studied. We have the actual recollections of most of the participants in both President Kennedy's and Premier Khrushchev's inner circle. The mounting tensions almost advanced to a nuclear war between the United States and the

Soviet Union, and it escalated due to faulty assumptions and misinformation on both sides.[10]

So, then, what is the opposite of gossip and cliques? A welcoming and respectful atmosphere is an excellent place to begin. I would have thought these are basic manners that our parents should have taught us long ago. Thus, I was astounded that at this same small agency, new employees, including me, were routinely ignored when the men and the women went out separately for the special Friday afternoon lunch. I think I had been working there nearly three months before one of the men noticed it with some embarrassment and invited me to join them. Soon after, several of us insisted on ending the practice of separate male and female Friday lunches and always made sure that new staff members were invited. That small gesture improved morale and staff bonding considerably, so why was such an obvious courtesy not part of routine agency practices? We might start with the fact that the leaders never joined the staff for lunch, so they did not set a good example. As I witnessed this staff's inner workings over the next several years, I saw that newcomers were often met with suspicion. Power, status, ego, and fear were frequently behind the destructive behaviors of staff and leaders. Lies and manipulation were not uncommon. Leaders and coworkers did not have each other's back. These were not bad people—some became friends—but beyond their own thoughtlessness (Do you have to be told to be welcoming to new people?), there was an organizational culture that encouraged insensitivity. Eventually, even though I believed in and loved the work, I, along with many others, felt immediate dread as I stepped across the threshold of the office each morning. It was not a respectful, cheerful, or welcoming environment.

I'm Right, You're Wrong

I have heard parents and bosses proclaim proudly, "It's my way or the highway." Needless to say, their children and their employees respectively will not feel listened to or respected. This is the height of ego and arrogance, as if anyone could always be right. You can guarantee that adults

10. David Gonzalez, "At Cuba Conference, Old Foes Exchange Notes on 1962 Missile Crisis," *New York Times*, October 14, 2004, A6. In 2002, senior government participants and historians met in Cuba to share what really happened during the Cuban Missile Crisis. Many were astounded at the misinformation and wrong-headed assumptions held by both parties. Thankfully, cooler heads prevailed within President Kennedy's and Premier Khrushchev's leadership circles.

embracing this philosophy had a parent who always had to be right, consequently making them feel they were always wrong. The ironic thing is that this child will grow up determined never to be wrong again, unconsciously becoming precisely what they detested in their parent.

Some bosses and coworkers appear to genuinely be listening and appear interested in your point of view, but you find over time that this is a cover-up. In the end, it seems that their opinions and decisions always prevail. They, too, have a difficult time seeing or accepting other points of view. They are even harder to work with because their intransigence hides beneath a pleasant or seemingly accommodating demeanor—the wolf in sheep's clothing. To both types of managers, I have four simple words for them: bad management versus teamwork. To be effective, the modern boss or manager must know how to create a dedicated team. The word "team" implies a cooperative and collaborative effort with each member carrying out an important role. It even indicates a level playing field among its members. An effective team requires a manager who knows how to challenge them, listen to them, and utilize their ideas. The point of a team is to develop more creative approaches to their work, which leads to a more efficient and productive work process. There can be no room for "my way or the highway" on a team, whether that comes from the leader or a team member. Such attitudes are team and productivity Terminators.

A useful rule in all communications is what I call the "Five Percent Rule." When you disagree with someone, always assume that they are at least 5 percent correct and you are 5 percent incorrect. That little toe in the door of inflexibility can lead to the wondrous discovery that the other person is often far more than 5 percent correct. It is an essential aspect of good communication. John Gottman, the marriage and family therapy researcher, calls it validation. This is simply accepting that the other person is sincere in their point of view, and if you stood in their shoes, you would understand why they feel that way. It does not mean you must agree with them; just that you accept the authenticity of their feelings about their perspective.[11]

I can't tell you how many times, as a psychotherapist and marriage and family therapist, I saw that two people could both be right even though their positions differed significantly. The sooner they could understand and accept this, the sooner a real dialog and resolution could be

11. John Gottman et al, *A Couples Guide to Communication* (Champaign, IL: Research Press, 1976), 17.

initiated. A typical example is the couple who both insist that the other partner doesn't listen to them. Their positions differ because each believes they are the good listener and the other partner is not, but they are both right and both wrong. They both want to be good listeners, but neither is listening well to the other. When they stop the finger-pointing and actually begin to "hear" each other, the wonders of good communication are unveiled. Both feel valued by the other. It works with couples and it works in the office. If you think about it, isn't it the way you would want to be treated by your boss or coworker? That you just might have a sensible point? That you are worth listening to?

If that doesn't work, I always recommend the "Cup of Coffee Rule." How many of our problems could be settled if two people sat down over a cup of coffee and actually attempted to listen to each other and reach an understanding? It is a peace offering time and requires good manners. Too bad Kennedy and Khrushchev didn't do this. Their coffee klatch could have avoided a lot of fear and pain for hundreds of millions.

Preventive Maintenance

One principle that reverberates throughout this whole section on style and communication is the simplest and most straightforward: Address issues early on. Perform preventive maintenance!

For leaders and subordinates, and for families and couples, resentment, anger, frustration, and hurt feelings cannot build if they are dealt with directly at the time of the grievance or disagreement. It is so much harder to resolve six months or six years of pent up feelings than five minutes or five hours of unresolved emotions. If the issue is not faced quickly, by the time it erupts, people tend to not only address the issue but also throw in the kitchen sink. The kitchen sink method[12] means that every even remotely related grievance and concern is thrown in for good measure. It totally knocks the two parties off track because it is hard to focus on the central issue when so many tangential issues keep rising from the grave. For the same reasons we noted in the section above about fear and feeling intimidated by authority figures (learned from parental programming), people are often afraid to confront an issue head-on at the moment it emerges. They often expect they will not be listened to and/or that the other person will react aggressively and punitively if they

12. Gottman, 36.

bring up why they are feeling hurt or angry. Successful organizations and leaders create an atmosphere of trust and safety so that preventive maintenance is the norm, and uncomfortable issues are not allowed to intensify and fester over time.

The Old Go Around

This was a tactic we all learned as kids. If you couldn't convince dad of something, go to mom. And, unless mom and dad presented a united front and kept good communication between them, it worked. We knew it was a done deal if mom said, "Go ask your father."

What is so hard about being direct and forthright with coworkers, employees, and bosses? It must be extremely difficult because it is most often the exception than the rule. There are a number of books describing dysfunctional organizations, and Lloyd Williams says it as well as anyone as he denotes the split in Western culture between the demands on individuality and the requirements of organizational conformity.

> In effect, people are asked to bring together individual expertise and strengths and still function as one collective group, one organization, or one team . . . Simultaneously, organizations and cultures struggle to meet perceived goals and yet avoid destruction of the individuals in the process . . . *Individuation* and *socialization* seem to be opposing forces within the person in the struggle to be whole and complete, to be able to handle stress, and to be sensitive to the needs of adapting to the changes in the person and the society. *This initiates dysfunction.*[13]

When I was a Family Therapist, all my training and experience pointed to the essential truth that the ways we communicate as adults have everything to do with how our parents and families communicated. This family stuff, our blueprint, is a most potent programming. If mom and dad were direct and forthright with each other and with their children, then that is the family practice and functioning. If mom and dad have couple problems and poor communication, they often triangle in the children to take on well-defined dysfunctional roles. Their child becomes

13. Lloyd C. Williams, *The Congruence of People and Organizations: Healing Dysfunction from the Inside Out* (Westport, CT: Quorum Books, 1993), 4–5. A related book on this topic is *The Addictive Organization: Why We Overwork, Cover Up, Pick Up the Pieces, Please the Boss and Perpetuate Sick Organizations* by Anne Wilson Schaef (San Francisco: Harper, 1990).

the Rescuer, Mediator, Clown, Problem Kid, Sick Kid, Daddy's Little Girl, Mommy's Little Boy, and so on as a means to help the parents focus away from the problems between them. If parents are harsh and judgmental in their responses to questions or to a child's attempts to speak his or her mind, then children will be resentful and fearful of parent-child communications. They will keep everything inside and hide their real feelings. Or they will be timid and fearful in their communications. Or they will be aggressive, harsh, and judgmental (like mom or dad) in their communications. The first two types learned to avoid direct communication and practice the go-around, which can include gossip. Similar results can be seen with a timid or manipulative parent who is not direct or clear in his or her communications. Are you beginning to recognize some traits in your coworkers, your bosses, your family, or yourself?

All of this is about teaching Lightworkers new and better ways of working together. An organization will remain dysfunctional and unhealthy if it does not practice some central principles of good communication and respect. Its employees must be committed to the same, but the leadership must provide the role modeling.

The most common way this behavior is shown in an organization is by going around the chain of command. For example, if you have a beef with your boss, instead of sitting down with him or her and attempting to resolve it, you talk about it with your coworkers. Essentially, you are triangling them into the conflict. Or you can go over the head of your boss to a higher manager and triangle him or her. There are many reasons for this manipulative behavior. However, for many people, they have been so adversely affected by authority figures who did not listen to them or punished them for being direct and assertive (like parents, bosses, and teachers), they are often discouraged and assume it will be just another bad outcome. The final dysfunction in this set piece occurs if the coworkers or the senior manager allow or encourage this triangling conduct.

In a healthy organization, coworkers and managers push you to speak directly with your boss and work it out. Of course, this assumes a boss who is open and fair-minded; someone who will listen. This is not always true, and, sadly, sometimes, it is the boss who is indirect and manipulative. There are moral victories that can be vital to your integrity, so even if the other person is unwilling to listen, you can at least stand up for yourself (without ego and without intent to harm or seek revenge). However, this can also lead to unwanted consequences (like increased tension with the boss, being labeled a troublemaker, or punitive repercussions) when there are high expectations of conformity from your boss or the organization. So, one must weigh carefully whether being direct and assertive is a good idea in an unfriendly management environment. Sadly, survival in a dysfunctional organization frequently requires dysfunctional self-protective responses.

In one corporation I worked in, it was the official corporate policy that an employee must attempt to resolve any issues with his or her direct superior before involving anyone else, and vice versa. If the matter could not be resolved, only then is the next higher manager called in to sit down with both parties in an attempt to work it through. It is a great policy. The only problem is that most senior managers did not follow it, which led to a lot of gossip, "go-arounds," and backbiting within the organization. It clearly demonstrated that for all the fancy management principles and ethics policies, organizations (like individuals) cannot just "talk the talk."

Walking the Walk

Recently, our church's Level II Ministry Course students provided a list of what they considered to be essential leadership characteristics during their "Living Leadership" module. It is a diverse group. It includes a former attorney (now a high school teacher), a senior investment banker, an art teacher, a graphic designer, a chef, a fashion designer, a healer, a secretary, and an artisan. They have a lot of experience with organizations, bosses, and employees; corporate, government, and entrepreneurial.[14] The leadership principles they recommended include:

- Humility: Arrogance and huge egos do not fit well with teamwork and power-sharing. To be a bona fide Facilitator Leader, one must check their ego at the door.
- Being authentic and genuine: From a spiritual perspective, we call this our "I AM." I am who I am. We are who we are. People quickly pick up when someone is "full of it," and they do not respect the person. If anything, lack of authenticity breeds the same in response.

14. Discussion in Church Ministry Course II about "Living Leadership" between Facilitator Instructor Thomas Norris and students Dan Katz, Mary Hill, Luciana Esposito, Sarah Bramham, Cate Norris, Elisa Rossi, Karen Matamoros, and Sujeiry Aguilera; Pembroke Pines, FL, November 16, 2009.

- Integrity and honesty: Your word must mean something, or your words will not be listened to. In these days of legalese, lawsuits, contracts for just about anything, the idea that my word is my bond has become increasingly rare. However, we sure appreciate those people who mean what they say and follow it up with action. Also, these leaders hold themselves accountable and are not afraid to admit when they are wrong.
- The ability to listen and actually hear: So many of us are developing our response to someone's words, even as they are speaking, so we miss a lot. Sometimes, we Type A's are even thinking several things at once (polyphasic thinking). It is an art to truly keep the mind still and just listen.
- Consistency: Whether one is parenting or leading, consistency is appreciated. Neither children nor adults like walking into minefield situations, where the rules change all the time, and no one ever quite knows where the mines are from day to day.
- Internal balance: Consistency is not just about management style and behavior but also temperament. It is very stressful to work with or for someone who is on a constant emotional roller coaster. Life is enough of a soap opera without adding to the drama.
- Compassionate: How many times have we witnessed a lack of compassion in our work lives? A loyal, long-time employee is laid off and given ten minutes to clean out his or her desk and then is escorted off the premises by security. This is almost the norm in corporate America today. It has happened to me, and it was a very humiliating experience for this loyal employee. How does a company handle an employee's serious illness or the serious illness of a close family member, stressful reactions to a divorce, single parenting, drinking or drug problems, maternity and family leave, and so on? Are there substantive support systems in place, or are people left to fend for themselves? Good leaders decide what the compassionate culture of their organization is going to be by their example and policies (policies that are actually followed). Good leaders lead from the heart.
- Intuitive: They feel and intuit the group process in a meeting or a class. They are tuned in and sensitive to the person they are listening to, the team they are working with, or the audience they are addressing. Shamanic and spiritual teachers report that they "feel" the

energies of a group and can actually "hear" what is going on within the "group mind," as well as within the individuals in the group. They also routinely receive spiritual messages and guidance from what might be called "Cosmic Consciousness" or "Cosmic Wisdom." Thus, it can be unnerving to those raised in Western ways of thinking when a shaman or spiritual leader interjects a comment that lays bare an underlying or unspoken issue, or the unexpressed feelings of the group or an individual in the group. With practice, the leader becomes confident in these "messages" and their uncanny accuracy.

- Healthy boundaries: What is the line between concern for someone and prying into their personal life? How do office affairs affect an organization? What is the line between a relaxed, informal atmosphere and a lack of discipline or self-discipline in staying focused on the job? What is the line between time on the computer for personal matters and taking time from the organization for inappropriate use of the computer (like long online chats, online games, or porn)? Why is it that so many organizations and individuals within organizations struggle with these issues? The question of appropriate boundaries is quite a minefield.
- Passion: The good leader is passionate about his or her work, team, and organization. A passionate leader can be the CEO or a low-level supervisor, but their motivation and enthusiasm are contagious. It creates a milieu of caring for the work and for each other. For a Lightworker, this passion is fueled by faith in self, in each other, and in the organization's work.
- Wisdom: Wisdom is not just about intellect and knowledge; it involves mind and heart working together. And, as we have all heard, a wise person knows his or her strengths and limitations.
- Strength (Backbone): They are secure enough to take a firm stand, when necessary, while also having the courage (and common sense) of knowing when to back down. They pick the right battles.
- Patience: Rome was not built in a day, and following the Buddhist Law of Nonpermanence, "This, too, shall pass." Discovering the tricky Yin (non-action) and Yang (action) line is an art well practiced. There is a time to relax and be still (reflect, contemplate, assess, sleep) and a time to seize the moment (awaken, act, move, decide). A good leader has a great feel for each moment.

- Respectful: It literally means full of respect. Loose cannons and hard asses need not apply. There is a time to be a maverick in the creative sense and a time to be tough, but neither has to be done without respect or revered as a superior management style. Good leaders have many tools in their management toolbox.
- Confidence: The crew and customers want to know that the ship captain has a pretty good idea of where she or he is going. As one student noted, "Once you know who you are, you aren't afraid to be who you are. You just can't be anyone other than yourself." In Humanistic Psychology, we call this a self-actualized person. This is another version of the I AM, and it is not ego-driven. Confidence is not about feelings of superiority, but feelings of security—secure in one's knowledge, skills, and talents, while unafraid to face one's limitations and gaps in knowledge and expertise.

Now that we have everyone walking on water, the perfect leader, I suppose it would be easy to criticize this as just a nice wish list, or simply a list of clichéd principles. But I disagree. I don't believe anyone can live up to these leadership principles every day of his or her life, but as ideals, they are something to strive for. They don't have to walk on water, and they don't have to be perfect, but that just keeps them more real and authentic. Argue with me if you will, but would you like to have a boss or coworker with these traits? Would you feel more confident in your CEO, President, or supervisor if they embodied these qualities? Could you imagine that any ship they are steering would follow a relatively straight course? Would you follow their lead? Would you wish to have those qualities yourself? This is really the Golden Rule in the workplace. Works there, too.

Facilitator Model of Leadership

There are specific qualities that go into this type of leadership, many mentioned above, and there is more than one leader in a Universalist organization—that Yin-Yang balance again. Although we focus on the Universalist Church below, the principles are pertinent to all postmodern organizations.

- After all the preceding discussion, it may not surprise you that the leaders are not the boss. The leaders are there to serve the organization, its employees, and those the organization serves. At the very least, we stand the old pyramid hierarchical model on its head. In a Universalist Church, the members are the boss. However, even that hierarchical, polarizing word "boss" is foreign to the Universalist experience. We are all on the same team, despite any role differences we might have.

- As administrators, the leaders are only leaders in so far as they facilitate the organization's activities and mission at the direction of the membership.
- Since many Universalist groups appear to be more "teaching" than "preaching" organizations, the leaders also facilitate educational activities and learning.
- The teacher leaders are facilitators of the group's learning in classes and workshops. They may have particular expertise and knowledge, but it is their job to mine the talent, experience, and knowledge of the student group as well. It is the facilitator teacher's job to assist the student in discovering their own "Teacher Within." General Systems Theory states that the whole is greater than the sum of its parts. We live by that concept. A class is more than a teacher and students. There is a "whole" far beyond that simple sum of teacher + students = class. It is the facilitator teacher's job to bring out the group knowledge. In many spiritual classes, there is far more going on than just learning about various spiritual issues. There is more than the content and the interaction, but a multidimensional aspect added through the meditations and higher teachings. These carry an energy all their own. When this is successful, the courses have become life-transforming for student and teacher and have taken on a unique "whole" energy of their own that could not have been predicted by the class demographics.
- The pastoral and spiritual counselor's role is to facilitate the empowerment of the counselee. They return them to mental, emotional, and spiritual health by developing their "Healer Within." They help them regain their decision-making abilities; learn how to love themselves (and others) again; restore hope, which means they believe they have a meaningful future; discover their life goals and skill-building; and develop their innate spiritual and intuitive abilities. The counselor helps them find their "Wise Counselor Within" and bring them back to life—out of the "dead zone." It is not the

counselor's job to rescue or do the work for the counselee. There are enough "wounded messiahs" around, and being a savior only leads to burnout and maintaining the counselee in a dependent posture.

- We recognize that committees may need to exist from time to time, but they, too, are run by these principles. They facilitate the outcome of whatever process they are asked to undertake, and any member may feel free to join any committee. All meetings will attempt to follow a consensus model. Many times, there will not even be a real chairperson, as we seem to operate well in a "round table" format.

So, we have come to the end of the chapter on Organizational Leadership. We have seen how structure and leadership dance together. Now let us complete the choreography by bringing in the Organizational Mission.

CHAPTER 19

Stay the Course

(On the Nature of Organizational Mission)

Purposes and Ethos

ANY SUCCESSFUL, HEALTHY MODERN organization must have a clearly defined Mission Statement, whether that's IBM, BMW, Pizza Hut, the Smithsonian Museum, a church, or a non-profit. A Mission Statement brings to light and life the organization's overall reason for existence, and it establishes the ethos of the organization. What is the purpose and the ethical culture of the organization? Sometimes a specialized organization, such as a church, also lives by other abiding principles—their founder's words, their particular commandments and laws, or their scriptures. As one example, our Universalist Church has a Mission Statement but is also guided by the twenty-eight principles in its *Universalist Spiritual Manifesto* (Appendix A). It is an essential mission piece in aiding the organizational wheel to stay round (balanced) and move forward. Since this is a spiritual book centered on Universalist ideas, for practical purposes, we will use this church's Mission Statement as an example. The primary principles of this chapter are relevant to all organizations, especially in observing how a Mission Statement interacts with, supports, and reinforces the organization's structure and leadership. Admittedly, it is not the perfect model for the tightly focused Mission Statements that business textbooks might recommend. It covers a lot because there is a lot to be covered. We are Universalists, after all.

Our Mission Statement

> *The Church of the Way of the Messiahs is a Universal Spiritual Teachings Church. It is our mission to share the Creator's message of love, tolerance, hope, joy, and peace with all. We are teachers and students of life and the One. We honor diversity and discover unity within diversity. We intend to constantly evolve without reliance on rituals and with only one truth—our love for each other and the One—to spiritually connect and not just to organize. We are helping bring light to the planet and bridge the differences between peoples, cultures, traditions, religions, and dimensions. We co-create networks and circles of light. We are a spiritual home to all seekers of Universal truth. We are the Many and the One, the One and the Many.*

So, even if it is not as neat and tidy as it should be, much more importantly, it was developed by the church members themselves. On top of that, it covers all the bases of *koinonia* (community), *martyria* (witness to creation and all its wonders), and *diakonia* (service and justice).

Utilizing the Facilitator Leadership Style and the Wheel and Hub Organizational Structure to translate ideas, goals, and plans into active mission is the real challenge for a Universalist church. The leadership and organizational models are mainly internal mechanisms, but the mission is an internal to external process—it reaches out to and into the world. In utilizing this Mission Statement as an example, we will consider what the themes of a Universalist mission might look like and some of the possible means to implement them. To accomplish this, each section of the Mission Statement is broken down, explained, and analyzed.

The Church of the Way of the Messiahs is a
Universal Spiritual Teachings Church.

Like any good Mission Statement, this states the name of the organization and its primary purpose.

It is our mission to share the Creator's message of
love, tolerance, hope, joy, and peace with all.

All Mission Statements are by nature more general than a goal, objective, or task. Here, the general philosophy of the organization is laid out. How do we implement that philosophy and theology? That is where the goals and objectives come into the picture. There are several avenues for sharing the message. Underscoring this section, I like to think Universalists are similar to the *Ani Walelu*, the Cherokee Clan of the Hummingbird. They will do anything, fly any direction, stand still, anything to bring peace to the earth.[1] Add to that love, tolerance, hope, and joy, and you wonder if there can be a more beautiful message to share.

Teaching, Learning, Praying, Meditating, Enjoying

Of course, there is a seriousness of purpose in living a spiritual life, but it doesn't have to be so serious. We also subscribe to the Gospel of Laughter and Humor since spiritual living means living life to the fullest, enjoying all that Creation offers. Thus, there are several ways to express a loving and spiritual life.

Naturally, as part of their work, every spiritual and religious organization has some type of regular "worship service" or "sacred gathering." In our Universalist Church, they are called Sacred Circles, which fits neatly with the church's Native American Medicine Wheel logo and the sacred geometry of circles discussed earlier. However, the name is unimportant, for sacred meetings come in many names and many forms. Our weekly Sacred Circles have minimal ritual and structure. They generally follow a four-part format: welcome and announcements; healing prayers and blessings for self, others, and the world; presentation and lively discussion of a spiritual topic, which as Universalists, can be on just about anything in the universe; and a group meditation related to the topic. We close with a prayer. We find that the prayers, blessings, and meditations are often the most compelling aspects of the Sacred Circle, and we have witnessed a number of healings and spiritual breakthroughs as a result.

Additionally, the church oversees The Light University, which provides various classes, courses, seminars, and workshops mirroring

1. Kim Flink (Seneca) and Walter Pathfinder (Cherokee) in a talk on "Native American Traditions" at Miami-Dade College, during a course on *Native American Traditions* taught by Thomas and Cathleen Norris (Fall 1999, Miami, Florida).

its Universalist theology and utilizing local, national, and international teachers. Thus, The Light University curriculum covers a wide variety of areas from healing modalities, to teachings on world religions, to spiritual skills, to yoga classes, and so on. Finally, a set of three one-year Ministry Courses, each building on the other, provides the training for church members to learn Universalist theology, receive leadership training, and explore how they wish to carry out their Lightwork mission.

Most organizations cannot survive if they do not offer diverse events and projects to build organizational unity and interest. Hence, we have monthly Reiki Healing Circles, Past Life Healing Circles, Mystical Movie Nights, charity work, and social activity nights for singles, couples, and families (canoe trips, parties, camping trips, bike trips, Tarot Fun Nights, and so on). These are mentioned because they provide an essential balance in the organization between the more serious elements of its mission versus the more hands-on and fun social activities.

As we progress through the rest of the Mission Statement, it will become clear how we share this message.

We are teachers and students of life and the One.

Denoting our Universalist character and rejection of the Great Guru model, we are students of the Creator, and both teachers and students of creation and created. Hence, we emphasize continuing education and learning through Sacred Circles (which are like weekly mini-workshops), The Light University, and attending workshops and courses through other spiritual and educational organizations as well. Anything to enhance our learning. This applies to all members, regardless of leadership or participant role. Life is a continuing and adventurous learning process for us. Of particular importance is the point that our Facilitator Leaders are teachers, not preachers. As a Universalist Church, we are disinterested in preaching to anybody. We figure that the message should sell itself and does not need arm-twisting, fear tactics, or manipulation to convince someone of the "rightness" of the message. That term "rightness" does not even work in our faith. Who are we to say what is "right" and what is "wrong"? Universalists tend to believe that someone will participate in the work and the message if they wish to. If they don't, it is not the path for them, and we respect that. Later, you will see how we honor diversity.

Specialized Missions

An aspect of the mission that has not been addressed to this point is the idea that not all Sacred Circle groups need to conduct themselves in exactly the same way. Universalists do not promote a cookie-cutter model. Each Circle is guided by its own individual mission, based on the local talents and passions of the leadership and members. However, it is expected that each Circle will address all three areas of *koinonia* (spiritual community and family), *martyria* (witness to creation and all its wonders), and *diakonia* (service and justice) in some manner, since that is the heart of who we are. A few examples will suffice.

- One of our Sacred Circle groups provides direct outreach to the LGBTQ (gay, lesbian, bisexual, transsexual, and queer) community. Their *koinonia* is the sense of support and community for each other. Their *martyria* involves celebrating the beauty and diversity of all creation (a personal witness to Universalism). Their *diakonia* is their advocacy for gay rights and service to the gay community.
- Another Sacred Circle group is composed mainly of local college students. Their needs and issues will be different from those of the Sacred Circle at the Assisted Living Center for seniors.
- One Sacred Circle group wishes to start something called The Children's Project, an advocacy and public awareness initiative to assist abused and neglected children. It is a project dear to their hearts, since many came from abusive or neglectful childhoods. Some members are artists, so they wish to especially reach out to these children through art classes.
- Some members have deep connections with Mother Earth and the plant and animal nations, so their work may develop along the path of a Green Ministry. They are particularly interested in ecology and Greenwise living. One member is developing a holistic urban and community gardening project through his university and our church to put his ideas to practical use. He hopes to teach others how to grow their own food organically, even in their own backyards.
- Another Sacred Circle group wishes its *diakonia* to center around domestic violence prevention, as a number of them have been victims of domestic violence or were raised in homes where it was an everyday fact of life.

- One member hopes to create a Sacred Circle group for single parents, focusing on support and parent education.
- One wealthier member plans to develop a spiritual clearinghouse for spiritual organizations and missions. His particular focus is on developing a mechanism within this clearinghouse for affordable spiritual retreats.

The list of possibilities goes on and on. Nor can we ignore a dream many of us have: to create a Light Charter School that teaches all the regular classes required by the state, but also teaches children Universalist and spiritual principles of living.

Network Advocacy

One particularly promising avenue is our concept of a Network Advocacy Model of action. For example, there are many areas of this country, and especially in other less-developed countries, where local people do not have access to, are savvy in, or understand how to accomplish specific community goals based on community needs. Since we believe in a two-pronged approach of socio-political and spiritual action, we are not wedded to strictly political or purely spiritual models of action. We realize Holy Spirit works differently from the traditional, worldly models of power and leadership. We do not have to be an elected mayor or president to be effective. We can be far more useful in the background by being a networker, an advocate for change, and a connector. Within our broad-based, multi-cultural church community, we have many contacts and a variety of resource skills.

There is a huge disconnect between the disadvantaged and the power elite when it comes to local projects. Many small community groups develop innovative education, ecological, and other community-based projects but have no access to, or understand how to, obtain grants or assistance from the appropriate government, business, or private resources. As a networker advocate, we can bring the two pieces together. In this way, we accomplish important liberation work without becoming too deeply involved in politics and without becoming the rescuers of the oppressed. We are facilitating change by encouraging their own empowerment. For us, it is not about being in a position of power, but being in a position to serve. It is about connecting the people of the margin to the people of the center and aiding people to move out of the margin.

This would be only one of many advocacy endeavors the church foresees taking. In this way, it will be moving to a new level of spiritual engagement, beyond the *koinonia* focus of its early years of development, which was limited to developing the spiritual family base. This new field of spiritual action for the sake of social justice and service to oppressed communities (*diakonia),* while avoiding the treacherous quicksand of politics, will surely test our creativity and courage.

Field of Dreams

As you can see, all of these ideas hope to facilitate some type of spiritual change and real world improvements. They are proactive. Wherever it takes us, as the church grows and the members grow into their leadership, we will see many more of these unique and compelling ideas take shape. Along with the new leadership and organizational models, this is the best antidote to institutionalization and bureaucratization. There is no uniform ritual or organizational mission beyond tolerance and service. This is co-creation at its best, and as one of our members paraphrased from the movie *Field of Dreams*, "If you build it, they will come."

We honor diversity and discover unity within diversity.

The essence of Universalism must be its honoring of diversity. As a religion of tolerance, there are no outsiders. The unity is seen in that we are all headed on the same Mother Earth path as we hurtle through the galaxy at some 69,000 miles per hour. We are all on the same Mother Ship headed the same way, even if we view our journey differently.

Through my many years in South Florida, I have witnessed the influx of Cuban refugees and Latin American and Caribbean immigrants in search of a better life. I never understood my "Gringo" brothers and sisters who were threatened by this. They felt a way of life—old "Miamuh"—was dying and that "they" were taking over with their strange customs and Spanish or island lingo. Indeed, Miami and South Florida were changing, and the Old South ways were dying, but that was happening everywhere as we neared the end of the 20th century. What emerged was a vibrant, multicultural, interracial, multi-lingual community evolving into an international hub for Europe, Latin America, and Asia. It is hard to become tired of the local treasures of food, music, culture, and languages in this community. I always chuckle at the thought that this "Gringo" Minnesota boy, raised in the Presbyterian and Lutheran churches, now heads a non-Christian, mystical Universalist Church with a membership that is three-quarters Latino and Caribbean. It is the same when I observe my World Religions classes. Nearly every ethnicity, race, culture, continent, and language are represented—it truly is Florida International University. Why this is not viewed as exciting, enriching, and enlivening to some is beyond me, but I guess that is why we are Universalists.

We intend to constantly evolve without reliance on rituals and with only one truth—our love for each other and the One—to spiritually connect and not just to organize.

Universalism may borrow many rituals and enjoy them thoroughly, whether it is a Full Moon Drumming Circle at the beach or a Universalist baptism of a newborn (with all her Fairy Godmothers standing up for the child), but there is not an over-reliance on them. They are often fun, exuberant expressions of love, community, and connection to Spirit, but we try not to make the mistake of putting the ritual on a pedestal and forgetting the larger message of Spirit. It is not the ritual that is so important, but what it signifies. So, Universalists keep their focus on the central truth in Universalism—our love for each other and our Source. Our main work is to spiritually connect in harmony with each other through the oneness of Creator, Creation, and Created. In doing so, we assist in raising the spiritual vibrational energies of each other and our planet. Organizing, organizations, and organizational structure, like rituals, are just a means to carry out that work. They are just the connecting pieces in a material world, not the work itself.

We are helping bring light to the planet and bridge the differences between peoples, cultures, traditions, religions, and dimensions.

By living our lives in a more joyful, vibrant, caring, and tolerant manner, we bring light to ourselves and those around us. It is a Universalist belief, and modern science is beginning to back this up, that we each carry a vibrational energy that not only affects us but those around us. I think of the times that I lose my temper (often over the computer), and afterwards, how I feel a little sick. The vibrational energy of anger does not suit me well anymore. It is imperative to my health and well-being and the sense of harmony of those around me that I find other, healthier ways to express my frustration.

HeartMath

When you think about it, if the vibrational energy of seven billion people is added together, it most surely has a powerful impact. Think, then, what the forces of fear and despair can accomplish versus the forces of courage, love, and hope. And who and what is impacted? Can these emotions have a physical impact on the world? If you think this is science fiction, I need only report the scientists' findings at the Global Coherence Initiative and HeartMath Institute. They have reported that the earth's magnetic field has a high resonance with the rhythms of the human heart and brain. For example, it seems linked to brain activity, memory, athletic performance, and mortality from strokes and heart attacks, as well as the incidence of traffic violations and accidents, depression and suicide. There is even evidence from the monitoring of the earth's magnetic field during 9/11 that the significant spike in the field just before, during, and after the event indicated a resonance with collective human emotions at that time around the world. We are creatures of our planet intimately tied to its energies and evolutionary history for millions of years. Why wouldn't our individual energies be connected to that of our planet?[2] The researchers add:

> When an event evokes stress responses, this could be viewed as a planetary incoherence (stress) wave. Conversely, a positive emotional wave could create a global coherence wave. This perspective is supported by research at HeartMath showing that emotions not only create coherence or incoherence in our own bodies, but also radiate outward like radio waves and are detected by the nervous systems of those around us.[3]

Just think about 9/11, the Indonesian Tsunami, and Haiti Earthquake, and you might imagine the global impact of emotions. Imagine a global coherence of calm, peace, and tolerance even in the midst of those terrible

2. Global Coherence Initiative, "The Global Coherence Initiative," accessed May 28, 2015, https://www2.vsb.bc.ca/NR/rdonlyres/086A35EA-09D5-4886-B4E8-68828041F24C/0/global_coherence_initiative_brochure.pdf.

3. Ibid.

tragedies, perhaps even preventing those tragedies. Who will be the calm leaders who assist in preventing or saving, healing, and rebuilding?

To round this section out, it is evident that Universalists help bridge the differences between peoples, cultures, and traditions since we are promoting respect and tolerance for all of these. If we could accomplish that bridging in our world, then war, discrimination, and poverty could, at last, become historical footnotes. A big task, to be sure, but one that every major spiritual teacher has proclaimed in some fashion. You have to start somewhere. Being a bridge or bridgewalker is as good a place as any.

You might wonder, how does one bridge dimensions? Through daydreams and night dreams, prayers, visions, and meditations, people from time immemorial have been able to enter other realms of consciousness. Some are lower vibrational realms, which as Lightworkers, we would not ordinarily wish to visit or bridge. Yet, others are higher realms where we can receive teachings, healings, and energies that raise our vibrations and the vibrations of our communities and planet. By forming a bridge with the latter, we draw down the higher energies, as well as invite the spiritual teachers from those realms to teach and assist in our planetary enlightenment.

Occasionally, we are guided to form temporary bridges to the lower dimensions to free those trapped there who desire to leave. We can also share our higher energies with those communities so they can accelerate their growth as well. Of course, this is only done at their request, as this is a free will exercise. I think of it as being a spiritual social worker and providing aid to individuals and communities torn by the lower vibrations of discord and division. Those dimensions can exist on planet Earth, even in the midst of our own usual dimensional level. We see evidence in places torn by war, poverty, and hatred. Alternatively, we see places filled with peace, sharing, and love, sometimes right next door. In the end, we recognize that we are all multi-dimensional beings, as is our planet, even if we cannot see it yet. We exist and work within many levels of physical-worldly and soul-level consciousnesses.

We co-create networks and circles of light.

As more and more people awaken to their true selves, they create circles of light. As these circles of light are called and guided to share and join in with other circles of light, other Lightworkers, they form islands of light. When there are enough islands of light and they begin to link together, a critical mass is reached and the awakening process accelerates for the whole planet. Some might call this ascension. So many religions speak of a Golden Age of peace and plenty, but it requires enough people and their combined light energies to outshine the darkness and birth this New Age.

We are entering a new time. In this time, since all are beloved, no one can be left behind unless they choose to be. The 14th Dalai Lama has promised to keep returning (reincarnating) until the last person on the planet is no longer suffering. What a beautiful bodhisattva[4] path of love and service. This is available to us as well. If we indeed are all brothers and sisters, then we need to care for each other as our brother's and sister's keeper, in answer to God's question to Cain (Genesis 4:9–10). Moreover, it is not just our human brothers and sisters, but all of creation that needs to be respected.

As Universalists, to further this, we are happy and willing to work with anybody and any group working toward raising the vibrational love energy of our families, communities, and planet. This may include religious organizations, spiritual groups, atheist humanitarian organizations, corporations, philanthropists, social justice efforts, environmental groups, and so on. In other words, anyone and any organization of good heart and intent. This is more of being a bridge. Our Sacred Circles and social justice projects are just two examples of circles of light, but there are many more examples around the world. Every spiritual bookstore; every church, temple, and mosque; every healing circle; every prayer and meditation group; every Sweat Lodge; every health clinic serving the poor; every corporation genuinely focusing on the environment or world health; and every advocacy group standing up for the oppressed are all potential circles of light. There are so many more that could be listed. Circles of light working together create islands of light. Islands of light working together build a world of light.

We are a spiritual home to all seekers of Universal truth.

It can be a jungle out there. For Lightworkers, there are not many spiritual way stations where you can catch your breath during the average workday at the office, driving in traffic, hurriedly shopping at the grocery

4. In Buddhism, a "bodhisattva" is a being who has cleared his or her karma and does not have to continue being reborn lifetime after lifetime—but still chooses to return to serve humanity.

store, paying bills, helping the kids with homework, catching your favorite show, and watching the 11:00 p.m. news. The Sacred Circle, the spiritual workshop, the yoga class, the prayer group, the church party all provide a refuge and a sanctuary from the world. This is a compelling aspect of *koinonia*. As so many have commented, upon attending one of the church's events, "I finally found a place where I could just be me—and even have fun."

For Universalists, our essential Universal truth is the deeply-felt quest for loving harmony on the planet and with the planet. The means to accomplish this are as diverse as human creative expression, so there is room for everyone in this quest.

We are the Many and the One, the One and the Many.

Just as we see God as partner, friend, and companion, so are our spiritual teachers and guides. As pantheists, we also believe everything is part of the Creatress-Creator, including us. Thus, when we say the Great Spirit is the Many and the One, we are reminded that we are part of a Universal God Community in Oneness. Each of us, then, is part of the Many, while we are also part of the One and part of each other's Oneness.

Afterword

AND THAT IS THAT. We have just begun the journey of definition, explanation, and sketching the blueprint in this book. It is only a beginning. I hope you have enjoyed the journey. Ho! Mitakuye Oyasin!

That said, we cannot finish without acknowledging the myriad of spiritual guides and Ascended Masters who guided this book through their teachings and direct revelations. These include Jesus, Gautama Buddha, Kuan Yin, Mother Mary, Kuthumi, St. Germain, Isis, White Buffalo Calf Woman, the Holy Spirit, and so many more. This might have seemed odd at first; but now that you've read the book, you should better understand how they could have helped write it.

APPENDIX A

A Universalist Spiritual Manifesto

THE UNIVERSALIST PRINCIPLES BELOW are the heart, lifeblood, and backbone of this new theology and this book. The best way that I can explain how they emerged is simply to tell the story. One evening in March 1997, I had just finished a seminary course on Christian Church History as part of my Master's Degree in Divinity program. I walked the few blocks to Unity-on-the-Bay in Miami, where Cate was conducting a meditation group. While waiting in the lobby for her, I felt the presence of what I call Holy Spirit. These 28 principles poured out onto the paper over the next hour, and few changes were required as they evolved into their final form. Our Universalist Church sees them clearly as a revelation from Spirit. You have seen them interspersed throughout the book with accompanying explanations and examples that expand upon their significance and meaning.

1. *There is one Divine Creation Spirit of All That Is, Seen and Unseen, Known and Unknown, Understood and Not Understood.*
2. *All that is of and from this Great Spirit is, in essence, good and perfect, even if we do not always understand the higher purpose of things that appear dark, shadowy, evil, or unjust. There is divine purpose in All That Is, and no lesson is imposed upon us without our free choice, permission, and participation, even if we are not always conscious of the choice at this physical level of consciousness.*
3. *We, humans, are gifted with free will by Great Spirit, and by our choices in this world, we find joy or suffering, lightness or darkness, peace or turmoil in our lives. Then as we awaken further, we begin*

to understand our free will choices and the reasons for the lessons, difficult or gentle, we have drawn to ourselves.

4. *Along with all our relations, we humans are Spirit, One with the Divine Creation Spirit, manifesting in this plane through the vehicle of the physical body.*
5. *The Divine Creation Spirit is the One and the Many, the Many and the One. The Divine Creatress-Creator is female and male, infinitely large and infinitely small, Spirit and Substance, Light and Dark, beyond understanding and wonderfully simple, Manifest and Unmanifest, Mind and Heart. The Great Spirit is All That Is.*
6. *All creations of Great Spirit have their own consciousness of self and purpose. Though it may differ from ours, their consciousness is nonetheless quite real and essential to the workings of the Whole. Thus, Mother Earth, all nature, and the heavens above are guides and messengers if we have but eyes to see and ears to hear.*
7. *Along with all our relations, we are constantly in Oneness with Great Spirit, knowingly or unknowingly, in lightness or in darkness, in the physical or in the spiritual, as we are all the divine manifestation of Great Spirit, and in All That We Are, we are the Many and the One, the One and the Many.*
8. *We are all Sons and Daughters of the Divine Creatress-Creator with all the love and inheritance of such, when we so choose. It is the height of arrogance to believe that a Divine Creation Spirit of All That Is, a Creatress-Creator of unconditional love and unlimited wisdom, would not love all creation, or would come to only one community or people, or favor one group over another, or one sex over another, or one person over another. We are all favored Sons and Daughters, equally and yet uniquely loved by Great Spirit, which is the beauty and mystery of the divine paradox of the Many and the One.*
9. *We will come to an understanding and a life whereby we recognize our Oneness with the Divine Creation Spirit, and dedicate our lives to the Divine Love, Will, Purpose, and Creation Work of Great Spirit, according to our unique talents, skills, and gifts. This is our Awakening, our Enlightenment, and begins the Conscious Path of Love and Service.*
10. *We recognize and affirm the limitless beauty and truth of the Divine Creation Spirit, the Holy Spirit, that reveals itself through the many*

religions and peoples of faith throughout history and throughout the world. We acknowledge that a Divine Creation Spirit of all nations, of all peoples, of all creatures appears in many forms of Revelation through Divinely-guided Teachers, oral and written scriptures, and individual inspiration among all the peoples of the world. We call these revelations, inspirations, and teachings the loving, universal, divine truths of Great Spirit that shine through time, culture, personality, history, and geography.

11. *We are here to co-create Light, Harmony, and Balance in all things of creation by example, teaching, charity, compassion, prayer and meditation, and the guiding principle of unconditional love.*

12. *We understand that the "fall of humanity from Grace" was a free will choice for teaching and learning purposes, experienced as individuals, as families, and as a community of peoples in our towns, provinces and states, nations, and world. This choice, manifested through the physical plane, will teach us much of all creation, both the Light and the Dark, and that through this "fall," that is, the acceptance of the shadow teachers of suffering, pain, ignorance, fear, and the illusion of death, we will learn from our experiences and grow in our understanding in order to return to the higher states of Spirit, Joy, and Grace; to the Oneness that we knew in the Beginning and which has always resided within us.*

13. *We honor and acknowledge the Great Christed-Buddhic-Yogic-Messianic Teachers and Masters, Messengers of Light and Love for all that have come to us, the Awakening Daughters and Sons of Great Spirit.*

14. *We honor the great spiritual teachers and guides not in-the-body that support and assist us in our growth as individuals, families, communities, nations, and world.*

15. *Those that serve darkness, whether in body or spirit, are adversaries and shadow teachers, often of great power and influence until we begin to see through them. Yet, even the darkest beings, as creations of Great Spirit, carry the divine spark at their center. As energy and part of Great Spirit's creation, the divine spark cannot be extinguished. Also, we have played all the roles of Light and Dark, good and evil. We have been "them." There is no elitism in this higher awareness. There are no Elect, or we are all Elect. One sign of a less-awakened soul is pride and a "holier than thou" belief. Eventually, and they have all*

time, all will remember who they truly are. Perhaps, Lucifer, unconditionally Beloved Son of the Creatress-Creator, shall simply be the last Prodigal Son to trudge home.

16. *The Divine Creatress-Creator is the essence of all-encompassing and unconditional love for all of Creation and for all beings. This is our model and ideal for our own participation in the world and in creation. Once Self-remembered and Self-realized, we are likewise the essence of this same love, for we have been told and shown that the greatest commandment is love.*
17. *We, humans, are all Christed-Buddhic-Yogic Beings and Messiahs, and can begin to express this as we are awakened to our true nature. We are all ministers, priests, priestesses, gurus, lamas, medicine men and women, and rabbis of love, faith, and truth. We will serve Great Spirit's creation of love in all pathways of life, each according to our talents and interests and calling.*
18. *By following the example of unconditional love through complete forgiveness of self and others, we heal our karmic patterns of darkness, suffering, blindness, ignorance, and fear, especially through the courage of Self-exploration and Self-discovery. Life is not about being perfect, although Great Spirit sees us in our perfection at all times. Mother Life is about experience, knowledge, growth, and love. By facing our Shadow Teachers and Shadow Selves with love and acceptance, and through genuine remorse for wrongs committed or imbalances created towards self or others, now and in any lifetime, we heal and grow.*
19. *All life is to be honored. All life has purpose and meaning for itself and the Divine Creation Spirit. Through the eyes of love and Great Spirit, there is no justifiable harm or injury done to another being, whether physical, emotional, mental, or spiritual. When we are in the heart of love and Creation, we no longer bring that disharmony into our lives or the world. We no longer perceive or accept separateness, nor believe that any human is higher than any other being in the eyes of Great Spirit. We know with all of our being that we are in Oneness with all beings and all creations, for we are all in Oneness with the Divine.*
20. *Death is an illusion. The release of our physical vehicle is simply a transition from one form of existence to another. It may be chosen as a moment of great joy as we directly reunite with our Creatress-Creator; are finally freed to explore other planes of existence; and to choose our*

next lessons and steps of spiritual growth. No physical death occurs without the higher self's permission, and there is a higher purpose in even the most tragic deaths.

21. *Suffering is an illusion. With enough clearing of the illusionary material we have accumulated over many lifetimes, and as our Higher Awareness increases, suffering can be released as we remember our Co-Creatress-Creator status, and the gift of creating our own lessons, destiny, and path. When each tragedy becomes a lesson, even a triumph, the pain is lessened and truly transformed. At the same time, the pain and suffering experienced at this level of existence is very "real" to us, so genuine compassion for the less fortunate and the oppressed is part of unconditional, non-judgmental love. Whatever the fancy, metaphysical explanations, there is no room for intellectual and philosophical distancing from the profound grief and pain of the Holocaust; of the abuse of children; of the genocidal wars against the Native Peoples around the world; of the effects of famine, poverty, and disease; of the oppression of women; of the effects of war; and the other harsh lessons of humanity. Even as the Buddha came to free the world from suffering; and Christ opened his heart to the thief, the prostitute, and the leper; and White Buffalo Calf Woman came to awaken her people to goodness and to Spirit, so we carry a responsibility to follow in their footsteps of compassion and understanding.*
22. *Evil is an illusion. In the higher planes, what has occurred here, in the physical plane, is seen and understood entirely differently. It is not duality, but Oneness. As part of our work here, all humans will choose to do evil for some time, until the lessons are learned, as roles are played on both sides as the oppressor and the oppressed, the power hungry and disempowered, and the abuser and the victim. Depending upon the soul's motivation and awareness, each choice of darkness or evil slowly or quickly leads to spiritual growth and the lifetimes where the commitment to the Light and to Love and Harmony becomes stronger. Remembering all that we have been and accepting responsibility for all that we have done, both in the Light and in the Darkness, leads to redemption of the Self and the return to Oneness.*
23. *As unconditional love, Great Spirit is All-forgiving. The God of fear and judgment is a human-made creation, and an earlier step in our evolution of spiritual understanding. It is easier to believe in that God than the far more difficult task of accepting responsibility for our own*

actions and the hells we can create in our own lives all by ourselves. Great Spirit is not an interfering parent. Interestingly, the hardest task is forgiving ourselves as we begin to remember and awaken, for we are still under the programming and illusion that we are bad, that the God of fear and judgment finds us unworthy and unsightly.

24. *It creates imbalance and disharmony to over-analyze and over-interpret the Divine Creation Spirit or Great Spirit's works. An equally wonderful name for the Divine Creation Spirit is "Great Mystery," a mystery far beyond our limited vision in the physical plane. StaYing only in the limited human mind, without the love and inspiration and reason of Divine Mind and Holy Spirit, has created much suffering throughout history in war and division. Divisiveness, separation, judgmentalism, nationalism, and theological hairsplitting were not the teachings of the divinely guided teachers who came to assist us. Splitting theological hairs over the "correct" beliefs, laws, and rituals, that is, in following what was thought to be the letter of the law, we have sorely missed the spirit of the whole thing. There is no justification for war against, hatred for, or separation from any of our Brothers and Sisters, and no divinely guided teacher would justify such.*

25. *Hell is a human-made creation. An all-loving, all-forgiving Creatress-Creator would have no need to punish its own beloved creations. We do a fine job of punishing ourselves all by ourselves.*

26. *All rituals, ceremonies, and places of worship, which honor life and the Divine Creation Spirit, and bring us into Great Spirit's presence, are worthwhile and respected. Whether simple or ornate, whether in temple, synagogue, church, sweat lodge, cave, or sacred mountain, they will be known by the divine revelation, inspiration, love, healing, and peace that they bring. Rituals, ceremonies, and places of worship are simply a means to focus our attention and to gather divine energies into our presence more directly and consciously. They are only meaningful if the celebrant moves beyond the action or place and allows them to be experiences felt from the level of the heart and soul.*

27. *There is room for both science and spirituality since both are creations of Great Spirit. Science attempts to explain the Mystery, and faith attempts to experience the Mystery. In the end, they will be one.*

28. *The whole point is the Gestalt, the Uniqueness, Partness, Wholeness, and Oneness of all things, whether viewed from a scientific, moral,*

artistic, legal, economic, spiritual, or philosophical perspective. The parts and the whole are equally necessary for the definition, effectiveness, and integrated beingness of anything, whether: human body, national constitution, power saw, government, Theory of Relativity, sculpture, star, molecule, law, universe, Divine Creatress-Creator. The Universe is not lonely. Rather, it is filled with the parts and the sum of all things infinitely expanding beyond infinite time and space. It is Divine Creation Spirit growing, and we are adventurously part of the continual rebirth and renewal of Creation.

APPENDIX B

The Little Church That Could

How has every religion started? With the revelation of the Creator and a meeting in someone's small home, in a cave, under a tree, on a mountainside meadow. In February 1992, Medicine Signs Spiritual Center was born in Miami, Florida in a modest two-story townhouse with a tiny backyard and flower garden. The name of the housing development, aptly enough, was "The Crossings," a pretty tree-lined community with a nearby lake ideal for contemplating quiet, star-filled evenings or jogging around on sunny days. The spiritual center's name derives from the Native American concept of "medicine." It is the sacred and personal life energy and power of each human being, animal, plant, mountain, star, ocean, and raindrop. It is the life energy of all things, and it is the power of Great Spirit expressed through each and every thing in the universe. Thus, Medicine Signs refers to the sacred power signs that are all around us every moment of our existence.

The spiritual center arose out of a call from Holy Spirit that something new was needed, a new or renewed spirituality. Some five years later, in March 1997, I began to receive revelatory messages that out of the spiritual center we were to form a church since we did all the things a church did anyway. I even received an additional name, *The Church of the Way of the Messiahs*. I resisted this notion, as did others in the center because we felt the word "church" was too "churchy" and many would associate the word "church" only with Christianity. However, our spiritual guidance, what we consider to be the voice of Holy Spirit, was quite firm. It further related that the energy of the name, *The Church of the Way of the Messiahs*, would have a powerful meaning for people seeking a new way. In retrospect, we all agree that this has turned out to be true, so we are glad we listened. As Spirit foretold, we are redefining and transforming the meaning of "church" back to its original *koinonia* and ecclesial community origins, signifying that a church is a spiritual family and a spiritual community. The church's name also connotes that we are all messiahs. Many of us may be Messiahs-in-kindergarten, or we may be lost or wayward or blind or rebellious Messiahs, but the Messiah Within, the Christ Within, the Buddha Within, the Avatar Within, the Yogi Within, the Goddess Within, the God Within, the Shaman Within remains an accessible God-potential for all people. This has contributed to the egalitarian, community theology of the church.

From these meager beginnings, the church began to grow with teaching work (classes and workshops) throughout South Florida, Florida, the United States, and the world (six continents). Since 1997, in addition to its meditation groups, spiritual classes and social activities, the church initiated weekly Sacred Circles (worship services) that have been held in Miami, Ft. Lauderdale and Orlando, Florida, and are continuing to expand. We like to keep things simple, so we are a home church, and our services naturally are held in the homes of our congregants or in spiritual centers, such as spiritual bookstores and apothecaries. Recently, the church instituted a Light University in which students are discovering their Higher Purpose and Spiritual Mission, and turning that learning and training into action. The church has come a long way since 1992. It has touched the lives of many thousands of people, so we are excited about what is yet to come and expanding our island of light.

Bibliography

"About Rudolf Steiner." *Steiner*. Accessed January 15, 2006, http://www.steinerbooks.org/aboutrudolf.html.

Abe, Masao. "Buddhism." *Our Religions*. Ed. Arvind Sharma. San Francisco: Harper, 1993, 69–137.

Al Suhrawardy and Allama Sir Abdullah Al-Mamun, *The Wisdom of Muhammad*. New York: Citadel, Copyright Philosophical Library, Inc., 2001.

Albanese, Catherine L. "Introduction: Awash in a Sea of Metaphysics." *Journal of the American Academy of Religion* 75:3 (September 2007): 582–88.

"An Unnatural Disaster," *The Mountain Eagle*. Accessed October 5, 2009, http://www.themountaineagle.com/news/2007/0829/Opinion/017.html.

Anderson, C. Alan and Deborah G. Whitehouse, *New Thought: A Practical American Spirituality*. New York: Crossroad, 2003.

"Angelus Silesius aka Johannes Scheffler." *The Columbia Encyclopedia*. New York: Columbia University Press, 2001. Accessed March 25, 2005, http://www.bartleby.com/65/an/AngelusS.html.

Antonio, Edward. "Black Theology." *The Cambridge Companion to Liberation Theology*. Ed. Christopher Rowland. Cambridge: Cambridge University Press, 1999, 63–88.

Armstrong, Karen. *A History of God*. New York: Alfred A. Knopf, 1994.

———. Muhammad. San Francisco: Harper, 1992.

Augustyn, Adam. "Quetzalcoatl: Mesoamerican God." *Encyclopedia Britannica*, https://www.britannica.com/topic/Quetzalcoatl.

Baigent, Michael. *The Jesus Papers*. San Francisco: Harper, 2006.

Barnes, William H,"Fundamentalism." *The Oxford Companion to the Bible*. Ed. Bruce M. Metzger and Michael D. Coogan. New York: Oxford University, 1993, 236–37.

Barrett, C.K. *The Gospel According to St. John*. London: SPCK, 1967.

Bauckham, Richard. "Jurgen Moltmann." *The Modern Theologians*. Ed. David F. Ford. Cambridge: Blackwell, 1997, 209–24.

Becker, Carol E. "In Any Age: Can We Hear God?" *New Age Spirituality*. Ed. Duncan S. Ferguson. Louisville, KT: Westminster/John Knox, 1993, 20–34.

Beckford, James A. "New Religious Movements and Globalization." *New Religious Movements in the 21st Century*. Ed. Phillip Charles Lucas and Thomas Robbins. New York: Taylor and Francis, 2004, 253–64.

Bender, Courtney. "American Reincarnations: What the Many Lives of Past Lives Tell Us about Contemporary Spiritual Practice." *Journal of the American Academy of Religion* 75:3 (September 2007): 589–614.

Benor, Ehud Z. "Meaning and Reference in Maimonides' Negative Theology." *Harvard Theological Review* 88:3 (July 1995): 339–60. Library and Information Resource Net, Infotrac, accessed March 25, 2005.

Blavatsky, Helena P. "What is Theosophy?" *Theosophy Library Online.* Accessed January 15, 2006, http://www.theosophy.org/tlodocs/WhatIsTheosophy.htm.

Blyth, Myra and Wendy S. Robins. *No Boundaries to Compassion? An Exploration of Women, Gender and Diakonia.* Geneva: World Council of Churches Program Unit on Sharing and Service, 1998. Accessed January 15, 2006, http://www.wcc-coe.org/wcc/what/regional/compas.html.

Boehmer, Heinrich. *Road to Reformation.* Trans. John W. Doberstein and Theodore G. Tappert. Philadelphia: Muhlenberg, 1946.

Bonhoeffer, Dietrich. "Sanctorum Communio." *Dietrich: Witness to Jesus Christ.* Ed. John de Gruchy. Minneapolis: Fortress, 1991, 43–71.

Bonino, Jose Miguez. "Marxist Critical Tools: Are They Helpful in Breaking the Stranglehold of Idealist Hermeneutics?" *The Bible and Liberation.* Ed. Norman K. Gottwald and Richard A. Horsley. Maryknoll: Orbis, 1993, 107–15.

Boorstein, Daniel. *The Discoverers.* New York: Random House, 1983.

Borg, Marcus J. *The Heart of Christianity: Rediscovering a Life of Faith.* New York: Harper Collins, 2003.

Bowie, Fiona "The Anthropology of Religion." *Introduction to World Religions.* Ed. Christopher Partridge. Minneapolis: Fortress Press, 2005, 19–22.

Bro, Harmon Hartzel. "New Age Spirituality: A Critical Appraisal." *New Age Spirituality.* Ed. Duncan S. Ferguson. Louisville: Westminster John Knox Press, 1993, 169–95.

Brown, Raymond. *An Introduction to the New Testament.* New York: Doubleday, 1997.

Brown, Judith. "The Pseudo Religion of Western Romantic Love." Class lecture, Florida International University, February 14, 2007.

Buddha, Gautama. *The Dhammapada.* Trans. Byrom Thomas. Boston: Shambhala Publications, 1993; and *The Dhammapada.* Trans. Harischandra Kaviratna. Pasadena: Theosophical University Press, 1989.

Buckland, Raymond. *Buckland's Complete Book of Witchcraft.* St. Paul: Llewellyn Publications, 1993.

"Bush, Congress: Low Approval." *Miami Herald.* July 16, 2008, 6A.

Byrd, Robert. "No More Excuses, Make the Mines Safer." Address to U.S. Senate, February 1, 2006, http://byrd.senate.gov/speeches/2006_february/mine_safety_bill.html.

Byung-Mu, Ahn. "Jesus and the Minjung in the Gospel of Mark." *Voices from the Margin.* Ed. R. S. Sugirtharajah. Maryknoll: Orbis, 1995, 85–104.

Capra, Fritjof. *The Tao of Physics.* New York: Bantam Books, 1984.

Carneiro de Andrade, Paolo Fernando. "Reading the Bible in the Ecclesial Base Communities of Latin America: The Meaning of Social Context." *Readings from This Place, Vol. 2.* Ed. Fernando Segovia and Mary Ann Tolbert. Minneapolis: Fortress Press, 1995, 237–49.

Chai-Yong, Choo. "A Brief Sketch of a Korean Christian History from the Minjung Perspective." *Minjung Theology.* Ed. Commission on Theological Concerns of the Christian Conference of Asia. Maryknoll: Orbis, 1981, 2–13.

Charlesworth, James H. "A Critical Comparison of the Dualism in IQS 3:13—4:26 and the 'Dualism' Contained in the Gospel of John." *John and the Dead Sea Scrolls.* Ed. James H. Charlesworth, New York: Crossroad, 1991, 76–106.

Chilton, Bruce. *Rabbi Jesus: An Intimate Biography*. New York: Doubleday, 2000.

Cobb, Jr., John B. "The Role of Theology of Nature in the Church." *In Liberating Life: Contemporary Approaches in Ecological Theology*. Ed. Charles Birch, William Eaken, and Jay B. McDaniel. (Maryknoll: Orbis Books, 1990): 358–61, Religion Online, religion-online.org.

Coffin, William Sloane. *Marcus J. Borg's The Heart of Christianity: Rediscovering a Life of Faith*. New York: Harper Collins, 2003.

Cohn, D'Vera. "Hispanics Declared Largest Minority." *Washington Post*, June 19, 2003, A: 01.

Collins, Randall. *Four Sociological Traditions*. New York: Oxford University Press, 1994.

Commission on Theology and Church Relations of the Lutheran Church—Missouri Synod.

Cone, James H. "A Black Theology of Liberation." *Readings in Christian Ethics*. Ed. J. Philip Wogaman and Douglas M. Strong. Louisville: Westminster John Knox, 1996, 358–61.

Conze, Edward. *Buddhist Scriptures*. New York: Penguin Books, 1959.

Crossan, John Dominic. "Past and Future." Chautauqua Institute Great Lecture Series, September 16, 2001, Chautauqua, New York.

Crossan, John Dominic. *The Gospel of Eternal Life*. Milwaukee: Bruce Publishing, 1967.

Crouch, Andy. "The Emergent Mystique." *Christianity Today* 48:11 (November 2004): 36–41.

"Southern Baptists change stance, say stopping global warming a biblical duty." *Dallas Morning News*, Local News/Religion, March 9, 2008, http://www.dallasnews.com/sharedcontent/dws/dn/religion/stories/031008dnnatsouthernbaptists.31bd4ca.html.

Davidson, F. *The New Bible Commentary*. Grand Rapids: Wm. B. Eerdmans Publishing, 1963.

Dawson Andre. "The Origins and Character of the Base Ecclesial Community: A Brazilian Perspective." *The Cambridge Companion to Liberation Theology*. Ed. Christopher Rowland. Cambridge: Cambridge University Press, 1999, 109–28.

Dawson, Lorne L. "Who Joins Religious Movements and Why: Twenty Years of Research and What We Have Learned." *Cults and New Religious Movements*. Ed. Lorne L. Dawson. Oxford: Blackwell, 2001, 116–30.

de Gruchy, John. "Introduction: Christology and Reality." *Dietrich Bonhoeffer: Witness to Jesus Christ*. Ed. John de Gruchy. Minneapolis: Fortress Press, 1986, 13–18.

Diaz, Ada Maria Isasi. *Mujerista Theology*. Maryknoll: Orbis Books, 1996.

Du Toit, Andrie B. "Canon." *The Oxford Companion to the Bible*. Ed. Bruce M. Metzger and Michael D. Coogan. New York: Oxford University Press, 1993, 98–104.

Eaglebear, Barrett. "Lectures on the oral teachings of the Lakota Elders." Various workshops and seminars, 1990–2004, Miami, FL.

Eck, Diana L. *A New Religious America*. San Francisco: Harper, 2001.

Egan, Harvey D. *An Anthology of Christian Mysticism*. Collegeville, MN: Liturgical Press, 1996.

Eisler, Riane. *The Chalice and the Blade*. San Francisco: Harper Collins, 1987.

Ellis, Peter Beresford. *The Druids*. Grand Rapids: Wm. B. Eerdmans, 1994.

Epstein, Perle. *Kaballah*. Boston: Shambhala, 1978.

Escobar, Michelle. "Defining the Role of Religion." *Religion 2011, Religion: Analysis and Interpretation*. (Miami: January 24, 2006), unpublished undergraduate student paper, Florida International University.

Falikowski, Anthony. *Moral Philosophy for Modern Life*. Scarborough: Prentice Hall Allyn and Bacon, 1998.

Fehr, Ernest Urs Fischbacher, Samuel Bowles, Herbert Gintis, Simon Gachter, et al. "International Effort Explores Evolution of Human Cooperation," Santa Fe Institute Update, December 2007, http://www.santafe.edu/events/update/files/12_07newsltr.pdf.

Fellowship West. "Christ Within," 2001, http://www.fellowshipnet.com/2within.html.

Ferguson, Marilyn. *The Aquarian Conspiracy*. New York: Putnam, 1980.

Finlayson, Alan and Jeremy Valentine. "Introduction." *Politics and Post-Structuralism: An Introduction*. Edinburgh: Edinburgh University Press, 2002, 1–20, Netlibrary, http://www.netlibrary.com/Reader.

Fisher, Mary Pat. *Living Religions*. Upper Saddle River: Prentice Hall, 2008.

Fitzgerald, Stephen. *Organizational Models*. Oxford: Capstone, 2002.

Flanders, Jr., Henry Jackson, Robert Wilson Crapps, and David Anthony Smith. *People of the Covenant*. New York: Oxford University Press, 1996.

Flink, Kim and Walter Pathfinder. "Native American and Seneca Traditions." Class lecture, Miami-Dade College, Fall 1999.

Fowler, James. "Stages of Faith." *Women's Spirituality: Resources for Christian Development*. Ed. Joann Whelks Conn. Mahwah: Paulist Press, 1986, 226–32.

Fox, Matthew. *The Coming of the Cosmic Christ*. San Francisco: Harper and Row, 1988.

Freud, Sigmund. *The Future of An Illusion*. Trans. W.D. Robson-Scott. Garden City: Anchor, 1964.

Gallup, George. "Americans' Belief in Psychic and Paranormal Phenomena is Up Over the Last Decade." *Gallup News*, June 8, 2001, http://home.sandiego.edu/~baber/logic/gallu.html.

Gandhi, Mohandas. "Mahatma Gandhi: A Century of Peaceful Protest." *Mahatma Gandhi News Digest 11* (September 17, 2006), http://www.gandhiserve.org/news/mgnd/news200609110917.html.

———. "Mohandas Gandhi Quotes." Brainymedia, August 2007, 24, http://www.brainyquote.com/quotes/authors/m/mohandas_gandhi.html.

———. quoted in *Satyagrha*, www.salsa.net/peace/satyagraha/quotes.

Gardner, Howard. *The Development and Education of the Mind: The Selected Works of Howard Gardner* (New York: Routledge, 2006), Netlibrary, http://www.netlibrary.com/Reader.

Gasperson, David. "The Polarization of Ministry." Class lecture, Florida Center for Theological Studies, Miami, FL, April 3, 2003.

Gerard, Scott. Interview by Thomas Norris, January 25, 2006, The Church of the Way of the Messiahs, Miami, FL.

"Giveaway: North American Indian Custom." *Britannica Online*, accessed July 15, 2008, http://www.britannica.com/EBchecked/topic/1080979/giveaway#tab=active~checked%2Citems~checked&title=giveaway%20—%20Britannica%20Online%20Encyclopedia.

Global Coherence Initiative. "The Global Coherence Initiative." Accessed May 28, 2015, https://www2.vsb.bc.ca/NR/rdonlyres/086A35EA-09D5-4886-B4E8-68828041F24C/0/global_coherence_initiative_brochure.pdf.

Gonzalez, David. "At Cuba Conference, Old Foes Exchange Notes on 1962 Missile Crisis." *New York Times*, October 14, 2004, A6.

Gonzalez, Justo L. *A History of Christian Thought: Volume Two*. Nashville: Abingdon, 1970.

Gottman, John et al. *A Couples Guide to Communication*. Champaign: Research Press, 1976.

Gragg, Alan. "Charles Hartshorne." *Makers of the Modern Theological Mind*. Ed. Bob E. Patterson. Waco: Word Books, 1973. *Religion Online*, accessed June 14, 2005, religion-online.org.

Greene, Brian. *The Fabric of the Cosmos*. New York: Alfred A. Knopf, 2004.

Greenwood, Robin. "Ordering the Church for Working with God's Life in the World." *Society for Promoting Christian Knowledge*, 2002, http://ministry.ireland.anglican.org/articles/greenwood.pdf.

Griffin, David Ray. "Introduction." *Knowing and Value: Toward a Constructive Postmodern Theology by Frederick Ferre*, xv-xviii. Albany: State University of New York Press, 1998.

Gutierrez, Gustavo. "A Theology of Liberation." *Readings in Christian Ethics*. Ed. J. Philip Wogaman and Douglas M. Strong. Louisville: Westminster John Knox Press, 1996, 341–44.

Gutierrez, Gustavo. "The Task and Content of Liberation Theology." *The Cambridge Companion to Liberation Theology*. Ed. Christopher Rowland. Cambridge: Cambridge University Press, 1999, 19–38.

Gutierrez, Gustavo. *We Drink from Our Own Wells: The Spiritual Journey of a People*. Trans. Matthew J. O'Connell. Maryknoll, NY: Orbis Books, 1984. (Reprinted, *Invitation to Christian Spirituality*, Ed. John R. Tyson. New York: Oxford Press, 1999, 448–51.)

Gyatso, Dalai Lama Tenzin. "A Talk with Western Buddhists." *A Policy of Kindness*. Ed. Sidney Piburn. Ithaca: Snow Lion, 1993.

———. "Dalai Lama Quotes," ThinkExist, accessed August 24, 2007, http://thinkexist.com/quotes/dalai_lama/.

———. *The Opening of the Wisdom Eye*. Wheaton: Quest Books, 1966.

Hall, Manly P. *The Secret Teachings of All Ages*. Los Angeles: Philosophical Research Society, 1988.

Harner, Michael. *The Way of the Shaman*. San Francisco: Harper, 1990.

Harris, Gardner. "Peanut Product Recall Grows in Salmonella Scare." *New York Times*, January 29, 2009, A15.

Hassan, Riffat. "Challenging the Stereotypes of Fundamentalism: An Islamic Feminist Perspective." *The Muslim World* 9:1 (Spring 2001): 55–69.

Hillel. Talmud, b. Sabb.31a, quoted by Robert A. Guleich. "The Golden Rule." *The Oxford Companion to the Bible*. Ed. Bruce M. Metzger and Michael D. Coogan. New York: Oxford University Press, 1993, 257–58.

Holland, Joseph. "An Excerpt from . . . Pax Romana in Postmodern Planetary Civilizations." 28th Plenary Assembly, Pax Romana. International Catholic Movement for Intellectual and Cultural Affairs, Paris, France, September 21, 2000.

Holland, Joseph. "The Evolution of Modern Industrial-Capitalist Society and the Birth of the Postmodern Electronic-Ecological Era." The Association for the Sociology of Religion Annual Conference, Pittsburg, PA, August 18, 1992.

Holland, Joseph. "The Postmodern Transformation of Religious Life: Prophetic-Mystical Lay Communities of Ecological, Societal and Spiritual Regeneration." The Annual Assembly of the Conference of Major Superiors of Men (Miami: St. Thomas University, 1990), Newport, RI, August 8, 1990.

Hopfe, Lewis M. and Mark R. Woodward. *Religions of the World.* Upper Saddle River: Prentice Hall, 2001.

"Inside Islam: What a Billion Muslims Really Think." Unity Productions, 2009.

Isherwood, Christopher. "Jain Data Base: Quotes." *Ramakrishna and His Disciples* (Hollywood: Vedanta, 1965), accessed August 24, 2007, http://www.ibiblio.org/jainism/database/index.html.

John of the Cross. *Dark Night of the Soul.* Grand Rapids: Calvin College Christian Classics Ethereal Library, 1994. Accessed January 20, 2006, htttp://www.ccel.org/ccel/john_cross/dark_night.html.

John Paul II. "Pope John Paul II Taught Love for Animals." *North American Liberation Press Office*, accessed August 8, 2005, http://www.animalliberationfront.com/Philosophy/Religion/PopeTaughtLoveAnimals.htm.

Johnson, Elizabeth A. *She Who Is.* New York: Crossroad, 1996.

Julian of Norwich. *The Revelation of Divine Love in Sixteen Showings.* Trans. M. L. del Mastro. Liguori: Liguori Triumph, 1994.

Kapleau, Philip. *The Wheel of Life and Death.* New York: Anchor Books, 1990.

Katha Upanishad 3:14. "Death as Teacher." *The Upanishads.* Trans. Eknath Easwaran. Tomales, California: Nilgiri, 1987.

Kelly, Walt. *Pogo: We Have Met the Enemy and He is Us.* New York: Simon and Schuster, 1987.

Kelsey, Morton. "The Former Age and the New Age: The Perennial Quest for the Spiritual Life." *New Age Spirituality.* Ed. Duncan S. Ferguson. Louisville: Westminster John Knox Press, 1993, 35–58.

Kim, Chang-Nack. "Korean Minjung Theology: An Overview." *Register* 85:2. Chicago Theological Seminary (Spring 1995): 1–13.

King, Jr., Martin Luther. "Letter from Birmingham City Jail." *Readings in Christian Ethics.* Ed. J. Philip Wogaman and Douglas M. Strong. Louisville: Westminster John Knox Press, 1996, 435–57.

Klassen, Pamela E. "Radio Mind: Protestant Experimentalists on the Frontiers of Healing." *Journal of the American Academy of Religion* 77:3 (September 2007): 651–83.

Kleinbaum, Adam, Toby Stuart and Michael Tushman. "Communication (and Coordination?) in a Modern, Complex Organization." *Working Knowledge.* Harvard Business School, July 31, 2008, 9, http://hbswk.hbs.edu/item/5991.html.

Kohn, Jerome. "Evil: The Crime Against Humanity." *Hannah Arendt Papers of the Library of Congress.* Accessed March 22, 2008, http://memory.loc.gov/ammem/arendthtml/essayc1.html.

Kohn, Sherab Chodzin. *The Awakened One: A Life of the Buddha.* Boston: Shambhala, 1994.

La Verdiere, Eugene. *The Beginning of the Gospel: Introducing the Gospel According to Mark: Volume Two.* Collegeville, MN: Liturgical Press, 1999.

Lao-Tzu. *Te-TaoChing.* Trans. Robert G. Henricks. New York: Ballantine, 1989.

LeBar, James J. *Cults, Sects, and the New Age.* Huntington: Our Sunday Visitor, 1989.

Lee, Yung Young. *The Trinity in Asian Perspective.* Nashville: Abingdon, 1996.

Lings, Martin. *Muhammad: His Life Based on the Earliest Sources*. Rochester: Inner Traditions International, 1983.

Linssen, Robert. *Living Zen*. Trans. Diana Abrahams-Curiel. New York: Grove Weidenfeld, 1958.

Lodahl, Michael. *Shekinah Spirit: Divine Presence in Jewish and Christian Religion*. New York: Paulist Press, 1992.

Ludwig, Theodore M. *The Sacred Paths of the East*. Upper Saddle River: Prentice Hall, 2001.

Lutzer, Erwin W. *Satan's Evangelistic Strategy for the New Age*. Wheaton: Victor Books, 1989.

MacGregor, Geddes. *Reincarnation in Christianity: A New Vision of Rebirth in Christian Thought*. Wheaton: Quest Books, 1989.

Maimonides. "Guide for the Perplexed, I, 59." Quote, Mary Pat Fisher, *Living Religions: Eastern Traditions*. Upper Saddle River: Prentice Hall, 2003.

Malik, Zahid. "War and Peace." *Review of Religions* 88:5/6 (May-June 1993). Accessed March 20, 2008, http://www.alislam.org/library/links/war_peace.html.

Mansfield, Victor. "The Rhine-Jung Letters: Distinguishing Parapsychological from Synchronistic Events—J.B. Rhine; Carl Jung." *Journal of Parapsychology* (March 1998), FindArticle, http://www.findarticles.com/p/articles/mi_m2320/is_n1_v62/ai_21227885#continue.

Marx, Karl. *Contribution to the Critique of Hegel's Philosophy of Law*. Moscow: Progress, 1957.

Masson, Jeffrey Moussaieff and Susan McCarthy. *When Elephants Weep*. New York: Delacorte, 1995.

McCutcheon, Russell T. "What is Religion." *Introduction to World Religions*. Ed. Christopher Partridge. Minneapolis: Fortress, 2005, 10–13.

McFague, Sallie. *Models of God: Theology for an Ecological New Age*. Philadelphia: Fortress, 1987.

McGinnis, Deborah. Interview by Thomas Norris, January 21, 2006, The Church of the Way of the Messiahs, Miami, FL.

McLaren, Brian. "Issues of Truth and Power: the Gospel in a Post-Christian Culture." Excerpt, "Emergent Evangelism," *Christianity Today* 48:11 (November 2004): 42–43.

Merton, Thomas. *Mystics and Zen Masters*. New York: Delta, 1967.

Meyer, Marvin W. *The Ancient Mysteries*. Ed. Marvin W. Meyer. San Francisco: Harper and Row, 1987.

Miller, Alice. *The Drama of the Gifted Child*. New York: Basic, 1981.

Min, Anselm Kyongsuk. *The Solidarity of Others in a Divided World*. New York: T & T Clark International, 2004.

Mindell, Arnold. *The Shaman's Body*. San Francisco: Harper, 1993.

Mitchell, Robert Allen. *The Buddha: His Life Retold*. New York: Paragon House, 1991.

Moise, Edwin M. *The Vietnam Wars*. Clemson: Clemson University Electronic Publication, 1998.

Montefiore, G. G. and H. Lowe. *A Rabbinic Anthology*. New York: Schocken, 1974.

Moody, Linda. *Women Encounter God*. Maryknoll: Orbis Books, 1996.

Murphy, Nancy and James W. McClendon, Jr. "Distinguishing Modern and Postmodern Theologies." *Modern Theology* 5:3 (April 1989): 191–214.

Nam-Dong, Suh. "Historical References for a Theology of Minjung." *Minjung Theology*. Ed. Commission on Theological Concerns of the Christian Conference of Asia. Maryknoll: Orbis Books, 1981, 155–82.

Norris, Cathleen. "On Defining Religion." Interview by Thomas Norris, January 21, 2006, The Church of the Way of the Messiahs, Miami, FL.

Norris, Thomas. *On the Nature of Universalism: The New Religion of Tolerance*. Doctoral dissertation, Florida Center for Theological Studies, Miami, FL, 2006.

———. "Six Decades Later: A Liberation Retrospective of Dietrich Bonhoeffer from the 21st Century." Unpublished paper, Florida Center for Theological Studies, July 30, 2006.

———. "Sociological Methodologies: The New Age and Christianity." Unpublished paper, Florida Center for Theological Studies, 2003.

———. *A Universalist Spiritual Manifesto*. The Church of the Way of the Messiahs, 1997.

Novick, Leah. "Encountering the Shechinah, the Jewish Goddess." *The Goddess Reawakening*. Ed. Shirley Nicholson. Wheaton: Quest, 1989, 204–14.

Nystrom et al. *Exploring World Religions*. Oxford University Press, 2009.

Order of Franciscans. "Franciscan Spirituality: An Invitation to Peacemaking from the Life of St. Francis—Reconciliation." Accessed on August 8, 2005, http://www.franciscanfriarstor.com/stfrancis/stf_blessing_of_animals.htm.

Origen. "Commentary on the Gospel of John (Book VI)." *Ante-Nicene Fathers, Gospel of Peter, Diatessaron, Testament of Abraham, Epistles of Clement, Origen and Miscellaneous Works: Volume Nine*. Ed. Allan Menzies. American Edition, 1896–97. Accessed August 8, 2005, http://www.newadvent.org/fathers/101506.htm.

Pacwa, Mitch. *Catholics and the New Age*. Ann Arbor: Servant, 1992.

Pagels, Elaine. *The Gnostic Gospels*. New York: Vintage Books, 1979.

Park, Sung. "Theology of Han (the Abyss of Pain)." *Quarterly Review* 9 (Spring 1989): 48–62.

Patterson, Stephen and Marvin Meyer. "Gospel of Thomas." *The Complete Gospels*. Ed. Robert J. Miller. San Francisco: Harper, 1994, 301–22.

Pew Forum on Religion and Public Life. "Many Americans Mix Multiple Beliefs." *Pew Research Surveys*, December 9, 2009, http://pewforum.org/docs/?DocID=490.

Pew Forum on Religion and Public Life. "U.S. Religious Landscape Survey: Religious Affiliation." *Pew Research Center*, 2009, http://religions.pewforum.org/reports.

Pine-Coffin, R. S. "Introduction." *Confessions by Saint Augustine of Hippo*. New York: Penguin, 1961, 11–18.

Pitts, Jr., Leonard. "What Robots We've Become." *Miami Herald*, October 3, 2007, 23A.

Planas, Ricardo. *Liberation Theology: the Political Expression of Religion*. Kansas City: Sheed and Ward, 1986.

Pontifical Council for Culture and Pontifical Council of Interreligious Dialogue. "Jesus Christ, The Bearer of the Water of Life: A Christian Reflection on the 'New Age.'" Vatican City, accessed January 19, 2006, http://www.vatican.va/roman_curia/pontifical_councils/interelg/documents/rc_pc_interelg_doc_20030203_new-age_en.html.

"Project Wittenberg: The Nature and Implications of the Concept of Fellowship." Concordia Theological Seminary, Walther Library, Fort Wayne, IN, April 1981, accessed August 1, 2005, http://www.iclnet.org/pub/resources/text/wittenberg/mosynod/web/fellow-2.html.

Pope John Paul II. "General Audience on Justice." Libreria Editrice Vaticana, The Vatican, November 8, 1978.

Prajna, Samani Charitra. "Jainism and Nonviolence." Class lecture, Florida International University, October 17, 2006, Miami, FL.

Price, James L. "Light from Qumran upon Some Aspects of Johannine Theology." *John and the Dead Sea Scrolls*. Ed. James H. Charlesworth. New York: Crossroad, 1991, 9–37.

Prophet, Elizabeth Clare. *Reincarnation: the Missing Link in Christianity*. Corwin Springs: Summit University, 1997.

Pui-Lan, Kwok. "Speaking from the Margins," quoted in "Appropriation and Reciprocity in Womanist/Mujersita/Feminist Work." *Feminist Theological Ethics*. Ed/ Lois K. Daly. Louisville: Westminster John Knox, 1994, 97–99.

Ramster, Peter. *In Search of Lives Past*. Somerset: Somerset Films and Pub, 1992.

Religious Movements Project. "'I AM' Religious Activity." University of Virginia, Charlottesville, 1997, accessed January 15, 2006, http://religiousmovements.lib.virginia.edu/nrms/iam.html.

Reuther, Rosemary Radford. "Eschatology and Feminism." *Lift Every Voice*. Ed. Susan Brooks Thistlewaite and Mary Potter Engel. Maryknoll: Orbis Books, 1998, 129–42.

———. "Feminism and Religious Faith." *Feminism and the Religious Experience* 3:2 (Winter 1986): 1–20.

Roach, John. "Does 'Intelligent Design' Threaten the Definition of Science?" *National Geographic News* (April 27, 2005), http://news.nationalgeographic.com/news/2005/04/0427_050427_intelligent_design.html.

Robinson, George. *Essential Judaism*. New York: Pocket, 2000.

Roof, Wade Clark. *Spiritual Marketplace*. Princeton: Princeton University Press, 1999.

Rowland, Christopher. "Introduction: The Theology of Liberation." *The Cambridge Companion to Liberation Theology*. Ed. Christopher Rowland. Cambridge: Cambridge University Press, 1999, 1–16.

Roy, Saberi. "The Psychology of Color: On studying the psychology of color as effects on human emotions and human cognition." E-Zine, accessed January 5, 2009, http://ezinearticles.com/?The-Psychology-of-Color&id=1488976.

Rumi, Jalal Al-Din and Shahram Shiva. *Hush Don't Say Anything to God: Passionate Poems of Rumi*. Trans. Shahram Shiva. Fremont: Jain Publishing, 1999. Accessed March 25, 2005, http://www.geocities.com/ostercy/rumi.htm.

Russell, Letty M. *Church in the Round*. Louisville: Westminster John Knox, 1993.

Sabatino, Charles J. "The Death of God: A Symbol of Religious Humanism." Horizons 10:2 (Fall 1983): 288–303.

Sams, Jamie. *Sacred Path Cards: The Discovery of Self Through Native Teachings*. San Francisco: Harper, 1990.

Savage-Rumbaugh, Sue. "Bonobos Know and Show Forgiveness." *Science and Theology News* 6:1 (September 2005): 9.

Schmidley, Dianne. *The Foreign Born Population in the United States: March 2002*. U.S. Census Bureau. Washington, D.C, accessed February 12, 2006, http://www.diversityresources.com/rc_sample/ForeignBornPop.pdf.

Schumann, H.W. *The Historical Buddha*. Trans. M.O.C. Walshe. London: Penguin Books, 1989.

Schwartz, Alan. "Concussion Trauma Risk Seen in Amateur Athlete." *New York Times*, October 22, 2009, B14; and "N.F.L. Data Reinforces Dementia Links." *New York Times*, October 23, 2009, D1.

Segundo, Juan Luis. *Liberation of Theology*. Maryknoll: Orbis, 1999.

Seltzer, Arthur. "The Kaballah and Reincarnation." Lecture, Temple Beth David, December 11, 2005, Miami, FL.

Sheldon, Lorraine. Interview by Thomas Norris, December 3, 2005, The Church of the Way of the Messiahs, Miami, FL.

Singh, Kirpal. *The Crown of Life: A Study in Yoga*. Bowling Green: Sawan Kirpal Publications, 1980.

Singh, Madanjeet. *The Sun: Symbol of Power and Life*. New York: Harry Abrams and UNESCO, 1993.

Smart, Ninian. *Dimensions of the Sacred*. Berkeley: University of California, 1996.

Sjoo, Monica and Barbara Mor. *The Great Cosmic Mother*. San Francisco: Harper and Row, 1987.

Southerland, Dan. *Transitioning*. Grand Rapids: Zondervan, 1999.

Steiner, Rudolf. "The Birth of Christ Within Us," Lecture, Berlin, December 27, 1914, http://wn.rsarchive.org/Lectures/19141227a01.html.

Stevenson, Ian. *Children Who Remember Previous Lives: A Question of Reincarnation*. Jefferson: McFarland and Company, 2000.

Stewart, Phil. "Vatican Reaffirms Catholic Primacy." *The Washington Post*. July 11, 2007, sec. A: 11.

Storm, Hyemeyohsts. *Lightningbolt*. New York: Ballantine, 1994.

———. "To All of Earth's People." Accessed March 4, 2010, http://peoplesfirecircleturtleisland.wordpress.com/2008/08/14/to-all-of-earths-people-by-hyemeyohsts-storm/.

Sutcliffe, Steven J. *Children of the New Age*. New York: Routledge, 2003.

Suzuki, Daisetz Teitaro. *Studies in Zen*. Ed. Christmas Humphreys. New York: Dell, 1955.

Tanner, Robert. "Governors want Bush to tighten borders." *Miami Herald*. February 27, 2006, sec. A, 3A.

Tarabishy, Ahmad Bakir. "Why Have Muslim Scholars Been Undervalued Throughout Western History?" *Islam for Today* (June 2005), http://www.islamfortoday.com/scholars.htm.

Teilhard de Chardin, Pierre. ThinkExist, accessed on March 23, 2006, http://en.thinkexist.com/quotation/you_are_not_a_human_being_in_search_of_a/257982.html.

The Gospel of Thomas: In The Other Bible. Ed. Willis Barnstone. San Francisco: Harper, 1984, 299–307.

"The Secret." Prime Time Productions, 2006.

Thera, Piyadassi. "The Buddha: His Life and Teachings." Buddha Dharma Education Association, accessed June 9, 2005, BuddhaNet.net.

Trust, Lucis. "About the Arcane School." Accessed March 20, 2008, http://www.lucistrust.org/en/arcane_school/introduction/about_the_arcane_school.

Tucker, Jim B. *Life Before Life: A Scientific Investigation of Children's Memories of Previous Lives*. New York: St. Martins, 2005.

U.S. Census Bureau, Population Division. *Interim Projections of Age, Race, and Hispanic Origin*. Washington, D.C. (2004), http://www.diversityresources.com/rc_sample/growth_uspop_hispanic.htm.

U.S. Mine Safety and Health Administration (MSHA). "Description of MSHA-Approved Technologies." Accessed November 8, 2010, http://www.msha.gov/techsupp/PEDLocating/MSHAApprovedPEDdescription.pdf.

Unitarian Universalist Association of Congregations. "History of Unitarian Universalism." Accessed March 20, 2008, http://www.unityonline.org/aboutunity/whoWeAre/index.html.

Unity Online. "Who We Are." Accessed March 20, 2008, http://www.unityonline.org/aboutunity/whoWeAre/index.html.

"Universalist Church of America." *Columbia Encyclopedia*, 2001–2008. Accessed March 20, 2008, http://www.bartleby.com/65/un/UnvrslCh.html.

Vallianatos, Angelos. "Creation, koinonia, sustainability and climate change: The Churches and Climate Change." *The Ecumenical Review*. World Council of Churches, April 1997, FindArticles, findarticles.com.

van Wijk-Bos, Johanna W. H. *Reimagining God*. Louisville: Westminster John Knox, 1995.

Vanderkam, James and Peter Flint. *The Meaning of the Dead Sea Scrolls*. San Francisco: Harper Collins, 2002.

"Vatican lists new sinful behaviors." CNN, March 12, 2008, http://www.cnn.com/2008/LIVING/wayoflife/03/10/vatican.updates.sins.ap/.

Vivekananda. "Vivrekananda's Quotes." Vivekananda Vedanta Network, Boston, Ramakrishna Vedanta Society, accessed August 24, 2007, http://www.vivekananda.org/quotes.aspx.

Vivekananda. "In Search of a Universal Religion." *Ahimsa Voices*. Berkeley: January 1997.

Waldrop, M. Mitchell. *Complexity: The Emerging Science at the Edge of Order and Chaos*. New York: Touchstone, 1992.

Walker, James R. "Walker's Outline of Oglala Mythology." *Lakota Belief and Ritual*. Ed. Raymond J. DeMAllie and Elaine A. Jahmer. Lincoln: University of Nebraska Press, 1991, 50–53.

Wall, Apryl. "Defining the Role of Religion." *Religion 2011, Religion: Analysis and Interpretation*. Unpublished undergraduate student paper, Florida International University, January 24, 2006.

Ward, Graham. "Postmodern Theology." *The Modern Theologians*. Ed. David F. Ford. Oxford: Blackwell, 1997, 585–602.

Weaver, Mary Jo. "Who is the Goddess and Where Does She Get Us?" *Journal of Feminist Studies in Religion* 5:1 (Spring 1989): 49–64.

Wenham, David. *Follower of Jesus or Founder of Christianity?* Grand Rapids: William B. Eerdmans, 1995.

Williams, Delores. *Sisters in the Wilderness: The Challenge of Womanist God-Talk*. Maryknoll: Orbis, 1995.

Williams, James. *Understanding Poststructuralism*. Chesham: Acumen, 2005.

Williams, Lloyd C. *The Congruence of People and Organizations: Healing Dysfunction from the Inside Out*. Westport: Quorum, 1993.

Wise, Michael, Martin Abegg, and Edward Cook. *The Dead Sea Scrolls*. San Francisco: Harper, 1996.

Woableza. "The Story of White Buffalo Calf Woman." Lecture, The Church of the Way of the Messiahs, October 1999, Miami, FL.

Woolger, Jennifer Barker and Roger J. Woolger. *The Goddess Within*. New York: Fawcett Columbine, 1989.

Woolger, Roger. *Other Lives, Other Selves*. New York: Bantam, 1988.

Yogananda, Paramahansa. *The Essence of the Bhagavad Gita*. Ed. Swami Kriyananda. Nevada City: Crystal Clarity, 2006.

Yogatmananda. "Reincarnation." Lecture, Florida International University, Center for Spirituality, December 5, 2005.

Younger, Susanna Oommen. "Gandhi: The Person and the Film." *Theology Today* 40:2 (July 1983): 169–73.

Zeidan, Adam. "Viracocha: Inca deity." *Encyclopedia Britannica*, accessed May 28, 2021, https://www.britannica.com/topic/Viracocha.

Index

www.ingramcontent.com/pod-product-compliance
Lightning Source LLC
LaVergne TN
LVHW050613100826
845148LV00011B/1572

* 9 7 8 1 6 6 6 7 3 0 0 9 8 *